U0959900

Development Process of China-Arab States Economic and Trade Relations Annual Report 2018

Jin Zhongjie
Major Contributor

中阿经贸关系发展进程 2018年度报告

社会科学文献出版社
SOCIAL SCIENCES ACADEMIC PRESS(CHINA)

Compiling Explanation and Acknowledgements

Guided by the Secretariat of China-Arab States Expo, this Report, with Jin Zhongjie as editor-in-chief, is organized and compiled by China Institute for Arab Studies at Ningxia University (see the following list of authors for members compiling the Report). With the long-term accumulation of knowledge on China-Arab states economic and trade relations, the members describe the progress, characteristics and development trend of China-Arab states economic and trade relations by using appropriate analysis tools.

The Chinese version of this Report is edited by Jin Zhongjie, proofread by Ding Liping. Chen Yuxiang and Lu Jiangang are responsible for coordination. Ma Boying, Zhang Juan, Jin Jiexiu, Ning Jiao, etc. translate this Report into English. Ma Boying provides excellent proofreading for the English version of this Report.

Sincere thanks go to all the members involved in compiling this Report for their efforts and professionalism as well as to the Secretariat of China-Arab States Expo for its support and assistance.

The view in this Report represents only the opinions of its author, and not the Secretariat of China-Arab States Expo.

List of Authors

Edited by

Jin Zhongjie (Professor of China Institute for Arab Studies at Ningxia University)

Proofread by

Ding Liping (Editor of Ningxia People's Publishing House)

Members of Editing Group

Sun Degang/Yu Yong (Researcher/Associate Researcher of Middle East Studies Institute at Shanghai International Studies University)

Xia Shuqin (Professor of School of Economics and Management at Ningxia University)

Yang Shaoyan (Professor of School of Economics and Management at Ningxia University)

Ma Xin (Associate Professor of Yinchuan Municipal Party School of CPC)

Wang Yongbao (Professor of School of Finance and Economics at Xi'an International Studies University and Guest Researcher of China Institute for Arab Studies at Ningxia University)

Cao Xiaoxiao (Associate Professor of School of Asian Languages and Cultures at Zhejiang International Studies University)

Yang Zishi (PHD Student of Ningxia University)

CONTENTS

Chapter 1 Special Report on Joint Construction of the Belt and Road by China and Arab States and Economic and Trade Cooperation between China and Arab States

The Arab world covers a vast territory, extending from the Indian Ocean all the way through the Red Sea and the Mediterranean to the Atlantic, with a total area of 13.13 million square kilometers and total population of about 400 million. It comprises 12 countries in west Asia and 10 countries in Africa. Those countries all have sea gates, providing convenience for seaborne trade. What's more, a majority of the countries boast extended coastline and rich marine resources and serve as the junction of the Land Silk Road and the Maritime Silk Road. They are also important contributors to construction of China-Arab States Cooperation Forum and Forum on China-Africa Cooperation.

The past six years have seen constant expansion of the bilateral and multilateral relations between China and Arab states with respect to joint construction of the Belt and Road. In 2014, Chinese President Xi Jinping attended the 6th Ministerial Conference of the China-Arab States Cooperation Forum, and proposed the joint construction of the Belt and Road between China and Arab states, and the "1+2+3" cooperation pattern; [①] In January 2016, Chinese government issued its first *China's Arab Policy Paper*. In the same month, Xi Jinping paid a state visit to Egypt and Saudi Arabia; in July 2018, Xi Jinping attended the 8th Ministerial Conference of the China-Arab States Cooperation Forum. China and Arab states reached an agreement to upgrade the China-Arab States cooperation – "strategic partnership". In the

① Ding Jun, *An Increasingly Broader Way of Cooperation between China and Arab States*, *Xinmin Evening News*, July 12, 2018, 23rd volume.

same month, Xi Jinping paid a visit to the United Arab Emirates, the first stop of international visit of state head since the 19th National Congress of the Communist Party of China. This visit played a positive role in promotion of the Belt and Road in the Middle East and China-Arab States economic and trade cooperation.

1.1 Joint Construction of the Belt and Road by China and Arab States: Direction, Path and Achievements

China and Arab states were both founders of the Ancient Silk Road, and are also builders of the Belt and Road of the new era. In the past six years, China and Arab states have been carrying out practical cooperation under the Belt and Road Initiative, with the top-level design constantly improved. Furthermore, the goal setting is becoming increasingly clear and the strategic cooperation is being implemented steadily. Based on the principle of achieving shared growth through discussion and collaboration, China always supports Arab states in playing a connecting and bridging role in construction of the Belt and Road, and is in support of the interconnection between Arab states. The Arab world is an important partner for China to launch strategic cooperation with developing countries in the Middle East and Africa. Both China and Arab states are developing countries, and they have the same priorities, namely, reform, development and stabilization. Furthermore, the two are both concentrating efforts on industrialization, informationization and intelligence, and are developing science and technology and improving people's livelihood. The Belt and Road Initiative brings about the best opportunity for reform and development of China and Arab states. In January 2016, Chinese government issued *China's Arab Policy Paper*, in which the Belt and Road construction is taken as the principal axis for overall planning of the "all-round, multi-layer, wide-ranging cooperation between China and Arab states". Moreover, a series of feasible schemes and measures have been proposed in *China's Arab Policy Paper* with respect to industrial production capacity cooperation, investment cooperation, trade, energy cooperation, infrastructure construction, aviation cooperation, cooperation in civilian nuclear area, financial cooperation, economic and trade cooperation mechanism and platform construction. [①] In July 2018,

① Liu Zhongmin, *Politics and Security Risks in Implementation of the Belt and Road Initiative in the Middle East and Countermeasures*, *International Review*, Volume 2, 2018, p.43.

President Xi Jinping of China pointed out at the 8th Ministerial Conference of the China-Arab States Cooperation Forum that: "China welcomes opportunities to participate in the development of ports and the construction of railway networks in the Arab world. China will support Arabs' efforts in building a logistic network connecting central Asia with East Africa, as well as the Indian Ocean and the Mediterranean.." ①

China-Arab States Cooperation Forum (hereinafter referred to as the "Forum") established in 2004 serves as an important platform for cooperation between China and Arab states. In the past 14 years since its establishment, the China-Arab States relation has gone through a steady development period of 7 years and a turbulent period of more than 7 years (since the "Arab Spring"). The Arab world is now divided into 3 major categories: The first category includes relatively stable countries such as Saudi Arabia, the United Arab Emirates, Qatar, Morocco, Jordan, Oman, Kuwait and other constitutional monarchy countries; the second category includes countries in transition, such as Egypt, Sudan, Djibouti, Iraq, Algeria, Lebanon, Tunisia and other republic countries; the third category includes countries in disorder, like Yemen, Syria, Somalia and Libya. ②

At the beginning of the outbreak of "Arab Spring", influenced by mainstream western media, a number of Arab states were busy handling domestic political affairs and tended to pay insufficient attention to international economic cooperation. However, after years of escalating, it turned out that the Arab states failed in democratic transition, which resulted in lower national identity, and rampage of splittism, terrorism and extremism. Economy has come to a halt and employment rate dropped to the lowest point, with increasingly serious inflation. Despite the difference between Arab states in political institution and development stage, they have all been concentrating efforts on economic transformation, and taking infrastructure upgrading, employment improvement and livelihood improvement as the priorities. They are now in support of China's the Belt and Road Initiative.

The joint construction of the Belt and Road by China and Arab states is the

---

① Xi Jinping, "Making Joint Efforts to Promote Strategic Partnership between China and Arab States in the *New Era* – Speech Delivered at the Opening Ceremony of the 8th Ministerial Conference of China-Arab States Cooperation Forum", *People's Daily*, July 11, 2018, Volume 1.

② Sun Degang, et al., *Theoretical and Case Study of China's Involvement in Governance of the Middle East after the Cold War*, Social Sciences Academic Press, 2018, p.30.

inevitable result of mutual benefit, equal cooperation and joint development. China and Arab states are developing counties, with population accounting for 1/4 of the global total. ① The two have set an example of "Africa-Asia Cooperation and South-South Cooperation". In the long-term development planning of China, China and Arab states both advocate economic diversification, and both give priority to infrastructure construction and livelihood improvement. In this new era, China is marching towards the "Two Century Goals", and has signed the Belt and Road agreement with 9 Arab states including Saudi Arabia, Sudan, Iraq, Oman, Qatar, Kuwait, Lebanon, Egypt and Morocco. It has also signed the cooperation documents on industrial production capacity with 5 Arab states, namely, UAE, Algeria, Saudi Arabia, Sudan and Egypt; seven Arab states including Saudi Arabia, UAE, Sudan, Oman, Qatar, Kuwait and Egypt have become founding members of the Asian Infrastructure Investment Bank. ② The economic and trade tie between China and Arab states has reached the historically closest point.

The Belt and Road Initiative is highly in accordance with the development strategy of Arab states, such as the "Economic Rejuvenation Plan" of Egypt, the "2030 Vision" of Saudi Arabia, UAE, Qatar and Bahrain, the "2025 Vision" of Jordan, the "2035 Vision" of Algeria, the "2020 Industrial Accelerated Development Plan" of Morocco, and the "Plan for 157 Key Reconstruction Projects" of Iraq. The Belt and Road Initiative has been playing a positive role in promoting policy communication, facility connection, trade contacts, accommodation of funds and mutual understanding between people of the two, and has enriched the "connotation" of China-Arab States "1+2+3" cooperation.

Based on similar development demands, China and Arab states have been making coordinating efforts in policy and projects under the Belt and Road Imitative. In the past 14 years since establishment of the "Forum", the trade volume between the two has increased more than 4 times, and the investment of China in Arab states has increased by a factor of 7. In addition, the amount of contracts for construction projects in Arab states signed by China has increased by 7 times. The number of Confucius Institutes and Confucius Classrooms opened in Arab states has reached 16. By now, there are already 26 pairs of

① Liu Baolai: "China-Arab States Cooperation Forum at the Historically New Starting Point", http://opinion.huanqiu.com/opinion_world/2018-07/12431973.html.

② "Declaration of Joint Construction of the Belt and Road by China and Arab States", China-Arab States Cooperation Forum, July 10, 2018, http://www.cascf.org/chn/zagx/gjydyl/t1577010.htm.

China-Arab States sister cities. ① Besides China-Arab States cooperation, China has also established close cooperation relation with the individual Arab states. By now, China has built up strategic relations of different types with 11 Arab states, including comprehensive strategic partnership with Algeria (2014), Egypt (2014), Saudi Arabia (2016) and UAE (2018); and strategic partnership with Qatar (2014), Jordan (2015), Iraq (2015), Morocco (2016), Sudan (2016), Djibouti (2017) and Oman (2018). ② The China-Arab States relation was upgraded from strategic partnership in 2010 to "a future-oriented strategic partnership of comprehensive cooperation and common development" in 2018. Arab states have become important partners for the Belt and Road construction.

The joint construction of the Belt and Road by China and Arab States plays a promoting role in communication of experience in country governance between the two. In the past more than 40 years since reform and opening up, Chinese people have been following the road of socialism with Chinese characteristics, and have accumulated rich experience in country governance. China is willing to share the experience with other developing countries with respect to the way to enhance the governing capacity of the governing party and establishment of the extensive united front relation, and the way to properly handle relation among reform, development and stabilization, the relation between livelihood and democracy, the relation between keeping independence and learning from foreign modes and the relation between inheriting national culture and coping with infiltration of western culture. ③ Some Arab states also have their own successful experience gained with their respective national conditions taken into consideration. China and Arab states are having dialogues on the basis of equality, and learning successful experience from each other in the process of the Belt and Road construction, in an effort to fulfill the 2030 sustainable development agenda of the United Nations. The success of Beijing in poverty

① Middle East Institute, Shanghai International Studies Institute and Research Center of China-Arab States Cooperation Forum, "Co-building the Belt and Road, Creating a New Starting Point for Collective Cooperation between China and Arab States – Achievements and Prospects of ' China-Arab States Cooperation Forum '", 2018, p.22, China-Arab States Cooperation Forum, http://www.chinaarabcf.org/chn/zagx/ltdt/P020180614580301500634.pdf.

② Li Weijian, "China-Arab States Strategic Partnership: Foundation, Current Situation and Trend", *West Asia and Africa*, 2018, Volum 4, pp.5-6.

③ Zhang Jianwe,"Strengthening Experience Communication in State Governnance and Deepening Cooperation Relation between China and Arab States", *Contemporary World*, 2014, Volume 12, pp.44-45.

alleviation, prevention and control of desertification, partner assistance, special economic zones, investment promotion, compulsory education, regional autonomy of ethnic minorities, food security and youth development can also be used as reference for Arab states; the successful experience of Arab states, such as construction of Dubai Free Trade Zone, is also of significant reference value for construction of free trade areas of Chinese port cities. In the process of the Belt and Road construction, China should offer necessary assistance to Arab states, so as to promote mutual improvement in economy and society between China and Arab States. In July 2018, Xi Jinping announced the decision of Beijing to grant another 600 million yuan to Syria, Yemen, Jordan and Lebanon as financial aid for local humanitarian reconstruction; furthermore, non-reimbursable assistance of 100 million yuan was granted to Palestine as financial aid for livelihood improvement; earmarked fund of 1 billion yuan was also established to support construction of stability safeguarding of Arab states. ① With assistance of China and the international community, Arab States will be able to shift from "blood transfusion" to "blood production" in their economic-social construction.

1.2 Progress Made in Economic and Trade Cooperation between China and Arab States in Recent Years

Despite the huge difference between China and Arab States in political institution, cultural tradition and ideology, the two share the same demands when it comes to livelihood improvement, economic development and employment promotion. Arab states enjoy a high natural population growth rate, and have a particularly large youth population, with young people aged below 30 accounting for 65% to 70% of the total population. As such, great efforts are needed for improving livelihood. The Belt and Road Initiative brings about opportunities for industrial upgrading of Arab States. "Interconnection" is an important characteristic of China-Arab States joint efforts in construction of the Belt and Road. Active promotion of five priority areas (namely, policy coordination, facility connection, trade liberalization, financial integration and people-to-people communication) is an important means of

① Xi Jinping,"Making Joint Efforts to Promote Strategic Partnership between China and Arab States in the New Era – Speech Delivered at the Opening Ceremony of the 8th Ministerial Conference of China-Arab States Cooperation Forum", *People's Daily*, July 11, 2018, Volume 1.

achieving the cooperation goals between two sides.

As of 2017, China has become the second largest trade partner of Arab States; in particular, China is the largest trade partner of 10 Arab states, including Bahrain, UAE, Qatar, Egypt, Jordan, Kuwait, Lebanon, Morocco, Oman and Saudi Arabia. The Arab League has become the seventh largest trade partner of China in the world. The economic growth of China and Arab States accounts for 1/8 of the world total. China and Arab states share similar demand in participating in international organizations like the International Monetary Fund, World Bank, Group of Twenty, Asia Infrastructure Investment Bank and International Energy Agency – to strive for an equal right of speech of developing countries in the international multilateral organizations.

China and Arab states are highly complementary in trade. Reciprocity is the guarantee for China-Arab States strategic partnership. As pointed out by President Xi, "China welcomes participation of Arab states in the First China International Import Expo to be held in November 2018 in Shanghai. In the 5 years to come, full coverage of CIIE and comprehensive trade and investment exhibitions by Arab States will be achieved." ① The active role taken by China in sharing development achievements with Arab States has been widely acclaimed.

For a long time, the China-Arab States trade has been limited to a few areas. Above 40% of energy import of China is from Arab states. Since the 21st Century, the economic and trade cooperation between China and Arab States has gone through 3 stages: The first stage started from 2000 and ended in 2013, which laid an emphasis on energy cooperation; the second stage started from 2014 after the 6th Ministerial Conference of China-Arab States Cooperation Forum, during which the cooperation between the two was centered on "1+2+3", with energy cooperation as the "principal axis", infrastructure construction and trade and investment facilitation as the "two wings", and nuclear energy, space satellite and new energy as the new breakthrough areas; ② the third

① Xi Jinping, "Making Joint Efforts to Promote Strategic Partnership between China and Arab States in the New Era – Speech Delivered at the Opening Ceremony of the 8th Ministerial Conference of China-Arab States Cooperation Forum", *People's Daily*, July 11, 2018, Volume.

② Gao Lanfang, "Strategic Choice of Ningxia to Involve in Construction of the Silk Road Economic Belt – With Discussion of Joint Construction of the Silk Road Economic Belt by China and Arab States", *Journal of Ningxia Party School*, 2014, Volume 6, p.104; Xi Jinping, " Expanding Silk Road Spirit and Deepeing China-Arab States Cooperation - Speech Delivered at the Opening Ceremony of the 6th Ministerial Conference of China-Arab States Cooperation Forum," *People's Daily*, June 6, 2014, Volume 2.

stage started in 2018, in which the China-Arab States cooperation features comprehensiveness and combination. Specifically, both economic and trade and industrial production capacity cooperation, bilateral cooperation and multilateral cooperation are involved.

In order to expedite trade facilitation between China and Arab States, China has established the joint trade committee system with 22 Arab states and the Gulf Cooperation Council, and has signed bilateral governmental agreement for economic, trade and technical cooperation with all Arab states. Since establishment of China-Arab States Cooperation Forum, noticeable growth has seen in trade volume of China and Arab states , direct investment flow of China in Arab States and amount of newly signed contracts for projects in Arab States. In 2004, the trade volume between the two was 36.7 billion USD, and in 2008, the amount topped 100 billion USD. In 2012, the amount exceeded 200 billion USD and in 2014, it reached 251.2 billion USD, with a year-on-year increase of 5.2%, accounting for 5.8% of the total foreign trade volume of China. In 2017, the trade volume between the two reached 191.352 billion USD, increased by 11.9% year on year. [①]

Energy cooperation is the priority among priorities of China-Arab States trade cooperation. In 2016, China imported crude oil of 151 million tons in total from the 6 member states of Gulf Cooperation Council and Iraq, accounting for 39.7% of the total crude oil import of China. In the same year, China imported crude oil of 160 million tons in total from all Arab oil producing countries, accounting for 41.93% of total crude oil import of China. [②] In 2017, China imported crude oil of 157 million tons from Arab states, accounting for 37.03% of the total crude oil import.

China-Arab States cooperation in economy and trade is now shifting from the traditional energy area to diversified and multidimensional areas, with agriculture, environment and cutting-edge technologies, becoming new growth points of

---

① Middle East Institute, Shanghai International Studies Institute and Research Center of China-Arab States Cooperation Forum,"Co-building the Belt and Road, Creating a New Starting Point for Collective Cooperation between China and Arab States – Achievements and Prospects of 'China-Arab States Cooperation Forum'", 2018, pp.14-15,China-Arab States Cooperation Forum, http://www.chinaarabcf.org/chn/zagx/ltdt/P020180614580301500634.pdf.

② Yang Yanhong and Tian Ranran, "A Study of Ecnomic and Trade Cooperation between China and Arab States under the Belt and Road Initiative, International Business ", *Journal of University of International Business and Economics*, Volume 3, 2018, p.63.

China-Arab States cooperation. By now, China has signed MOU for agriculture or established agricultural working groups with Oman, Palestine, Syria, Egypt, Algeria, Sudan and Mauritania, and has signed bilateral environmental cooperation documents with Morocco, Egypt and Jordan. Furthermore, China has been spreading experience in peaceful use of nuclear energy among Arab states by offering training courses on reactor technology and small and medium sized reactors ①, thus laying a solid foundation for nuclear energy cooperation between the two in the future. In 2015, the China-Arab States Environmental Cooperation Forum was held, at which MOU was signed; in 2016, the China-Arab States Seminar on Desertification Control was held in Sudan; in an effort to strengthen communication and cooperation and regulate related work, China released the *Supporting Construction of the Green Belt and Road: Building China-Arab States Green Development Partnership* in 2016 and released the *Planning for Cooperation in Ecological Environment Protection along the Belt and Road* in 2017. ② In addition, the telecommunication enterprises in China established partnership with UAE, Saudi Arabia, Egypt and Qatar in terms of international roaming, international direct dialing and international data traffic. Huawei and ZTE are cooperating with telecommunication enterprises of nearly 20 Arab states in areas such as fixed network, wireless network and intelligent terminals. ③

In the process of economic and trade cooperation between China and Arab states, the two have been attaching great importance to construction of the bilateral and multilateral cooperation mechanism. A benign interaction mechanism in which "cooperation is discussed on a multilateral basis and

① "Outcome Document of the 10th Senior Officials Meeting of China-Arab States Cooperation Forum", ministry of Foreign Affairs of the People' s Republic of China, May 29 to 30, 2013, https://www.fmprc.gov.cn/zalt/chn/gylt/zywj/t1051545.htm.

② Middle East Institute, Shanghai International Studies Institute and Research Center of China-Arab States Cooperation Forum, "Co-building the Belt and Road, Creating a New Starting Point for Collective Cooperation between China and Arab States – Achievements and Prospects of 'China-Arab States Cooperation Forum'", 2018, p.19, China-Arab States Cooperation Forum, http://www.chinaarabcf.org/chn/zagx/ltdt/P020180614580301500634.pdf.

③ Middle East Institute, Shanghai International Studies Institute and Research Center of China-Arab States Cooperation Forum, "Co-building the Belt and Road, Creating a New Starting Point for Collective Cooperation between China and Arab States – Achievements and Prospects of 'China-Arab States Cooperation Forum'", 2018, pp.15-16, China-Arab States Cooperation Forum, http://www.chinaarabcf.org/chn/zagx/ltdt/P020180614580301500634.pdf.

implementation is discussed on a bilateral basis" has been realized, and the entrepreneur exchange visit mechanism between China and Saudi Arabia, China and UAE and between China and Algeria has been established. China has founded the bilateral business affairs council with Egypt, Morocco, Tunisia and UAE respectively. From 2005 to the present, 7 sessions of China-Arab States Entrepreneur Conference has been held; four organizations, including China-Arab Joint Chamber of Commerce, FGCCC, China-Africa Joint Chamber of Commerce and Industry and Arab Banking Union, have established the multilateral industrial and commercial cooperation mechanism, with 28 cooperation agreements signed with the related business associations and organizations, trade investment promotion organizations and large enterprises of Arab states. In a bid to promote China-Arab States cooperation in economy and trade, and expedite implementation of the Belt and Road Initiative in the Middle East, the four state-owned banks of China have successively started to run business in the Middle East. For instance, the Agricultural Bank of China has set up branches in Dubai; Bank of China in Bahrain, the Industrial and Commercial Bank of China in Qatar, Saudi Arabia, Kuwait and Iraq. [①]Besides, China and Arab states cooperation in civil aviation keeps making progress. Direct flights from China to 7 Arab states, including UAE, Algeria, Saudi Arabia, Iraq, Oman, Qatar and Egypt, have been opened. The number of flights exceeds 180 a week.

1.3 Progress in Industrial Production Capacity Cooperation between China and Arab States

Production capacity cooperation is an important part of China and Arab states cooperation in economy and trade, and is also one of the key areas of joint efforts made by China and Arab States in the Belt and Road construction. In June 2014, Xi Jinping proposed the "1+2+3" cooperation pattern for China and Arab states at the 6th Ministerial Conference of China-Arab States Cooperation Forum, in which the China and Arab States cooperation in production capacity forms a critical part. From January to April 2017, the number of foreign contracts signed between Chinese enterprises and countries along the Belt and

① Zhao Lei,"' Top Four State-owned Banks' Expediting Placement in the Middle East", *China Economic Weekly*, 2013, Volume 15, pp.53-55.

Road reached 1,862, with a total contract amount of 31.85 billion USD. Among the countries along the Belt and Road, member states of the Gulf Cooperation Council constitute one of the largest project contracting markets. Besides growth in number, the structure of construction projects is also being constantly optimized, shifting gradually from labor intensive type to a combination of labor, technology and capital intensive types. The business scope has also been expanding from ordinary housing construction and road and bridge building to areas such as industry, energy, communication and petrifaction. ① In 2016, the amount of contract for projects in Arab states signed between Chinese enterprises and Arab states was 40.4 billion USD, with a year-on-year increase of 40.8%, bringing a turnover of 33.6 billion USD, increasing 10.6% year on year. As of 2017, the total amount of contract for construction projects in Arab states signed between the two reached 32.805 billion USD.

China and Arab states have launched a number of major projects in areas such as production capacity coordination, petroleum refining and port infrastructure construction; China and Arab States have set up China-Arab States Technology Transfer Center under the framework of the Forum, and have signed the agreement for "Beidou" Navigation Satellite System. Furthermore, agreements have been concluded on establishment of the Training Center for Peaceful Use of Nuclear Energy and Clean Energy Center; China and Arab States have launched the technological partnership, and the two are going to set up 10 national joint labs in areas including new energy, health, modern agriculture and communication. China has carried out bilateral aviation cooperation with 5 countries including Egypt, Algeria, UAE, Saudi Arabia and Sudan. Particularly, China successfully launched No. 1 Communications Satellite of Algeria in 2017; the China-Arab States Beidou Center was founded in Tunisia in 2018. In 2017, the first batch of 30 key projects under production capacity and investment cooperation between China and Saudi Arabia were finalized, among which 8 projects have already been commenced. ② The main areas

① Liu Xinlu and Xu Ting, "China-Arab States Economic and Trade Cooperation from the Belt and Road Perspective", *Chinese Muslims*, 2018, Volume 1, p.31.

② Middle East Institute, Shanghai International Studies Institute and Research Center of China-Arab States Cooperation Forum,"Co-building the Belt and Road, Creating a New Starting Point for Collective Cooperation between China and Arab States – Achievements and Prospects of 'China-Arab States Cooperation Forum'", 2018, p.12,China-Arab States Cooperation Forum, http://www.chinaarabcf.org/chn/zagx/ltdt/P020180614580301500634.pdf.

of cooperation between China and member states of Gulf Cooperation Council include energy, steel and iron, building material, construction machinery, hardware and chemical engineering. Representative projects are Phase II EPC of MGS between SEPCO and Saudi Aramco, BGP Project of China National Petroleum Corporation and communication engineering project of China Communications Services Corporation Saudi Arabia. ①

As of 2018, significant progress has been made in a number of key infrastructure construction projects under the Belt and Road Initiative in Arab states undertaken by Chinese enterprises, represented by project preparation of Algeria Central Port, suburban railway of "10th of Ramadan" of Egypt, national main electric power transmission line of Egypt, glass fiber production line of Egypt, Moonlet Assembly and Integration Test Center of Egypt, Container Wharf of Phase II, Khalifa Port, UAE, expansion of Friendship Port of Mauritania, "Mohammed VI Bridge" of Morocco and achievements in cooperation under the Belt and Road between China and Morocco, the Lusai Stadium of Qatar, Atalate Oil Shale Power Plant of Jordan, Suhail Independent Power Plant of Oman, Upper Atbara Water Control Project of Sudan and Yanbu Oil Refinery of Saudi Arabia. ②

Important milestones have been achieved in production capacity cooperation between China and Algeria. By the end of October 2017, with joint efforts of Chinese engineers, the Ganntas Tunnel in north Algeria saw its holing-through, reducing the traveling time from Oran to Algiers from 4 hours to 2 hours only. It laid a solid foundation for construction of trunk railways in north Algeria③, and demonstrated the great cooperation potential in production capacity between China and Algeria.

Currency circulation between China and Arab states provides financing support for production capacity cooperation between China and Arab states as well as implementation of the Belt and Road. Arab states play a positive role in construction of Asia Infrastructure Investment Bank. Representatives from

① Liu Xinlu and Xu Ting,"China-Arab States Economic and Trade Cooperation from the Belt and Road Perspective", *Chinese Muslims*, 2018, Volume 1, p.31.

② "Declaration of Joint Construction of the Belt and Road by China and Arab States", China-Arab States Cooperation Forum, July 10, 2018, http://www.cascf.org/chn/zagx/gjydyl/t1577010.htm.

③ "China Completed the 'Engineers' Disaster', the Longest Tunnel in North Africa, within 7 Years", http://dy.163.com/v2/article/detail/DTLGCL8D0511DTU9.html.

Saudi Arabia and Egypt are respectively serving as directors of the Middle East Region and Africa Region of AIIB. By now, AIIB has approved 4 projects involving participation of Arab states — the Merchants' Wharf and Work Zone of Port of Duqm of Oman, Preparation Project for Oman Railway System, Wide-band Infrastructure Project of Oman and PV Power Generation Project of Egypt, with a total loan commitment amount of 663 million USD, accounting for 15.67% in total amount of projects approved by AIIB. ① Besides, in order to support industrialization of the Middle East, China has set up earmarked loan of 15 billion USD and concessional loan of 10 billion USD, and has jointly set up joint investment fund of 20 billion USD with UAE and Qatar. ②

With industrial upgrading of Arab states, in particular Saudi Arabia, Egypt, UAE, Qatar, Kuwait, Algeria and Morocco that have proposed economic diversification strategy in the medium and long-term development planning of China, their reliance on single-product economy has reduced. This has brought about favorable conditions for China to invest in production capacity of Arab states. In addition, the Arab world is an important destination of overseas investment of China. The investment from China is driving upgrading of production capacity of Arab states. In 2012, the flow of investment of China in Arab states was 890 million USD and the year-end stock was 7.2 USD; at the end of 2016, the direct investment stock of China to Arab states was 15.1 billion USD; in 2017, the flow of direct investment of China to Arab states was 1.26 billion USD, increasing by 9.3% year on year. In 2014, the amount of newly signed contracts for construction projects in Arab states undertaken by Chinese enterprises reached 35.9 billion USD, with a year-on-year increase of 23%, accounting for about 1/5 of the total amount of construction projects signed by Chinese enterprises across the world; in 2017, the amount of newly signed contracts for construction projects in Arab states undertaken by Chinese

① Middle East Institute, Shanghai International Studies Institute and Research Center of China-Arab States Cooperation Forum,"Co-building the Belt and Road, Creating a New Starting Point for Collective Cooperation between China and Arab States – Achievements and Prospects of 'China-Arab States Cooperation Forum'", 2018, pp.12-13, China-Arab States Cooperation Forum, http://www.chinaarabcf.org/chn/zagx/ltdt/P020180614580301500634.pdf.

② "Declaration of Joint Construction of the Belt and Road by China and Arab States", Beijing, July 10, 2018, China-Arab States Cooperation Forum, http://www.cascf.org/chn/zagx/gjydyl/t1577010.htm.

enterprises reached 32.805 billion USD. [①]

China has also established research centers and technical training centers as intelligence support for China and Arab states cooperation in production capacity. For example, the settlement of China-Arab States Research Center on Reform and Development at Shanghai International Studies University, the settlement of Overseas Traditional Chinese Medicine Center of Shanghai University of Traditional Chinese Medicine in Morocco, and the settlement of China-Arab States Beidou Navigation Satellite System Excellence Center in Tunisia, as well as establishment of China-Arab States Technology Transfer Center, Training Center for the Peaceful Use of Nuclear Energy and Training Center for Clean Energy are all considerable progress made in technology and experience change and production capacity cooperation between China and Arab states.

Both China and Arab states lay emphasis on production capacity cooperation in economic and trade cooperation zone in Arab states. The two have been concentrating efforts on construction of China Industrial Park of Jizan Economic City of Saudi Arabia, China-Oman (Duqm) Industrial Park, China-UAE Production Capacity Cooperation Demonstration Park, China-Egypt Suez Economic and Trade Cooperation Zone and China-Sudan Agricultural Cooperation Development Zone. As for facility connection, Chinese enterprises have been extensively involved in construction and investment of ports of Arab states, and are undertaking projects such as road, railway, oil pipeline and water supply pipelines. Taking port construction for example, as of 2018, Chinese enterprises have participated in nearly 10 ports in Arab states, including Djibouti Port, Sudan Port, Jeddah Port, Port Said and Port of Ain Sukhna of Egypt, Hamdaniya Port, Port Tangier and Port Casablanca, and Friendship Port in Mauritania. Arab states have thus become the focus of port diplomacy of China with countries along the Maritime Silk Road. [②]

---

① Middle East Institute, Shanghai International Studies Institute and Research Center of China-Arab States Cooperation Forum, "Co-building the Belt and Road, Creating a New Starting Point for Collective Cooperation between China and Arab States – Achievements and Prospects of 'China-Arab States Cooperation Forum'", 2018, pp.14-15, http://www.chinaarabcf.org/chn/zagx/ltdt/P020180614580301500634.pdf.

② Sun Degang,"Theory and Practice of China's Port Diplomacy", *World Economics and Politics*, 2018, Volume 5, pp.22-24.

A prospective view is taken for production capacity cooperation between China and Arab states, with high-tech cooperation and advantageous production capacity as the new cooperation areas. Since launching of the Talented Young Scientist Program by the Ministry of Science and Technology of the People's Republic of China in 2013, totally 123 scientific researchers from Arab states have undertaken short-term scientific research in China; in December 2014, President Xi Jinping of China and President Sisi of Egypt witnessed the signing of the *MOU for Joint Construction of China-Egypt Joint Lab of Renewable Energy* between the Ministry of Science and Technology of the People's Republic of China and the Ministry of Scientific Research of Egypt. In 2015, the China-Arab States Technology Transfer Center was officially inaugurated; in 2015 and 2017, two sessions of China-Arab States Technology Transfer and Innovation Cooperation Conference were successively held; in 2016, Xi Jinping announced launching of the "China-Arab States Scientific and Technological Partnership Program" during his visit to the Headquarters of Arab League; in March 2016, the Joint Lab of Renewable Energy co-built by China and Egypt was inaugurated in Egypt. At present, construction of the Joint Lab is progressing steadily. The Ministry of Science and Technology of the People's Republic of China and the overseeing authority of science and technology of Arab states are negotiating about co-building of labs in areas with shared interest. By now, 7 countries, including Egypt, Morocco, Algeria, Saudi Arabia, Jordan, Tunisia and Libya have signed inter-government agreement for scientific and technological cooperation with China. In particular, Egypt, Morocco and Saudi Arabia have established the scientific and technological cooperation mechanism with the Ministry of Science and Technology of the People's Republic of China. ① The cooperation in science and technology improves sustainability of China-Arab States cooperation in production capacity.

In recent years, Arab states have also increased investment in China. In December 2015, China and UAE reached an agreement to establish the "China-UAE Mutual Investment Fund" of 10 billion USD. The investment of UAE in China is mainly made in areas including advanced manufacturing industry,

---

① Middle East Institute, Shanghai International Studies Institute and Research Center of China-Arab States Cooperation Forum, "Co-building the Belt and Road, Creating a New Starting Point for Collective Cooperation between China and Arab States – Achievements and Prospects of 'China-Arab States Cooperation Forum'", 2018, pp.18-19, http://www.chinaarabcf.org/chn/zagx/ltdt/P020180614580301500634.pdf.

renewable energy and energy, health-care and medical equipment, agriculture, biological technology, innovative technology, hotel and port. Sultan, chairman of DP World, has signed an agreement with chairman of the Qingdao Port Group, according to which DP World is going to investment 636 million USD in building an intelligent container wharf at Qingdao Port with services including remote loading and unloading. In addition, DP World also invested 1.2 billion USD in construction of a new port in Tianjin, which had been completed in 2018. ① In 2018, President Xi Jinping and Vice President Wang Qishan successively paid a visit to UAE to further promote the investment of Arab states in China.

In February 2019, a delegation led by Crown Prince Salman of Saudi Arabia visited China, and reached an extensive consensus with China with respect to coordination between the Belt and Road Initiative and "2030 Vision" of Saudi Arabia and co-building of "China-Pakistan Economic Corridor". A massive deal of 28 billion USD was signed between the two sides. Saudi Aramco and China North Industries Company have reached an agreement to invest 10 billion USD to build oil refining and petrochemical enterprises in Panjin of northwest China, incorporate Aramco Petrochemical Engineering Joint Ventures and build up a refining with daily production capacity of 300,000 barrels of petroleum. ②

To sum up, the economic and trade cooperation between China and Arab states have expanded to a number of areas. The first area is the traditional energy and new energy cooperation, including petroleum, natural gas, nuclear energy, solar energy and green and low-carbon energy, with "energy +" as the focus; the second area is production capacity cooperation in the infrastructure area, including road, building, port, smart city, industrial parks and science and technology city. China has participated in construction of a central business district of the new administrative capital of Egypt with total investment of 3 billion USD. The Project includes construction of a 385m-high skyscraper, which will be the highest building in Asia upon completion; ③ the third area is high

① www.port-m.com," DP World to Invest 1.9 Billion USD in China", http://www.21pi.cn/news/show.php?itemid=6944.

② "Crown Prince of Saudi Arabia Visits China and Signs a Massive Deal of 28 Billion Yuan, Showing His Support for the Belt and Road Initiative," www.cankaoxiaoxi.com, February 24, 2019, http://www.cankaoxiaoxi.com/china/20190224/2372626.shtml.

③ Yang Fuchang, "Shared Development Direction Guarantees Sustainable Development of China-Arab States Relation", *Global Times*, July 9, 2018, Volume 14.

technology, including aviation, bio-pharmaceuticals, new materials, "internet +", artificial intelligence, big data, electronic commerce and joint R&D. Assistance in satellite launching offered by China to Algeria and the joint moon exploration and Mercury exploration plan between China and Saudi Arabia are continuation and expansion of the "Aerial Silk Road" between China and Arab states.

Ningxia plays a key role in promoting economic and trade cooperation between China and Arab states. Since 2010, the Ministry of Commerce, China Council for the Promotion of International Trade and the People's Government of Ningxia Hui Autonomous Region have held 3 sessions of China-Arab States Cooperation Forum and 3 sessions of China-Arab States Expo.① As of the end of 2017, the implementation rate of the 108 investment projects signed at the 2015 China-Arab States Expo had reached 70.4%, with paid-in investment of 27.21 billion yuan. ②

1.4 Conclusion

Since the Belt and Road Initiative was proposed by President Xi Jinping at the 6th Ministerial Conference of China-Arab States Cooperation Forum in 2014, the Arab states have gradually shifted from the pursuit of political transformation to development paths that are suitable for their respective national conditions, which are highly corresponding with the development strategy of China. In the past five years, Arab states has generally attached considerable importance to industrialization, informationization and industrial diversification as priorities of government work. The cooperation areas between China and Arab states have also expanded from traditional energy area to broader areas including infrastructure, production capacity cooperation, new energy, finance, aviation, ocean and high technology, and the experience exchange on state governance

① Middle East Institute, Shanghai International Studies Institute and Research Center of China-Arab States Cooperation Forum, "Co-building the Belt and Road, Creating a New Starting Point for Collective Cooperation between China and Arab States – Achievements and Prospects of 'China-Arab States Cooperation Forum'", 2018, p.16, http://www.chinaarabcf.org/chn/zagx/ltdt/P020180614580301500634.pdf.

② Yang Yanhong and Tian Ranran,"A Study of Ecnomic and Trade Cooperation between China and Arab States under the Belt and Road Initiative", *International Business – Journal of University of International Business and Economics*, Volume 3, 2018, p.65.

and policy communication between the two have moved forward noticeably. The relation between China and Arab states has upgraded from strategic cooperation to strategic partnership, and the two have set a successful example for "Asia-Africa Cooperation" and "South-South Cooperation. These are all of great significance for fulfillment of 2030 Sustainable Development Agenda of the United Nations and propaganda of "new security outlook" and "promoting peace with development" proposed by China.

Political mutual trust forms the basis of economic and trade cooperation between China and Arab states. China has been working on peace and development in the Middle East, and is hoping to play a positive role in promoting peaceful and stable development of the region. China has been providing substantial support for the just cause of the people of Palestine and advocates founding of an independent State of Palestine with complete sovereignty, with East Jerusalem as the capital and the 1967 boundary as the foundation. Furthermore, China is in support of the Middle East peace process with the "two-state solution" and "Arab Peace Initiative" as the basis. On November 29, 2017, the Commemoration Meeting of "International Day of Solidarity with the Palestinian People" was held by the United Nations, and Xi Jinping sent a congratulatory telegram to the Meeting. On the other hand, Arab states are generally in support of the One-China principle, and stand on the side of China when it comes to Taiwan and South China Sea issues related to the sovereignty, security and development benefit of China.

To sum up, the joint construction of the Belt and Road by China and Arab states and the economic and trade cooperation between two sides are playing a positive role in promoting the interconnectivity among developing countries in Africa and Asia in economy and trade, and boosting the internal trade facilitation and industrial upgrading of developing countries. The "promoting peace with development" idea proposed by China aims to resolve any conflicts, serves as a new solution to conflicts between Arab States and embodies the new concept and practice of "promoting security by comprehensive governance, striving for security through diplomatic negotiations and guaranteeing security with economic and trade cooperation."

Chapter 2 Special Report on Economic Development of Major Economies in Arab World

2.1 Selection of Research Objects

2.1.1 Brief Introduction to Arab World

In this Chapter, Arab world are taken as research objects. Located in western Asia and northern Africa, Arab states lie in the junction of Asia and Africa , of which the African part accounts for 72% and the Asian part accounts for 28%. Its location is of strategic importance. There are 22 countries (including the 21 countries of League of Arab States and Syria which were terminated in 2011), namely, Algeria, UAE, Oman, Egypt, Palestine, Bahrain, Djibouti, Qatar, Kuwait, Lebanon, Libya, Mauritania, Morocco, Comoros, Saudi Arabia, Sudan, Somalia, Tunisia, Syria, Yemen, Iraq and Jordan. Arab states covers an area of 13.13 million square kilometers, accounting for 9.53% of the world's land area. Its total population exceeds 359 million (2017, data from the UN report) with a labour force of 146 million people, accounting for 4.91% of the world's total population. More than 90% of the population in the Arab states believe in Islam. The Gulf Cooperation Council (referred to as the GCC, including Saudi Arabia, UAE, Oman, Kuwait, Qatar, and Bahrain) of Arab states is considered as the center of the Islamic cultural circle and is one of the major bases for energy production and export. Oil and gas reserves account for 45% and 23% of the global total, respectively. Most Arab states have a tropical desert climate with hot summers, mild winters, and little rains all year round.

2.1.2 Major Economies in Arab States

The Middle East is vast in territory. The economic development level of different Middle East countries varies considerably, with enormous internal difference. At present, its economy has continued to recover, but the economic growth is slowing down. The increased uncertainties and unstable factors have brought new challenges to Chinese enterprises in conducting foreign investment cooperation.

In this chapter, a number of major economies in the Middle East with close economic and trade tie with China are selected. The overall development of their national economy is then described separately in terms of economic aggregate, economic growth, economic benefit, economic structure and petroleum economy, so as to allow enterprises to better understand the change of economic development of the Middle East countries, master the major economic development policies of various countries and the main focus of national economic development as well as their the business environment, and enhance the ability to "go global" and the level of overseas operations; furthermore, it also aims to provide basis for China to formulate and implement science-based and desirable policy towards the Middle East, improve the relation between China and the Middle East countries, expedite the Belt and Road construction and maintain the interests of China in the Middle East. For the above purposes, six gulf countries, Saudi Arabia, UAE, Oman, Kuwait, Qatar, and Bahrain, one traditional regional power, Egypt, and two important countries of the North Africa, Algeria and Morocco, have been selected as the research objects. All of them are main trade partners of China in the Middle East.

2.2 Economic Development of Gulf Countries

The Gulf countries, led by Saudi Arabia, are playing a substantial role in the regional economic cooperation in the Middle East, and serve as the critical driving force for regional economic development. Those countries have a small population and have to face labor shortage. Petroleum industry is their pillar industry. They are earning zillions by getting the utmost out of the rich petroleum and natural gas resources. Furthermore, thanks to their high industrialization level and economic integration degree, they have developed from a trade zone to the Gulf Common Market. The data shows that its market size has exceeded 1.6 trillion USD and it is expected to reach 2 trillion USD in 2020. The general economic development is good and the income is at the world leading level.

Table 2.1 Ranking of 6 Gulf Countries among Middle East Countries in Terms of Economic Development Indicators in 2017 (Fixed price USD of 2010)

Country	GDP		GDP growth rate		Per Capita GDP	
	Amount (100 million USD)	Ranking	Growth rate (%)	Ranking	Amount (USD/ person)	Ranking
Saudi Arabia	6849.94	2	-0.74	19	20796.32	7
UAE	3872.59	4	0.79	17	41197.17	2
Qatar	1733.87	9	1.60	16	65696.39	1
Kuwait	1387.62	10	-2.87	21	33545.62	4
Oman	748.50	13	-0.27	18	16144.41	8
Bahrain	330.03	17	3.88	8	22111.48	6

Data source: World Bank

2.2.1 Saudi Arabia

The economy of Saudi Arabia develops under a typical petroleum-based economy mode. The petroleum export accounts for 40% of the GDP, 80% of the government revenue and more than 90% of the foreign currency earnings of Saudi Arabia. In terms of the economic aggregate, in 2017, the GDP of Saudi Arabia was 683.827 billion USD, with a relatively larger economic scale, ranking the second place in the Middle East. Specifically, the value added of the primary industry was 17.393 billion USD, that of the secondary industry was 307.697 billion USD, and that of the tertiary industry was 358.737 billion USD. In terms of economic growth, there was a drop of 0.74% in 2017, ranking the 19th place in the Middle East. Saudi Arabia was facing economic challenges such as low growth rate, high unemployment rate and inflation. In terms of economic structure, in 2017, the value added of the primary industry accounted for 2.54% of the GDP; that of the secondary industry accounted for 45%, and that of the tertiary industry accounted for 52.46% (decreased by 1.7% compared with that of the previous year). This indicates that the economic structure of Saudi Arabia was going through adjustment. However, petroleum profit accounted for more than 26% of the GDP, which was still a large proportion. The industrial structure needs further improving. In terms of economic benefit, the gross national income of the year was 695.6 billion USD, while the per capita GDP throughout the year was 20,796.32 USD, dropping by 2.73% year on year, ranking the 7th place in the Middle East. In terms of open economy, in 2016, the total foreign trade volume of Saudi Arabia was 337.4 billion USD; the balance of foreign exchange reserves at the end of 2017 was 488.9 billion USD; the balance of current account was -23.8 billion USD. This indicates a slight decrease of the net foreign property, which may pose an impact on growth of the foreign exchange reserve and the external income and expenses. In terms of reform and development, to cope with the petroleum related economic crisis, the government of Saudi Arabia proposed the "2030 Vision" in April 2016. The "2030 Vision" includes the following development goals: the industrial sector shall be established by using the low-price energy of Saudi Arabia; the heavy reliance on subsidies shall be overcome by improving the water resource and power management level; developing small public investment funds and strategic investment; developing agriculture and entertainment industry; building 16 nuclear reactors to replace petroleum power generation; increasing the proportion of non-petroleum export GDO from 16% to 50%, and reducing the proportion of non-petroleum income in the total income from 10% to 70%; increasing the localization rate of weapons from 2% to 50%; reducing unemployment rate from 11% to 7.6%; and driving the position of Saudi Arabia in the world economic ranking from the 19th place to the 15th place. In order to fulfill the "2030 Vision", the government of Saudi Arabia has released a series of supporting measures on the policy implementation level. The specific measures involve 3 aspects. The first one is to cut government expenditure and expand revenue sources. The main measures include suspension of housing allowance, reduction of petroleum price subsidy in Saudi Arabia, retrenching expense on new automobiles, furniture and other equipment and raising prices of electricity and petroleum. The second is to strengthen the economic opening. The main measures include establishment of free economic zones, encouraging development of commerce, finance industry and high-tech industry, such as energy and water, transportation, bio-technology, food industry, electronic technology, advanced manufacturing industry, media and entertainment industry and robot, renewable energy and future transportation solutions. The tourist market should also be open to foreign visitors to boost development of tourism. Cooperation with universities in Saudi Arabia should be encouraged and comprehensive financial training provided for students to expedite talent nurturing. The third is to concentrate efforts on development of private economy. The main measures include reorganization of most of the state-owned sectors, selling stock of state-owned petroleum companies and complete privatization of international airports. ① At present, Saudi Arabia is concentrating efforts on implementation of economic diversification, and remarkable achievements have been made in non-petroleum industries such as light industries. However, the economic effects are poorer than expected. Considering defects in the economic system and systematic obstacles facing the development of productive force, a complete industrial structure should be established based on a balance among industry, agriculture and service industry.

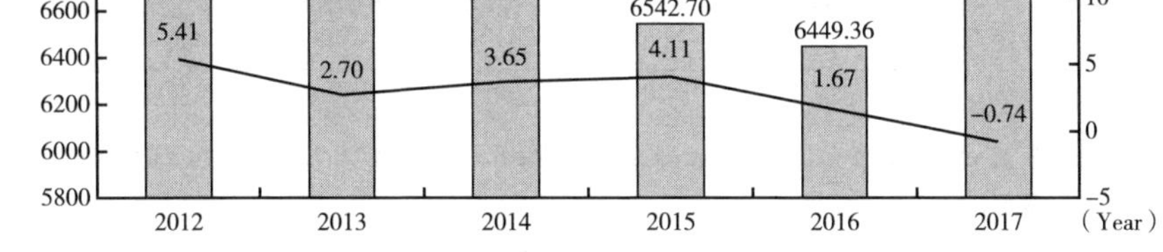

Figure 2.1 Saudi Arabia's GDP and Its Growth Rate from 2012 to 2017

Data source: World Bank

Note: The GDP is calculated based on the current price USD; the growth rate is calculated based on the fixed price USD of 2010.

① Lin Haihong, "Economic Transformation of Saudi Arabia: Vision and Challenges", *International Studies*, 2018, Volume 3.

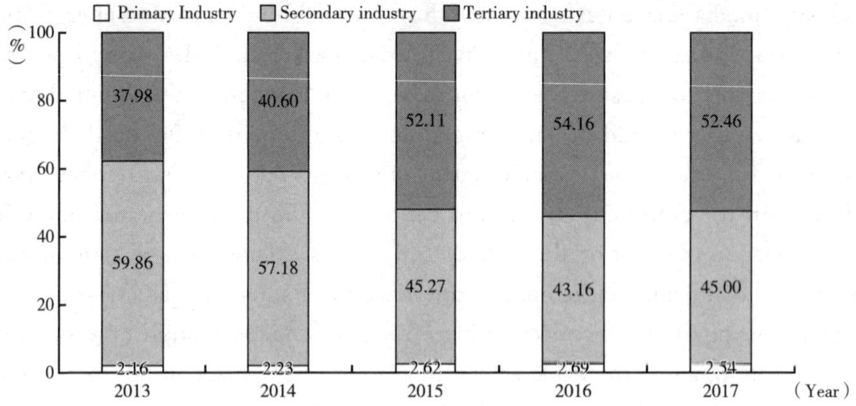

Figure 2.2 Proportion of Value Added of Three Industries in GDP of Saudi Arabia from 2013 to 2017

Data source: World Bank, calculated on the current value of USD

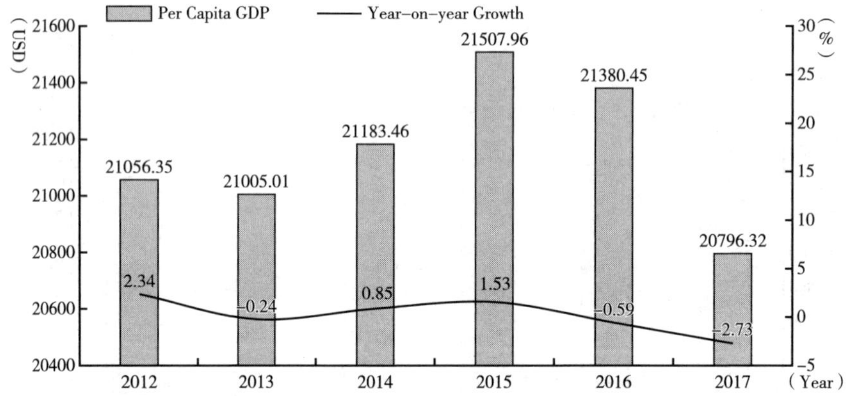

Figure 2.3 Per Capita GDP of Saudi Arabia and Its Growth Rate from 2012 to 2017

Data source: World Bank

Note: The per capita GDP and its growth rate are both calculated based on the fixed price USD of 2010.

2.2.2 United Arab Emirates

UAE is one of the Middle East's most successful countries in economic modernization. It is doing great jobs in areas such as tourism, commerce, trade, transportation and aviation. According to the *Global Tourist Competitiveness Report of 2015*, UAE was ranked the 24th place among the 141 candidate countries, 4

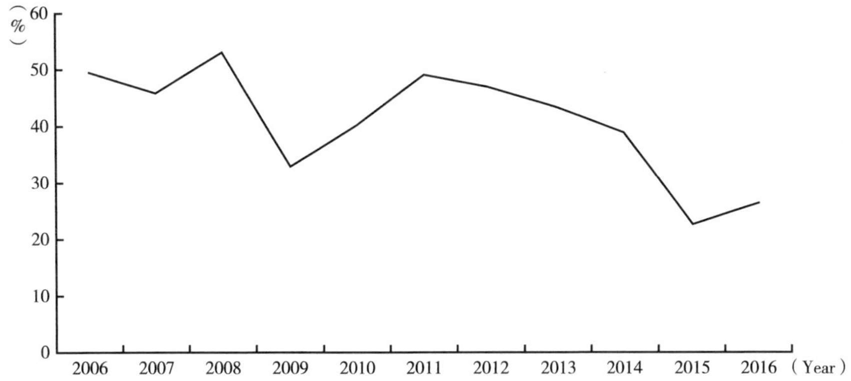

Figure 2.4 Petroleum Rent of Saudi Arabia from 2006 to 2016

Data source: World Bank

Note: Petroleum rent refers to the proportion of petroleum profit in GDP. Petroleum accounts for a considerable proportion in fiscal revenue of petroleum producing countries.

places higher than in 2014. According to the 2016 World Logistics Performance Index released by the World Bank, UAE was ranked the 13th place globally in terms of logistics performance index among the 160 countries, being the No. 1 in the Middle East. At present, non-petroleum economy has become the core of UAE's economic development,① contributing to more than 75% of its GDP. In terms of economic aggregate, in 2017, the GDP of UAE was 382.575 billion USD, ranking the 4th place in the Middle East. Specifically, the value added of the primary industry was 2.919 billion USD, and that of the secondary industry and the tertiary industry was respectively 166.79 billion USD and 212.865 billion USD. In terms of economic growth, the year-on-year growth in 2017 was 0.79%, which was quite low, ranking only the 17th place among the Middle East countries. In terms of economic structure, in 2017, the value added of the primary industry accounted for as little as 0.76%, and there was a heavy reliance on import of grain crop; the value added of the secondary industry was 43.6%, with a year-on-year increase of 2.15%; the value added of the tertiary industry was 55.64%, decreasing by 2.14% year on year. This indicates a need for improvement of the industrial structure. In terms of economic benefit, the gross

① Han Lu, Lin Meng, et al., "Development of Non-petroleum Economy of UAE and Suggestions on China-Arab States Cooperation", *International Economic Cooperation,* 2017, Volume 4.

national income of the year was 385.4 billion USD, and the per capita GDP of the year was 41,197.17 USD, dropping by 0.61% year on year, ranking the 2nd place in the Middle East. This indicates a considerable economic strength, and shows it is a highly wealthy country. In terms of economic opening, the total foreign trade volume of UAE in 2016 was 510.9 billion USD. In terms of external policy, there is a close tie between UAE and Saudi Arabia; in terms of domestic policy, UAE has maintained a highly coordinated relation with the member states of Gulf Cooperation Council, and the political situation has been generally stable. From the perspective of reform, UAE has proposed the “2021 Strategic Planning”, according to which efforts have been concentrated on development of modern service industry. The economic competitiveness of UAE is going to grow year on year. At present, UAE is taking measures to improve its investment environment, and its economy is seeing rapid development. The number of construction projects is enormous, with heavy reliance on reported production equipment, machinery equipment and building materials. According to the 2017 business environment index released by the World Bank, UAE was ranked the 26th place in terms of business environment, jumping 8 spots compared with that in 2016. The main reason was the detailed investment management and various constraints on foreign investment sectors imposed by UAE, as well as the complete legal institutions and great efforts taken by UAE in cracking down on defraud, bribery, fake and forged commodities, money laundering and other illegal behaviors in the economic and financial area, and in protection of investors. Furthermore, UAE is a low-tax country, and no enterprise income tax and individual income tax, value added tax and stamp duty is collected in UAE. The federal government of UAE generally imposes import duty of 5% on general commodities and some agricultural products and drugs are even duty free, with heavy duty imposed on articles of luxury. For instance, the tax imposed on tobacco is 50% to 70%.① Considering the encouraging market and financial environment and stable political situation of UAE, more and more investors from various countries will turn to UAE.

① “Report on Analysis of Economy and Business Environment Risks of UAE (2017)”, *International Finance*, 2018, Volume 9.

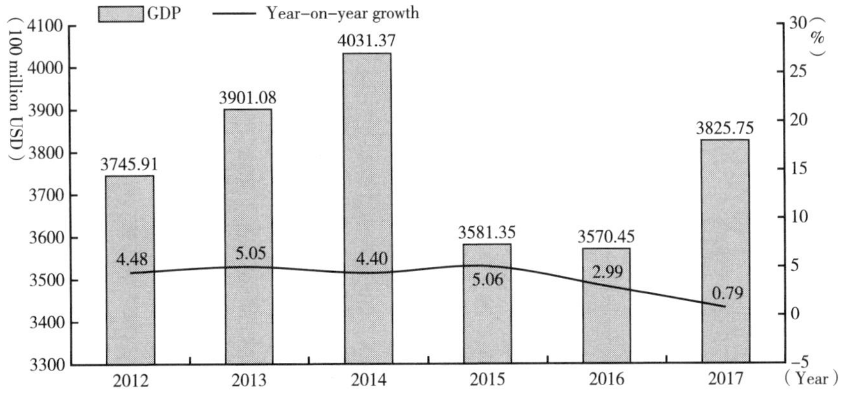

Figure 2.5 GDP of UAE and Its Growth Rate from 2012 to 2017

Data source: World Bank

Note: GDP is calculated based on the current price USD; the growth rate is calculated based on the fixed price USD of 2010.

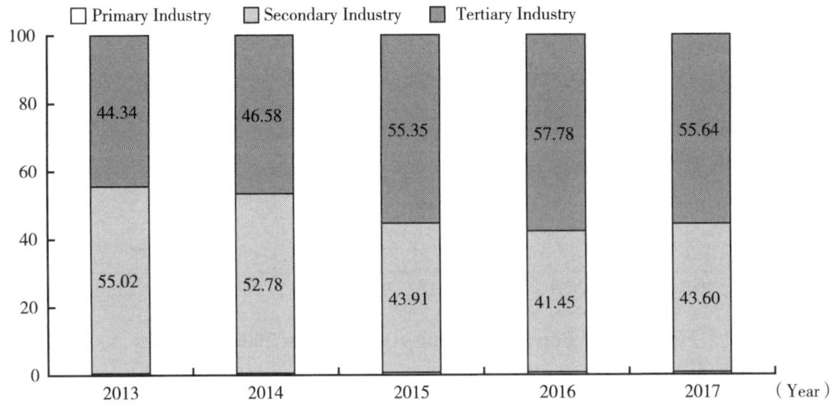

Figure 2.6 Proportion of Value Added of Three Industries in GDP of UAE from 2013 to 2017

Data source: World Bank, obtained by calculation based on the current value of USD

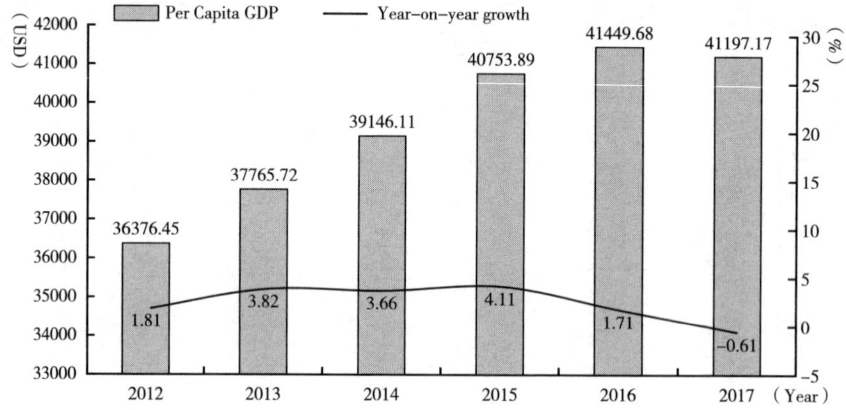

Figure 2.7 Per Capita GDP of UAE and Its Growth Rate from 2012 to 2017

Data source: World Bank

Note: The per capita GDP and its growth rate are both calculated based on the fixed price USD of 2010.

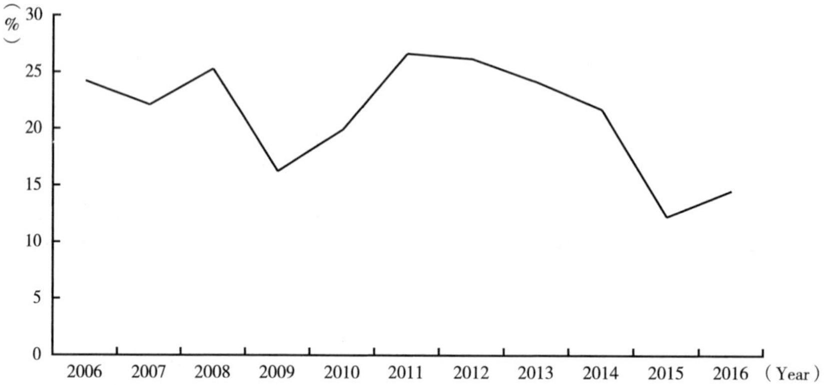

Figure 2.8 Petroleum Rent of UAE from 2006 to 2016

Data source: World Bank

2.2.3 Oman

Oman is a typical resource-exporting country. The oil and gas industry is the backbone of the national economy. Its output value accounts for nearly 30% of

GDP, and its export revenue accounts for nearly 70% of the government's fiscal revenue. In terms of economic aggregates, in 2017, Oman's GDP was 72.643 billion USD, ranking 13th in the Middle East. In terms of economic growth, in 2017, the figure was down 0.27% from the previous year and ranked 18th in the Middle East. In terms of economic structure, in 2016, the added value of the primary industry was 1.97%; that of the secondary industry was 47.17%; and that of the tertiary industry was 50.86%. In terms of economic benefits, the annual gross national income was 70.1 billion USD, and the annual per capita GDP was 16144.41 USD, down 4.82% from the previous year, ranking 8th in the Middle East. From the perspective of an open economy, Oman's foreign trade in 2017 totaled 53.9 billion USD, maintaining a trade surplus. The major trading partners of Oman include China, United Arab Emirates, Japan, India, Saudi Arabia, South Korea, the United States, the European Union and so on. Its main export commodities are oil and natural gas; the main imported goods are transportation tools, mechanical and electrical products, metal and minerals, chemical products, light industrial textiles, food and agricultural products. In 2017, Oman's inflation rate was 0.58%. From the perspective of reform, in recent years, it has fully promoted the strategy of economic diversification, vigorously optimized the environment for attracting investment by special economic zones and industrial parks such as China-Oman (Duqm) Industrial Park, and focused on major projects such as new airports and expressways to improve the infrastructure, actively support the development of manufacturing, logistics, tourism, fisheries and mining five non-oil and gas industries. *The Global Competitiveness Report 2017-2018*, released by the World Economic Forum shows that Oman ranks 62nd among the world's most competitive 137 countries and regions. In World Bank's *Doing Business 2018*, Oman ranks 31st in the ranking of entrepreneurial procedures and 71st in the ranking of business convenience.① This will boost market sentiment and promote it as a strong economic activity area.

2.2.4 Kuwait

Kuwait's economy is generally dominated by the oil, natural gas and petrochemical industries, and its structure is relatively simple. Fifty percent of its GDP and 85%

① Chinese Academy of International Trade and Economic Cooperation, etc., "A Guide to Foreign Investment and Cooperation by Country (Region)", *Oman (2018 Version).*

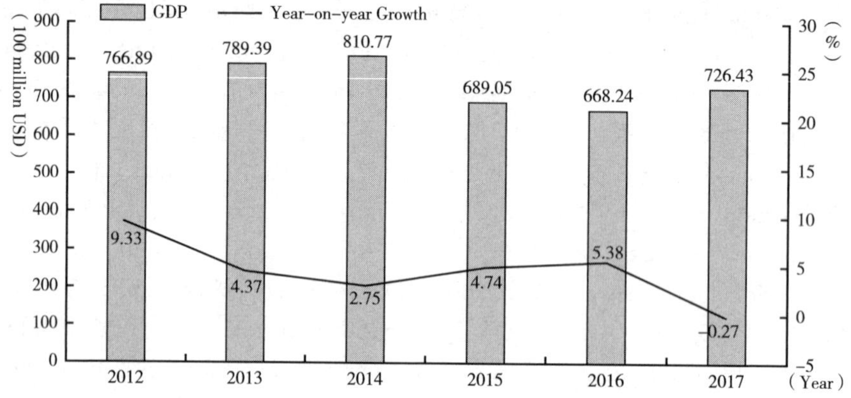

Figure 2.9 Oman's GDP and Its Growth Rate from 2012 to 2017

Data source: World Bank

Note: GDP is calculated based on the current price USD; the growth rate is calculated based on the fixed price USD of 2010.

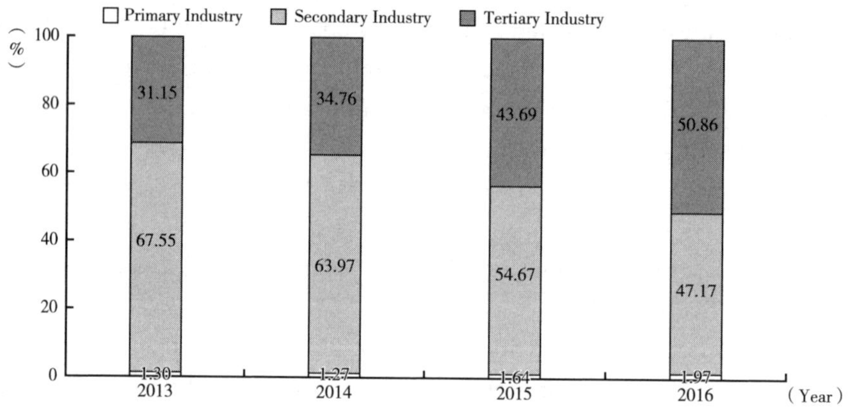

Figure 2.10 Proportion of Value Added of Three Industries in GDP of Oman from 2013 to 2017

Data source: World Bank, calculated on the current value of USD

Note: The 2017 data is missing.

of government revenue come from oil. Therefore, the government emphasizes the development of multiple economies to alleviate the dependence on the oil economy. It is more open to the outside world. In *the Global Competitiveness Report* 2017-2018 released by the World Economic Forum, Kuwait ranks 52nd out of 137 countries. In

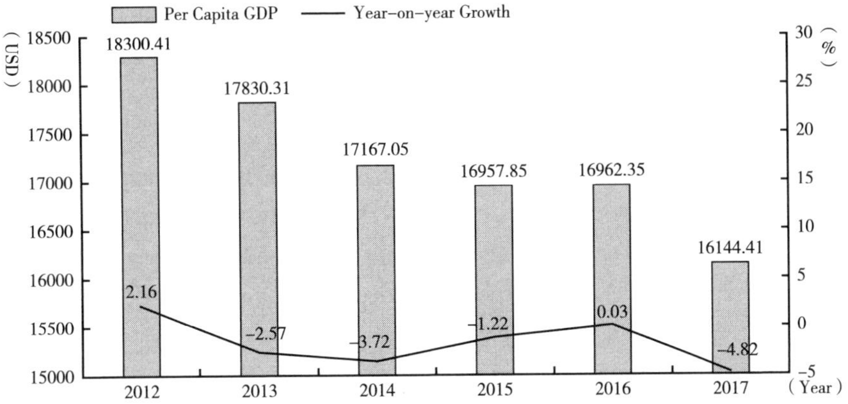

Figure 2.11 Per Capita GDP of Oman and Its Growth Rate from 2012 to 2017

Data source: World Bank

Note: The per capita GDP and its growth rate are both calculated based on the fixed price USD of 2010.

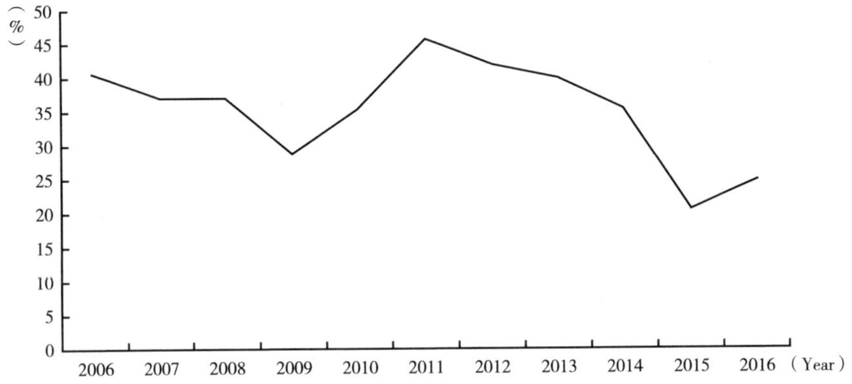

Figure 2.12 Petroleum Rent of Oman from 2006 to 2016

Data source: same as the figure 2.4

the World Bank's *Doing Business* 2018, Kuwait ranks 96th out of 190 economies, up 6 places from the previous year. Ranking of various indicators: it ranks 149th in terms of opening convenience, ranks 129th in terms of construction permit convenience, 97th in power supply convenience, 70th in registered property convenience, and 6th in tax convenience.① In terms of economic aggregates, Kuwait's GDP in 2017 was

① Chinese Academy of International Trade and Economic Cooperation, etc., "A Guide to Foreign Investment and Cooperation by Country (Region)", *Kuwait (2018 Version).*

120.126 billion USD, ranking 10th in the Middle East. In terms of economic growth, it was down 2.87% from the previous year, ranked 21st in the Middle East. From the economic structure point of view, in 2016, the proportion of the value added of the primary industry was small (0.56%), but the government attaches importance to the development of agriculture, mainly on vegetables production. Its agricultural and livestock products rely on imports. Kuwait is rich in fishery resources, like prawns, groupers and yellow croaker. The added value of the secondary industry was 51.64%, accounting for 4.3%. The proportion of added value of the tertiary industry was 47.8%, accounting for a substantial increase of 4.27%. From the perspective of economic benefits, the annual gross national income was 139.1 billion USD, and the annual per capita GDP was 33545.62 USD. Although it was decreased 4.84% than the previous year, Kuwait still ranked fourth in the Middle East. From the perspective of an open economy, Kuwait's foreign trade in 2017 totaled 88.4 billion USD, showing a surplus in overseas trade. Its major export commodities are petroleum and other fuels, minerals, chemicals, plastics and rubber products, transportation equipment, jewellery, etc.; the major imported goods are machinery and electrical products, metal products, vehicles and their components, chemicals, clothing and textiles, etc. As of the end of 2017, its foreign exchange reserves totaled 36.89 billion USD. The current account balance was 7.6 billion USD, and it grew faster. At the same year, its fiscal balance was in deficit and debt increased. The inflation rate in Kuwait in 2017 was 1.5%. From the perspective of reform, in order to attract foreign investment, it has enacted a series of relevant laws and regulations, and formed a relatively complete legal framework for encouraging foreign investment. Its overall tariff level is low. The import tariffs for general commodities are unified at 5%; for food, daily necessities, medicines, and machinery and equipment imported by newly established enterprises, tariffs are exempted; industrial products from some GCC countries and some agricultural products enjoy duty-free treatment. The focus of the Kuwait Development Plan 2015-2020 is to advance the economic reform process and implement large-scale strategic projects. The key areas for attracting investment are high-tech industries, including electronic network construction, telecommunications, environmental protection, and advanced petroleum technologies. Kuwait is not willing to encourage investment in industries with excess capacity, such as hotel industry. In recent years, Kuwait has engaged in infrastructure construction and civil engineering projects, and has successively launched a number of large-scale infrastructure projects and a number of urban road construction and renovation projects, which has brought opportunities for foreign companies to expand the project contracting and labor market in the local area.

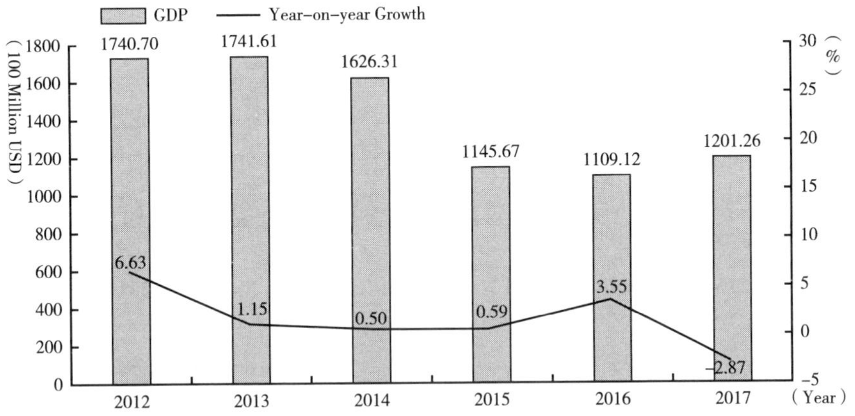

Figure 2.13 Kuwait's GDP and Its Growth Rate from 2012 to 2017

Data source: World Bank

Note: GDP is calculated based on the current price USD; the growth rate is calculated based on the fixed price USD of 2010.

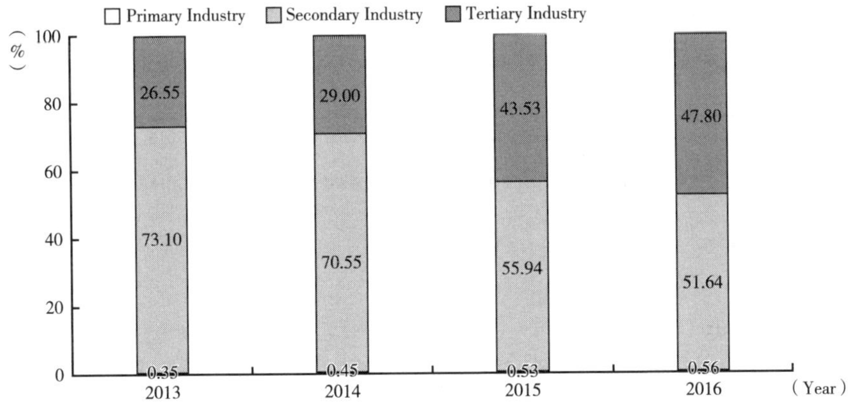

Figure 2.14 Proportion of Value Added of Three Industries in GDP of Kuwait from 2013 to 2017

Data source: World Bank, calculated on the current value of USD

Note: The 2017 data is missing.

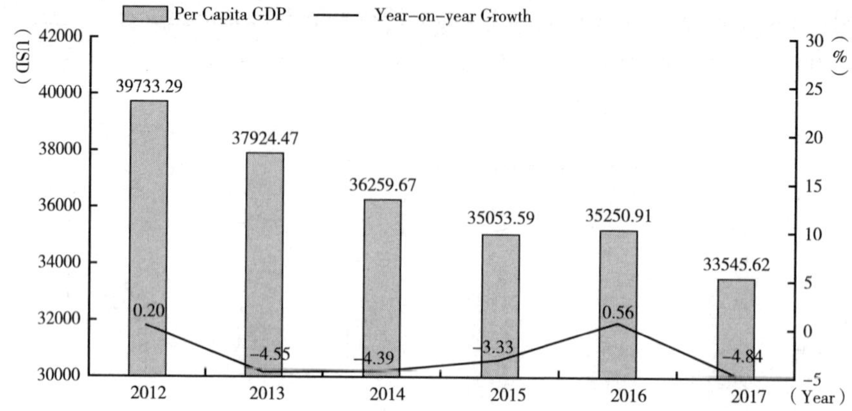

Figure 2.15 Per Capita GDP of Kuwait and Its Growth Rate from 2012 to 2017

Data source: World Bank

Note: The per capita GDP and its growth rate are both calculated based on the fixed price USD of 2010.

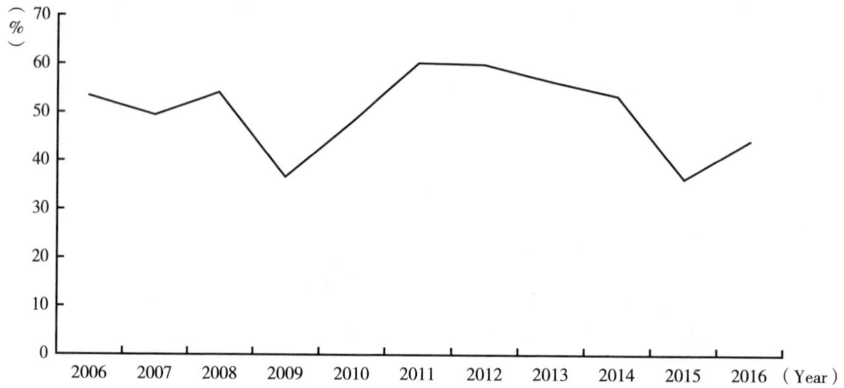

Figure 2.16 Petroleum Rent of Kuwait from 2006 to 2016

Data source: same as the figure 2.4

2.2.5 Qatar

Qatar is rich in oil and gas resources. Rapid development of the oil and gas industry ensure Qatar's high economic growth and huge wealth. Its per capita GDP ranks among the best in the world. Qatar chose an export-oriented economic development model. It has an increasingly sound legal and regulatory system, and the business environment continues to improve. According to *the*

Global Competitiveness Report 2017-2018 released by the World Economic Forum, Qatar ranks 25th among the most competitive 137 countries and regions in the world. In the World Bank's *Doing Business* 2018, Qatar's business environment ranks 83rd out of 190 countries.

In terms of economic aggregates, in 2017, Qatar's GDP was 167.605 billion US dollars, ranking 9th in the Middle East. In terms of economic growth, in 2017, it increased by 1.6% over the previous year and ranked 16th in the Middle East. In terms of economic structure, in 2016, its primary industry added value was 0.18%. The major agricultural products included fruits, vegetables, poultry, dairy products, beef and fish, and food crops were dependent on imports. The second industry added value was 51.9%, the proportion decreased by 6.6%; the tertiary industry added value of 47.92%, accounting for a substantial increase of 6.58%. From the perspective of economic benefits, the annual gross national income is 167.2 billion USD, and the annual per capita GDP is 65696.39 USD. Although it had decreased compared with the previous year, it still ranked first in the Middle East. This far exceeds the income level of the general developed countries and belongs to high-level rich countries, and its strength is very strong. From the perspective of an open economy, Qatar's foreign trade in 2016 totaled 89.4 billion USD, experiencing trade surplus generally. In 2017, its top four trading partners were: Japan (13.49%), South Korea (11.5%), China (10.9%), and India (10.09%). The major export products includes crude oil, gasoline, liquefied gas, condensate, urea, ethylene, etc.; the main imported products are aircraft and helicopter parts, construction materials and engineering machinery and accessories, transportation network equipment and accessories, food and so on. The Qatar current account balance in 2017 was 6.4 billion USD, and the surplus grew rapidly. Qatar's inflation rate in 2017 was 0.4%. From the perspective of reform, in preparation for the 2022 World Cup and the "2030 National Vision Plan", Qatar has implemented an economic diversification strategy to encourage foreign investment in non-oil and gas industry development in recent years, emphasizing support for food security projects, SME development, and development and construction of economic districts and free zones, etc. Qatar's economy is gradually transforming from a single oil and gas industry to diversified development. In 2017, the proportion of non-oil and gas sectors increased further, reaching 67.3%. In the future, the government of Qatar will give priority to ensuring the construction of World Cup venues and related infrastructure projects, and vigorously encourage such industries as finance, construction, processing and manufacturing, aviation shipping, logistics, tourism and business services. Investment opportunities in these industries will open up a broader space for foreign participation and investment.① Foreign capital is allowed to enjoy preferential policies in Qatar in a bid to improve the investment environment and attract foreign capital and technology. For example, foreign investors can lease land for a long time in the local area, and enjoy tax-free concessions such as investment capital income tax and import equipment tariffs. Foreign-funded funds can be freely remitted. In addition, for the industries that encourage investment by the government such as agriculture, industry, health, education, and tourism, foreign investors may hold more than 49% of the total project investment up to 100% of the shares. The implementation of these preferential policies provides guarantees and preferential treatment for foreign capital and will promote the sustainable development of Qatar's economy.②

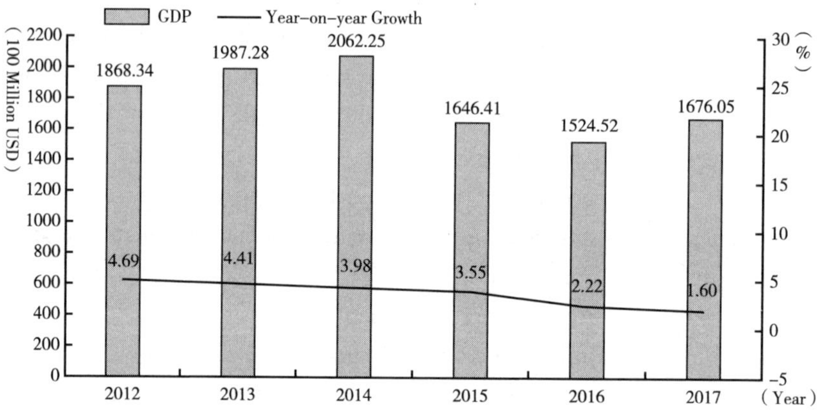

Figure 2.17 Qatar's GDP and Its Growth Rate from 2012 to 2017

Data source: World Bank

Note: GDP is calculated based on the current price USD; the growth rate is calculated based on the fixed price USD of 2010.

---

① Chinese Academy of International Trade and Economic Cooperation, etc., "A Guide to Foreign Investment and Cooperation by Country (Region)", *Qatar (2018 Version)*.

② Jiang Yingmei, " Qatar's Economic Development Strategy and the Construction of the Belt and Road," *Arab World Studies*, 2016, Volume 6.

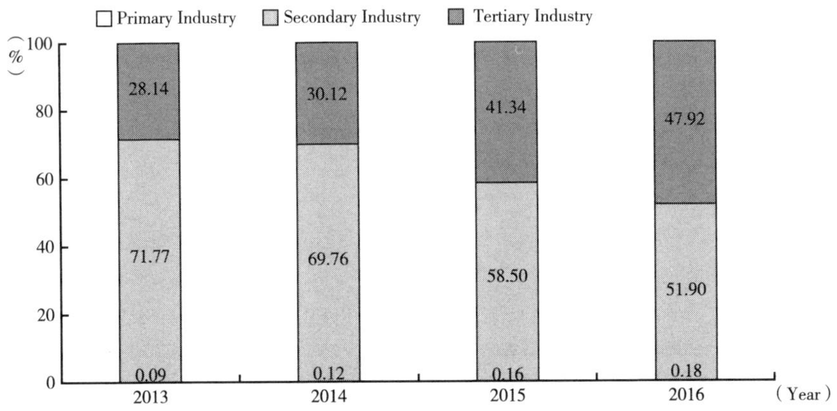

Figure 2.18 Proportion of Value Added of Three Industries in GDP of Qatar from 2013 to 2017

Data source: World Bank, calculated on the current value of USD

Note: The 2017 data is missing.

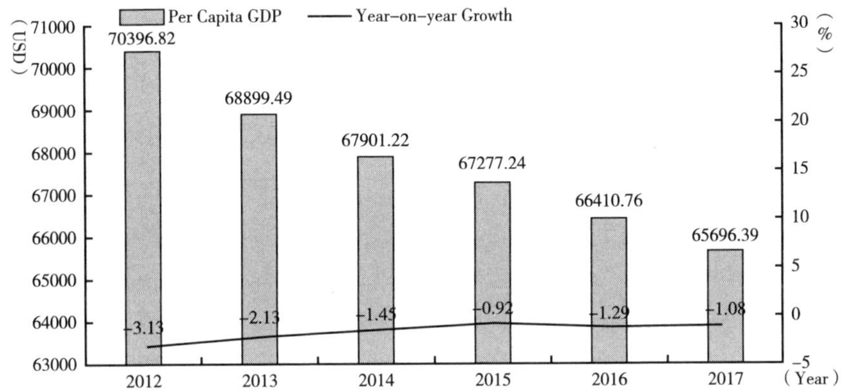

Figure 2.19 Per Capita GDP of Qatar and Its Growth Rate from 2012 to 2017

Data source: World Bank

Note: The per capita GDP and its growth rate are both calculated based on the fixed price USD of 2010.

2.2.6 Bahrain

Bahrain is the first country in the GCC to discover oil. Since the end of the 1970s, Bahrain has begun to implement a free and open economic policy, actively promoted the economic diversification strategy, and focused on the development of industries such as finance, trade, tourism and exhibitions, and reduced excessive dependence on

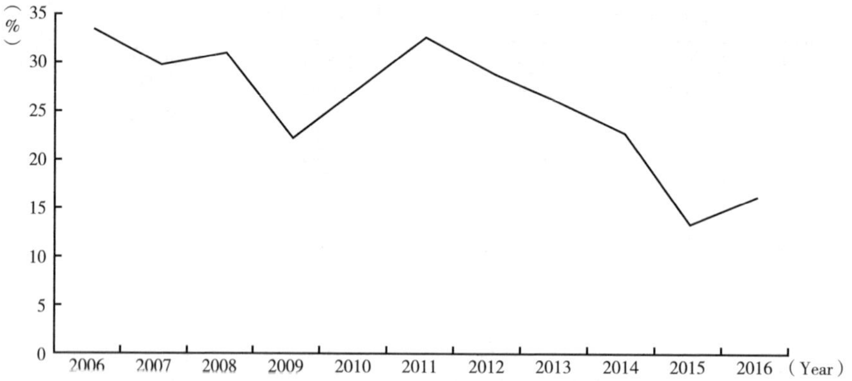

Figure 2.20 Petroleum Rent of Qatar from 2006 to 2016

Data source: same as the figure 2.4

the oil and gas industry. Currently, it has become one of the financial centers of the Gulf region. According to *the Global Competitiveness Report* 2017-2018, released by the World Economic Forum, Bahrain ranks 44th among the 137 countries and regions with the most competitiveness in the world. *Doing Business* released by the World Bank shows that Bahrain ranks 66th among the 190 economies in the world. ①

From the perspective of economic aggregates, Bahrain is in a small scale. In 2017, Bahrain's GDP was 35.307 billion USD, ranking 17th in the Middle East. Among them, the added value of the primary industry was 103 million USD, the added value of the secondary industry was 14.637 billion USD, and the added value of the tertiary industry was 20.568 billion USD. In terms of economic growth, 2017 increased by 3.88% compared with the previous year. Economic growth mainly relied on the promotion of non-oil industry, ranking eighth in the Middle East. In terms of economic structure, in 2017, the value added of Bahrain's primary industry accounted for only 0.29%. It shows that the scale of its agriculture is very small, mostly relying on imports. The added value of the secondary industry was 41.46%. Smelting and petrochemical are important industrial sectors of Bahrain. Petrochemical products, pellet iron ore, aluminum wire, aluminum plate and other resource products are their superior products; large mechanical and electrical products, textiles, building materials, home appliances and light industrial products are mainly imported. The

① Chinese Academy of International Trade and Economic Cooperation, etc., "A Guide to Foreign Investment and Cooperation by Country (Region)", *Bahrain (2018 Version)*.

added value of the tertiary industry was 58.25%, a decrease of 1.99 percentage points from the previous year. Due to the relatively open and relaxed social environment in Bahrain, the transportation is relatively convenient, and the service industries such as hotel catering, tourism and finance are relatively developed. There are more than 10 exhibitions of larger scale every year. At present, Bahrain has become an important exhibition center in the Middle East. From the perspective of economic benefits, the per capita GDP for the whole year was 22,111.48 USD, nearly 180 USD lower than the previous year, ranking 6th in the Middle East. From the perspective of an open economy, Bahrain's major trading partners include Saudi Arabia, China, the United States and the United Arab Emirates. Affected by the downturn in international oil prices, Bahrain's fiscal deficit has risen sharply. In 2017, the fiscal deficit accounted for more than 10% of GDP. As of the end of 2017, Bahrain's foreign exchange reserves were approximately 2.17 billion USD, and the public debt balance was 29.7 billion USD, accounting for 84% of GDP. In 2017, Bahrain's inflation rate was 1.4%.

From the perspective of reform and development, Bahrain has set up a special economic development conference for comprehensively formulating and supervising the implementation of Bahrain's economic development strategy, creating a good business environment to attract more foreign direct investment, and providing information consulting services for overseas investors. In recent years, the government has adopted a series of measures to increase revenues and reduce expenditures; on the other hand, it has further promoted economic transformation, especially the opportunities brought about by the digital process, and continuously promoted the development of the non-oil sector and the petroleum sector. Specifically, Bahrain is no willing to encourage heavy industrial enterprises coming in; its technological transformation will focus on five areas of finance, tourism, light industry, logistics and technology; in the next few years, the Bahrain government plans to upgrade some areas of infrastructure, and invest in a broader data ecosystem to help the new data industry cluster thrive.[①] The Bahrain government welcomes foreign investors to participate in local infrastructure investments. In terms of financing conditions, foreign-funded enterprises are required to enjoy the same treatment as local enterprises in Bahrain. In terms of taxation, Bahrain is a low-tax country, and the tax system is relatively simple. There is no income tax,

---

① Zhou Zhiyu," Digital Transformation of Bahrain Accelerated by Fluctuating Oil Price", *Commercial Economics Review*, 2018, Volume 12.

and the business cost is lower than the surrounding markets such as Dubai and Qatar. Only customs duties are imposed on imported goods. Investing in exclusive industrial zones can enjoy more favorable treatment, including cheap industrial land, preferential labor measures, and exemption of import tariffs on raw materials and equipment. Bahrain hopes to provide an environment of sustainable growth and fair competition that will put the economy on the right path.

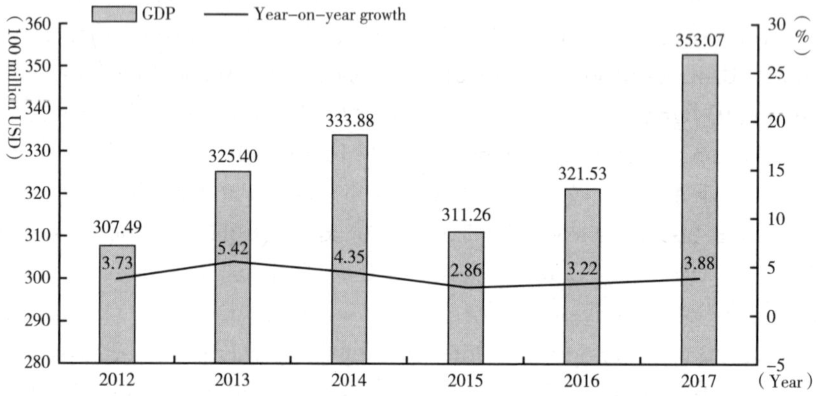

Figure 2.21 Bahrain's GDP and Its Growth Rate from 2012 to 2017

Data source: World Bank

Note: GDP is calculated based on the current price USD; the growth rate is calculated based on the fixed price USD of 2010.

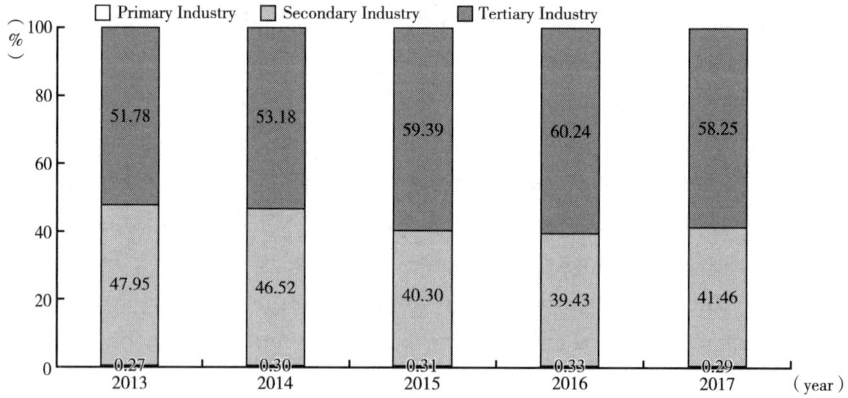

Figure 2.22 Proportion of Value Added of Three Industries in GDP of Bahrain from 2013 to 2017

Data source: World Bank, calculated on the current value of USD

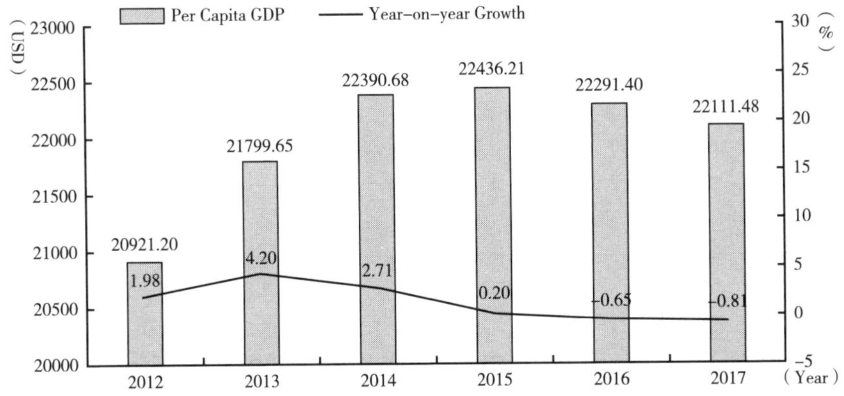

Figure 2.23 Per Capita GDP of Bahrain and Its Growth Rate from 2012 to 2017

Data source: World Bank

Note: The per capita GDP and its growth rate are both calculated based on the fixed price USD of 2010.

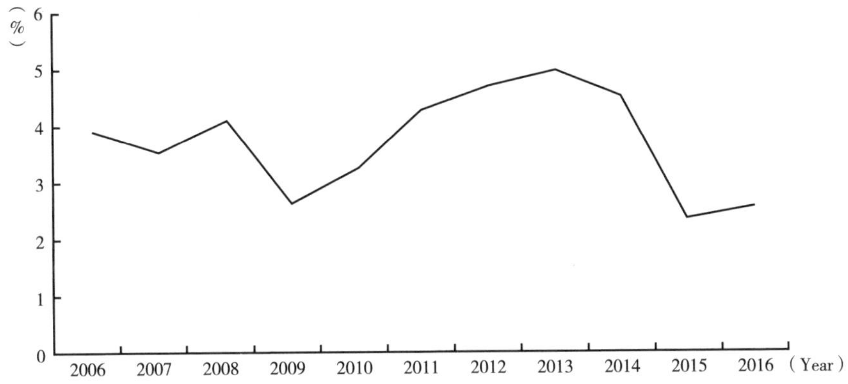

Figure 2.24 Petroleum Rent of Bahrain from 2006 to 2016

Data source: same as the figure 2.4

2.3 Economic Development of Traditional Regional Powers

2.3.1 Overview of Egypt's Economic Development

Egypt is one of the top 6 economies of the Middle East, and also an important traditional power of the region. As a key supporting country of the Middle East, its importance is not to be underestimated.

Table 2.2 Ranking of Egypt among Middle East Countries in Terms of Economic Development Indicator in 2017 (fixed price USD of 2010)

Countries	GDP		GDP growth rate		Per capita GDP	
	Amount (100 million USD)	Ranking	Growth Rate (%)	Ranking	Amount (USD/ person)	Ranking
Egypt	2717.22	6	4.18	5	2785.37	18

Data source: World Bank

Egypt has a big agricultural population and rich tourist resources, with tourist income being a major source of foreign exchange. Compared with other Middle East countries, Egypt has maintained a remarkable economic growth rate in recent years. However, domestic turbulence, high unemployment rate, and slow economic recovery are making economic development difficult. In terms of economic aggregate, in 2017, the GDP of Egypt was 235.369 billion USD and the economic scale shrank drastically, ranking the 6th place in the Middle East. Specifically, the value added of its primary industry, secondary industry and tertiary industry was respectively 27.033 billion USD, 79.439 billion USD and 128.897 billion USD. In terms of economic growth, the year-on-year growth rate of 2017 was 4.18%, ranking the 5th place in the Middle East. In terms of economic structure, it is still a developing country. In 2017, the proportion of the value added of its primary industry was 11.49%, and that of the secondary industry and the tertiary industry was respectively 33.75% and 54.76%. In terms of economic benefits, the comprehensive national strength of Egypt is growing constantly. The per capita GDP of the year was 2,785.37 USD, with a year-on-year increase of 2.19%, ranking the 18th place in the Middle East. The gross national income of the year was 230.9 billion USD. In terms of economic opening, in 2017, the total foreign trade volume of Egypt was 92.2 billion USD; the balance of current amount was -9.3 billion USD, showing a drop of its net foreign property. From the perspective of reform and development, the government of Egypt released the "2030 Vision of Egypt". At present, efforts are being concentrated on construction of economic and trade and investment cooperation projects that are closely related to livelihood. A great number of major projects have been launched one after another. However, according to *Global Competitiveness Report* 2017-2018 released by the World Economic Forum, Egypt ranks 128th out of 190 countries and regions. Furthermore, the ranking of cross-border trade, tax burden, and ability to perform are all after 160. This shows that Egypt needs to be improved on six major issues affecting the business environment, including policy sustainability, inflation, corruption, inefficient government and bureaucracy, low labor education, and financial market access.

2.3.2 Specific Indicators of Economic Development in Egypt

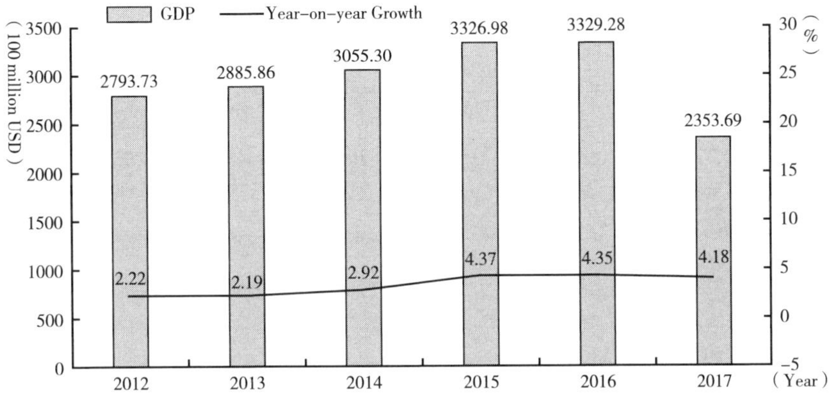

Figure 2.25 GDP of Egypt and Its Growth Rate from 2012 to 2017

Data source: World Bank

Note: GDP is calculated based on the current price USD; the growth rate is calculated based on the fixed price USD of 2010.

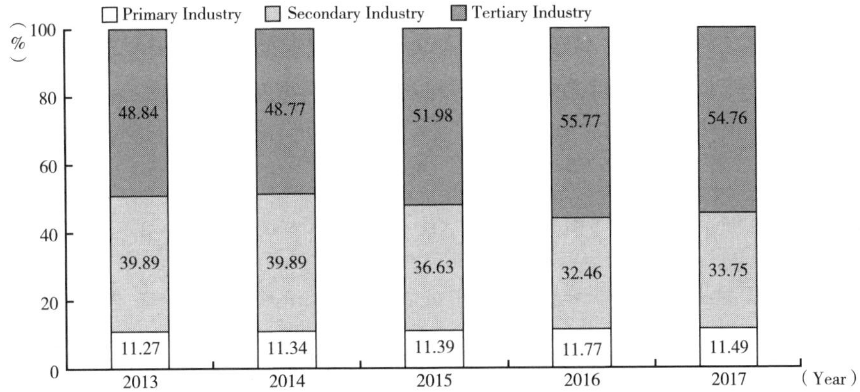

Figure 2.26 Proportion of Value Added of Three Industries in GDP of Egypt from 2013 to 2017

Data source: World Bank, obtained by calculation based on the current value of USD

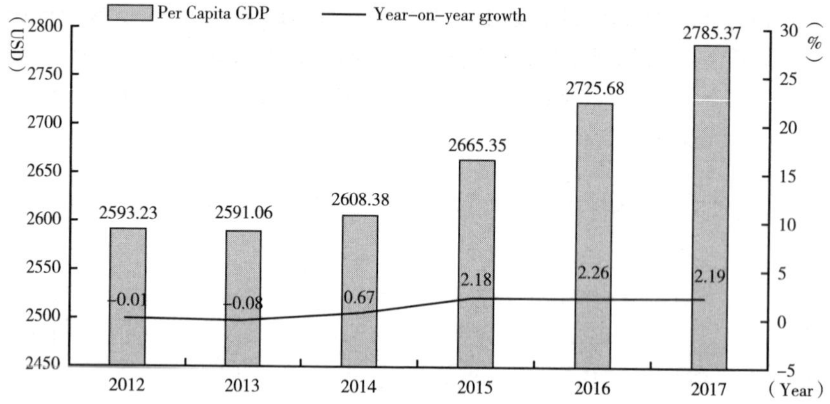

Figure 2.27 Per Capita GDP of Egypt and Its Growth Rate from 2012 to 2017

Data source: World Bank

Note: The per capita GDP and its growth rate are both calculated based on the fixed price USD of 2010.

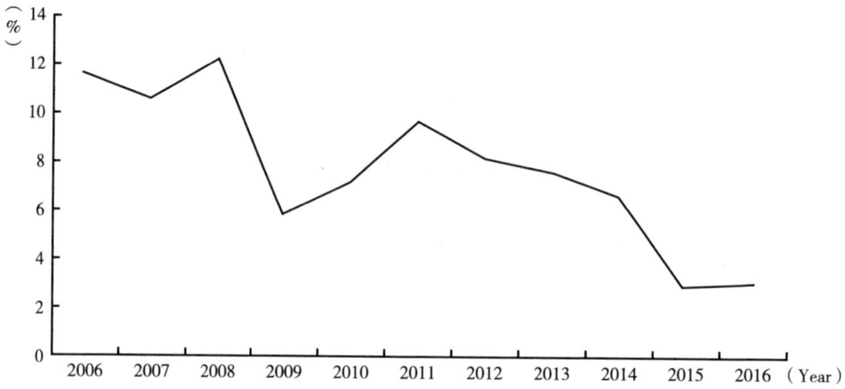

Figure 2.28 Petroleum Rent of Egypt from 2006 to 2016

Data source: same as the figure 2.4

2.4 Economic Development of Major North Africa Countries

Algeria and Morocco are two major developing countries of North Africa, with rich tourist resources and favorable geological locations, exerting influence on Europe, America, inland market of Africa and Arab world. These make them a desirable starting point for developing global trade. They have the potential to serve as the supporting point of the Belt and Road Initiative and insufficient importance has been attached to these two countries.

Table 2.3 Ranking of the Two Major Countries in Middle East Countries of 2017 in Terms of Economic Development Indicator (fixed price USD of 2010)

Country	GDP		GDP growth rate		Per capita GDP	
	Amount (100 million USD)	Ranking	Growth rate (%)	Ranking	Amount (USD/ person)	Ranking
Algeria	1714.67	8	1.70	15	4825.18	14
Morocco	1010.60	11	4.10	6	3292.45	16

Data source: World Bank

2.4.1 Algeria

The economic development of Algeria is lagging behind to a certain extent. In terms of economic growth, in 2017, its GDP was 170.371 billion USD, ranking the 8th place in the Middle East. In particular, the value added of the primary industry was 20.896 billion USD, and that of the secondary and tertiary industries was respectively 61.811 billion USD and 87.664 billion USD. In terms of economic growth rate, the year-on-year growth rate of 2017 was 1.7%, which was quite low, ranking the 15th place in the Middle East. In terms of economic structure, in 2017, the proportion of the value added of the primary industry was 12.26%, and that of the secondary industry and tertiary industry was respectively 36.28% and 51.46% (decreased by 1.37% year on year). Labor intensive industries are still accounting for a large proportion, and the industrial structure is not reasonable, entailing further adjustment. In terms of economic benefit, the per capita GDP of the year was 4,825.18 USD, dropping by 0.05% year on year, ranking the 14th place in the Middle East. The gross national income of the year was 167.9 billion USD. In terms of economic opening, in 2017, the total foreign trade volume was 81.2 billion USD; in 2016, the balance of current account was -26.2 billion USD, indicating a slight decrease of net foreign property. In terms of reform and development, the economic reform is currently being implemented, and efforts are being concentrated on industries such as petrochemical engineering, light industry and tourism. Measures such as industrial diversification and privatization are being taken in an effort to boost economic development. In particular, cooperation with foreign capital has been strengthened in areas such as petroleum, natural gas, power, communication and housing, so as to achieve a win-win result on the basis of equality and reciprocity. Furthermore, the overall investment environment of Algeria is discouraging. It takes both time and efforts to handle procedures related to banking, customs, taxation and visa, posing considerable constraints on economic and trade activities of foreign investors in Algeria. At present, the import payment ways have been expanded and domestic infrastructure construction has been enhanced. A new regulation designed to promote investment has also been introduced. Implementation of this regulation is part of the development strategy of Algeria. It aims to revitalize economy by improving the overall business environment of the country and reduce import quantity and improves export diversity by attracting direct investment from foreign investors. According to the new regulation on investment introduced by Algeria, investment projects are entitled to tax reduction and exemption to different extents depending on their geological location and contribution to the economic and social development of Algeria; extra preference is given to investment projects in prioritized development areas and those creating jobs; special subsidy is granted to investment projects with great significance to the national economic development. The constantly improving domestic environment is to bring about a more favorable investment environment for foreign investors in Algeria.①

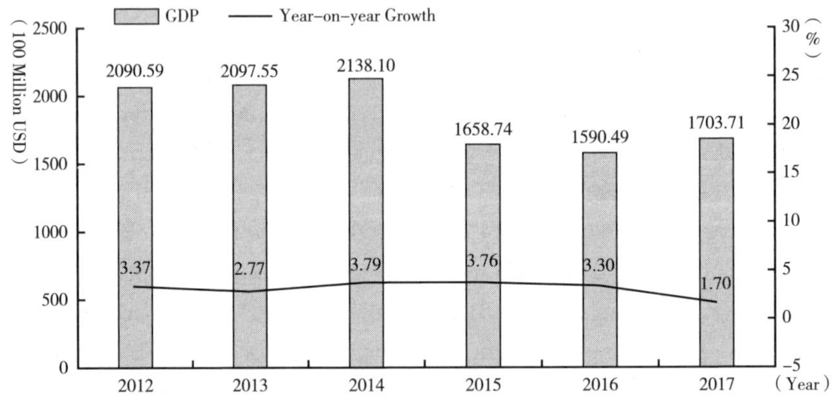

Figure 2.29 Algeria's GDP and Its Growth Rate from 2012 to 2017

Data source: World Bank

Note: GDP is calculated based on the current price USD; the growth rate is calculated based on the fixed price USD of 2010.

① Abudenu Helifei and Wang Xiaobo, "*Investment Guide for Algeria*", *China Investment*, 2017, Volume 20.

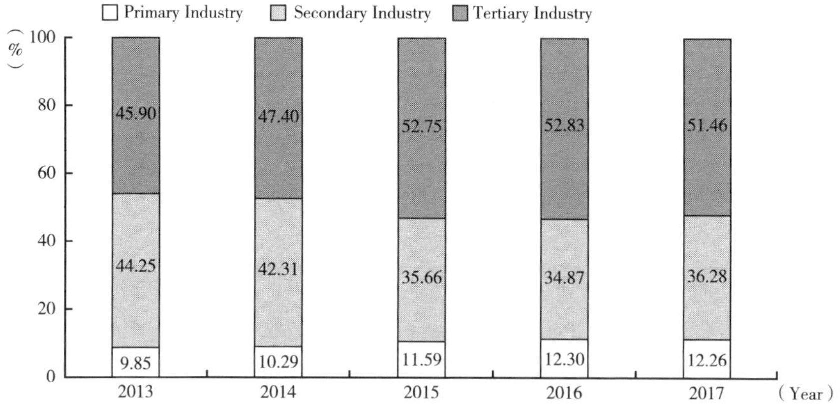

Figure 2.30 Proportion of Value Added of Three Industries in GDP of Algeria from 2013 to 2017

Data source: World Bank, obtained by calculation based on the current value of USD

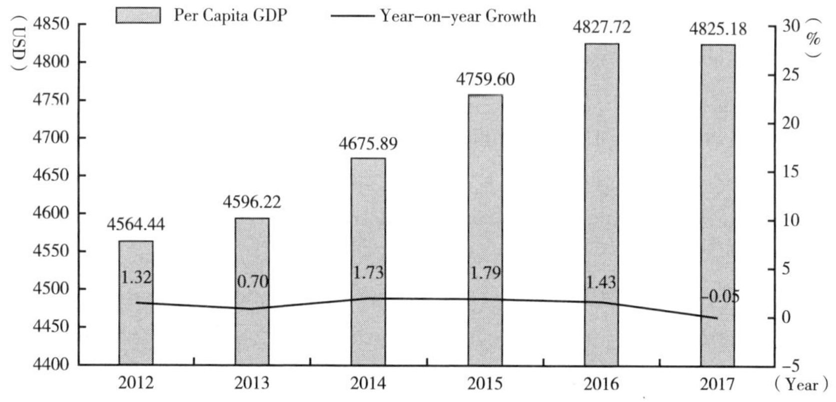

Figure 2.31 Per Capita GDP of Algeria and Its Growth Rate from 2012 to 2017

Data source: World Bank

Note: The per capita GDP and its growth rate are both calculated based on the fixed price USD of 2010.

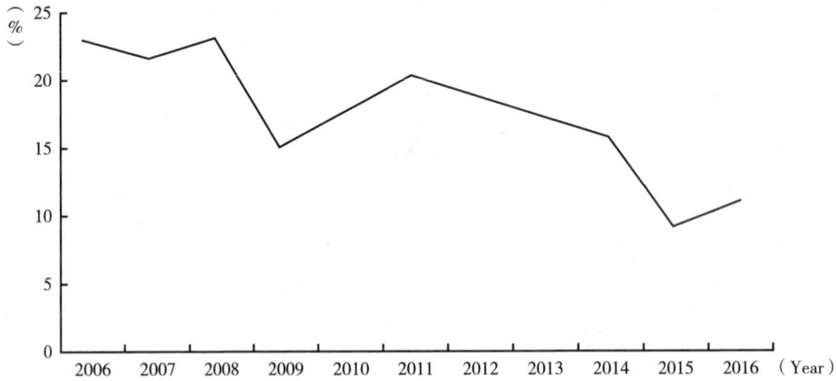

Figure 2.32 Petroleum Rent of Algeria from 2006 to 2016

Data source: same as the figure 2.4

2.4.2 Morocco

Unlike other Gulf countries with exceptional advantages in petroleum resources, Morocco has an unfavorable economic development condition. Its economy is dominated by agriculture, and is sustained by relying on export of raw materials and primary agricultural products. In the past 6 years, the economy of Morocco has seen steady and positive development, with an average annual growth rate of 2.13%. In terms of economic growth, the overall scale is small. In 2017, the GDP of Morocco was 109.139 billion USD, ranking the 11th place in the Middle East. Specifically, the value added of the primary industry was 14.25 billion USD, and that of the secondary and tertiary industries was respectively 27.913 billion USD and 66.977 billion USD. In terms of economic growth rate, the year-on-year growth rate of 2017 was 4.1%, ranking the 6th place in the Middle East, which was among top ones throughout Asia. It was also higher than the global GDP growth rate, making it one of the countries on the African Continent with promising economic development. In terms of economic structure, in 2017, the proportion of value added of the primary industry was 13.06%. That of the secondary and tertiary industries was respectively 25.58% and 61.36%, an industrial structure predominated by the service industry. However, it is still an agricultural country. In terms of economic benefit, its strength has been enhancing constantly. The per capita GDP of the year was 3,292.5 USD, with a year-on-year growth of 2.73%, ranking the 16th in the Middle East. The gross national income of the year was 107.1 billion USD. From the perspective of economic opening, in 2016, the total foreign trade volume of Morocco was 64.6 billion USD. The exported commodities mainly included minerals, air-crafts, spacecrafts and their parts and components, as well as premium agricultural products, livestock and fishery products; the balance of current account in 2017 was 3.95 billion USD, with surplus. From the perspective of reform and development, in recent years, Morocco has been actively implementing enterprise privatization and liberalization of trade, and has increased investment in infrastructure. Many major projects in areas such as telecommunication, road, water supply and dams are initiated every year. An increasing number of satellite towns are under construction, indicating huge project contracting market potential. This has also mitigated the unemployment of Morocco, and contributed to development of related industries of Morocco like warehousing, transportation and import & export. According to the *African Economic Outlook* of 2017, Morocco has become the African country with the greatest investment appeal, and is also one of the top 5 African countries in terms of investments abroad.

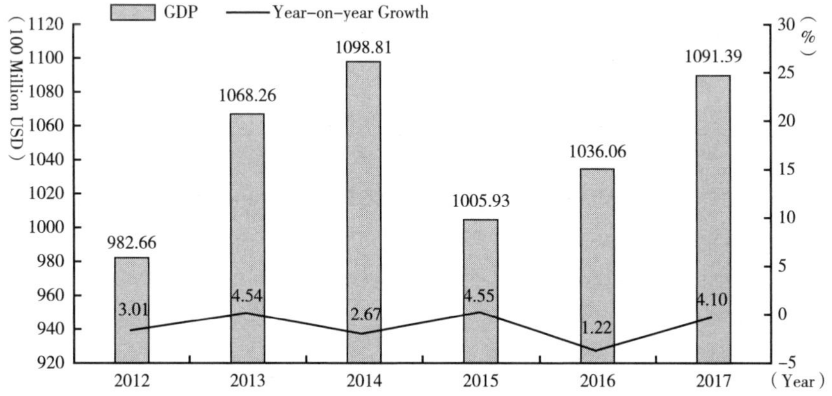

Figure 2.33 Morocco's GDP and Its Growth Rate from 2012 to 2017

Data source: World Bank

Note: GDP is calculated based on the current price USD; the growth rate is calculated based on the fixed price USD of 2010.

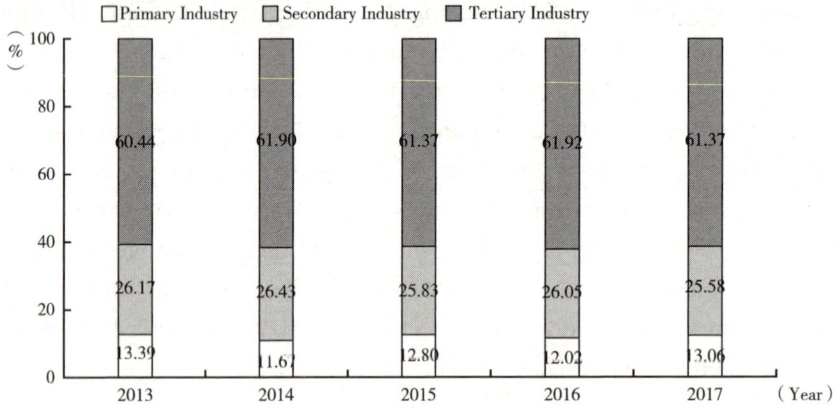

Figure 2.34 Proportion of Value Added of Three Industries in GDP of Morocco from 2013 to 2017

Data source: World Bank, obtained by calculation based on the current value of USD

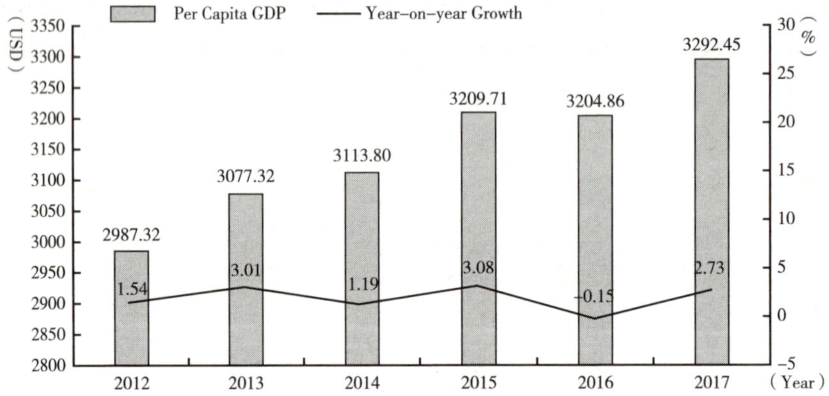

Figure 2.35 Per Capita GDP of Morocco and Its Growth Rate from 2012 to 2017

Data source: World Bank

Note: The per capita GDP and its growth rate are both calculated based on the fixed price USD of 2010.

Chapter 3 Special Report on Economic and Trade Cooperation between China and Arab States

In 2017, with steady recovery of global economy and rise of economic growth rate, the post-crisis profound adjustment stage was brought to an end. According to data released by the World Bank, the global economic growth rate was over 3% in 2017. The world economy is seeing better days. Despite the many risks and challenges facing global economy against the recovery of world economic growth rate, such as protectionism and prevailing reverse globalization trend and excessively high global debt level, countries are pushing forward the global macroeconomic policy coordination and responding actively to those risks and challenges. In particular, the initiative proposed by China to establish the new-type international relations and build the community with shared future for mankind has been well received by people of many countries. China has pointed out the direction of economic globalization. The Belt and Road Initiative put forward by China serves as a platform for exploring new spaces and areas for international cooperation, and provides motive force for economic development of countries along the Belt and Road.

The United States has announced its decision to quit the *Trans-Pacific Partnership Agreement* (TPP), and the negotiation between the US and the EU with respect to the Transatlantic Trade and Investment Partnership (TTIP), and that between the United States and China with respect to the *Bilateral Investment Treaty* (BIT) have come to a halt. Furthermore, countries all over the world are stoking the fire of protectionism. Nonetheless, according to the data released by World Trade Organization (WTO), the growth rate of total world goods export turned from a negative one to a positive one. The growth of international trade was reflected by rise in both price and quantity.

Given the above facts, China and Arab states have overcome a number of difficulties in their economic and trade cooperation, and the cooperation level has improved to a certain extent. This has contributed positively to the Belt and Road construction, and laid a solid foundation for the two to achieve a win-win result and build a community of shared future.

3.1 Basic Information on China's Foreign Arab States: Trade with Arab States

3.1.1 Basic Information on China's Foreign Trade

In 2017, China saw an economic growth rate as high as 6.9%, contributing to 15% of the world economy. In 2015 and 2016, there had been consecutive decrease of total export-import volume of China (the total export-import volume of 2015 tumbled to less than 4 billion USD, with a reduction rate of 8.35%; in 2016, the drop continued, and the total export-import volume was only 3,685.558 billion USD). However, in 2017, the total export-import volume of China reversed the downward trend and went up to 3,974.795 billion USD, with a year-on-year growth rate of 7.85%. In particular, the amount of exports reached 2,263.371 billion USD, increasing by 7.9% year on year; the amount of imports reached 1,711.424 billion USD, increasing by 7.78% year on year. Moreover, the balance of trace continued to be favorable, with a volume of favorable balance of 551.947 billion USD.

As for the position of China in international trade, the China's total export-import volume of China accounted for 17.6% of the world's trade volume in 2007. In 2010, this figure went up to 21.7%. Then in 2017, it raised again to 25.2%. As for export, the export volume of China became the world No. 1 in 2010, exceeding that of the United States, Germany and Japan; China's export volume accounted for 12.3% of the world's total exports. In 2017, the export volume of China accounted for an even larger part in the world's trade volume, reaching 13.96%. As for import, the import volume of China ranked the 3rd place in 2010, after only the United States and Germany, accounting for 6.7% of the world's total. In 2017, China ranked the 2nd place in terms of import volume in the world, second only to the United States. Its import volume accounted for 7.07% of the world's total import volume. The above data indicate that China has been gaining more prominence in international trade.

Table 3.1 China's Foreign Trade Volume and Its Growth Rate from 2010 to 2017

Index / Year	Import and export		Export		Import		Balance of trade	
	Total amount (100 million) USD) (%)	Year-on-year change (%)	Amount (100 million USD) (%)	Year-on-year change (%)	Amount (100 million USD) (%)	Year-on-year change (%)	Amount (100 million USD)	Year-on-year change (%)
2010	28668.98	35.18	15777.64	31.30	12891.34	40.25	2886.30	2.17
2011	35191.68	22.75	18983.88	20.32	16207.8	25.73	2776.08	-3.82
2012	37240.51	5.82	20487.82	7.92	16752.69	3.36	3735.13	34.55
2013	40014.58	7.45	22090.07	7.82	17924.51	6.99	4165.56	11.52
2014	41566.47	3.88	23422.93	6.03	18143.54	1.22	5279.39	26.74
2015	38096.63	-8.35	22734.68	-2.94	15361.95	-15.33	7372.73	39.65
2016	36855.58	-3.26	20976.37	-7.73	15879.21	3.37	5097.16	-30.86
2017	39747.95	7.85	22633.71	7.90	17114.24	7.78	5519.47	8.29

Data scurce: Obtained by calculation and reorganization based on data in the International Trade Database of the United Nations

Note: Taking China as the reporting state.

3.1.2 Basic Information on Foreign Trade of Arab States

The overall situation in the Middle East continued to be complicated in 2017, reflected by frequent security issues. However, thanks to steady rise of petroleum price, there was a slight rise in export trade volume of Arab states, ending the downward trend of export volume observed since 2014 due to factors such as drop in the petroleum price. In 2017, the export volume of Arab states reached 674.4687 billion USD, increasing by 7.67% year on year. Even so, the Arab states' export volume still failed to recover to its above-1-trillion USD level of 2012. Furthermore, the import volume of Arab States dropped further to 609.374 billion USD, with a decrease rate of 9.63%. This has mainly resulted from the fiscal contractions caused by the slowdown of fiscal revenue and economic growth of Arab States. The total import-export volume of Arab states was 1,283.843 billion USD, with a slight year-on-year drop. In 2010, the export volume of Arab States accounted for 5.71% of the world's total export volume. In 2017, this figure lowered to 4.59%. In 2010, the import volume of Arab States accounted for 3.73% of the worlds' total. Then in 2017, this figure rose to 3.86%. Generally speaking, there has been little change of Arab States' position in international trade.

3.2 China's Foreign Trade with Arab States

3.2.1 Scale and Growth Rate of China-Arab States Bilateral Trade

In 2017, there was a moderate rise of bilateral trade volume of China, reaching 191.757 billion USD, with a growth rate of 12.12%. Specifically, China's export to Arab States was 98.673 billion USD, dropping by 1.99%. China's export from Arab states reached 93.084 billion USD, increasing by 32.30%. There was a balance of trade (export minus import) of 5.589 billion USD, 24.729 billion USD less than that of the previous year. This indicates that the balance of trade between China and Arab states was reducing, considerably (See Table 3.3 and Figure 3.1). In 2016, Arab states were the 7th largest exporter to China. China's imports from Arab states accounted for 4.43% of the total import volume. Arab states were the 5th largest importer from China, accounting for 4.80% of the total, following the United States, EU, Hong Kong and Japan. In 2017, Arab States were the 7th largest exporter of China, accounting for 5.44% of the total, following the EU, South Korea, Japan, the United States, Germany and Australia. Arab States were the 6th largest importer from China, accounting for 4.4% of the total, following, EU, Korea, Japan the United States ,Germany and Australia.

Table 3.2 Arab States' Foreign Trade Volume and Its Growth Rate from 2010 to 2017

Index / Year	Import and export		Export		Import		Balance of trade	
	Total amount (100 million USD)	Year-on-year change (%)	Amount (100 million USD) (%)	Year-on-year change (%)	Amount (100 million USD) (%)	Year-on-year change (%)	Amount (100 million USD) (%)	Year-on-year change (%)
2010	13439.29	24.02	7960.126	34.32	5479.169	11.59	2480.957	144.16
2011	17392.17	29.41	10906.28	37.01	6485.896	18.37	4420.379	78.17
2012	19446.23	11.81	12289.56	12.68	7156.672	10.34	5132.887	16.12
2013	19903.86	2.35	12088.3	-1.64	7815.563	9.21	4272.736	-16.76
2014	19208.59	-3.49	11205.41	-7.30	8003.181	2.40	3202.229	-25.05
2015	14392.32	-25.07	7090.995	-36.72	7301.324	-8.77	-210.329	-106.57
2016	13007.05	-9.63	6264.124	-11.66	6742.926	-7.65	-478.802	-127.64
2017	12838.43	-1.30	6744.687	7.67	6093.74	-9.63	650.947	235.95

Data source: Obtained by calculation and reorganization based on data in the International Trade Database of the United Nations

Note: There is no data with Arab country as the reporting country. As such, all countries in the world are regarded as reporting countries for the purpose of the table.

Table 3.3 Overall Condition of Trade between China and Arab States from 2010 to 2017

Index / Year	Import and export		Export		Import		Balance of trade	
	Total amount (100 million USD)	Year-on-year change (%)	Amount (100 million USD) (%)	Year-on-year change (%)	Amount (100 million USD) (%)	Year-on-year change (%)	Amount (100 million USD) (%)	Year-on-year change (%)
2010	1368.58	34.37	629.37	16.00	739.21	55.32	-109.83	-264.77
2011	1843.58	34.71	758.61	20.53	1084.96	46.77	-326.35	197.13
2012	2224.20	20.65	912.79	20.32	1311.41	20.87	-398.62	22.14
2013	2388.97	7.41	1013.52	11.03	1375.45	4.88	-361.93	-9.20
2014	2510.51	5.09	1138.21	12.30	1372.30	-0.23	-234.09	-35.32
2015	2025.41	-19.32	1150.40	1.07	875.01	-36.24	275.38	-217.64
2016	1710.29	-15.56	1006.74	-12.49	703.56	-19.59	303.18	10.09
2017	1917.57	12.12	986.73	-1.99	930.84	32.30	55.89	-81.57

Classification basis: HS3

Data source: Obtained by calculation and reorganization based on data in the International Trade Database of the United Nations

Note: Taking China as the reporting state.

Table 3.4 Ranking of Major Import and Export Trade Partners of China in 2016 and 2017

Ranking	Countries and regions	China's export to various countries in 2016 (100 million USD)	Proportion (%)	Countries and regions	China's import from various countries in 2016 (100 million USD)	Proportion (%)
1	The United States	3856.78	18.39	EU (27 countries)	2079.82	13.10
2	EU (27 countries)	3383.06	16.13	South Korea	1589.75	10.01
3	Hong Kong	2872.52	13.69	Japan	1456.71	9.17
4	Japan	1292.68	6.16	USA	1351.20	8.51
5	Arab League	1006.74	4.80	Germany	861.09	5.42
6	South Korea	937.07	4.47	Australia	708.95	4.46
7	Germany	652.14	3.11	Arab League	703.56	4.43
Ranking	Countries and regions	China's export to various countries in 2017 (100 million USD)	Proportion (%)	Countries and regions	China's import from various countries in 2017 (100 million USD)	Proportion (%)
1	The United States	4303.28	19.01	EU (27 countries)	2447.95	14.30
2	EU (27 countries)	3711.73	16.40	South Korea	1775.53	10.37
3	Hong Kong	2792.11	12.34	Japan	1657.94	9.69
4	Japan	1372.59	6.06	USA	1544.42	9.02
5	South Korea	1027.04	4.54	Germany	969.40	5.66
6	Arab League	986.73	4.36	Australia	950.09	5.55
7	Vietnam	716.17	3.16	Arab League	930.84	5.44

Classification basis: HS3

Data source: Obtained by calculation and reorganization based on data in the International Trade Database of the United Nations

Note: Taking China as the reporting state.

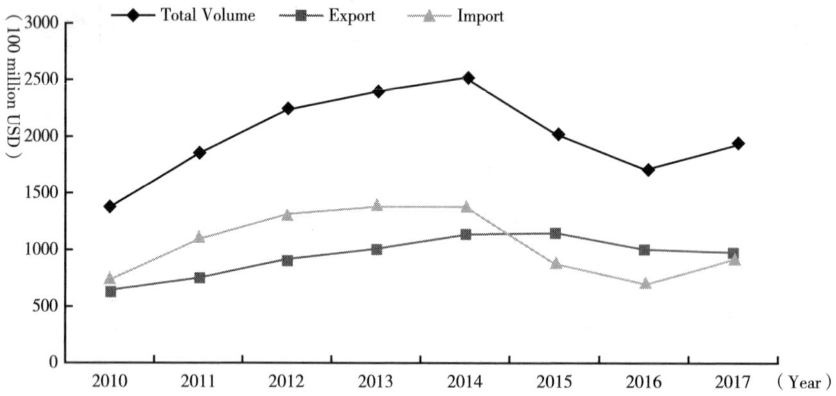

Figure 3.1 Trend of Trade between China and Arab States from 2010 to 2017

As shown in Figure 3.1, there was an overall trend of rapid growth of bilateral trade between China and Arab States during 2010 and 2014. In 2014, the bilateral trade volume in 2014 was 251.051 billion USD, the highest level during this period. In 2015, the bilateral trade volume dropped drastically by nearly 50 billion USD. This downward trend was not reversed until 2017. In 2017, there was a remarkable recovery of import volume, which drove up the total bilateral trade volume.

3.2.2 Basic Information on Import and Export between China and Major Trade Partners in Arab States

As shown in Table 3.4, the largest trade partner of China in Arab States in 2017 was Saudi Arabia, with a trade volume of 50.137 billion USD, followed by UAE, with a trade volume of 41.035 billion USD. The 2nd through 8th places were respectively Iraq, Oman, Kuwait, Egypt, Qatar and Algeria. In particular, the trade volume between China and Iraq, Oman, Kuwait and Egypt exceeded 10 billion USD, being respectively 22.144 billion USD, 15.699 billion USD, 12.048 billion USD and 10.828 billion USD. In the largest 10 trade partners, the one with the greatest growth rate of trade volume with China was Qatar, with growth rate of 46.2%, followed by Kuwait and Iraq, being respectively 28.56% and 21.60%. In terms of export, China's export to UAE was the highest, being 28.724 billion USD, followed by Saudi Arabia, being 18.375 billion USD. The third and fourth places were respectively Egypt and Iraq, being respectively 9.486 billion USD and 8.33 billion USD. The one with the greatest growth rate was Qatar, being 11%, followed by Iraq with a growth rate of 10.37%. In terms of import, the largest exporter to China in the region was Saudi Arabia. In 2017, the import volume was 31.762 billion USD, followed by Iraq, Oman, UAE and Kuwait, with import volume of 13.814 billion USD, 13.383 billion USD, 12.311 billion USD and 8.935 billion USD respectively. China's import from these 5 countries accounted for as much as 86.16% of the total import from Arab states. This was mainly because that China's import from Arab States involved mainly crude oil, and these 5 countries were important crude oil exporters to China. It should be noted that almost all of them, except for UAE, have a trade surplus with China.

Generally speaking, compared with that in 2016, there was only a little change of foreign trade between China and its main trade partners in Arab states. However, growth rate of import and export indeed changed. In 2016, there was negative growth of both import and export between China and its seven largest trade partners. However, in 2017, only the trade with Egypt saw negative growth. The trade with other countries all saw positive growth.

The six countries of the Gulf Cooperation Council were still the largest regional trade partner of China in the Arab world. In 2017, the bilateral trade volume between China and the Gulf Cooperation Council states was 128.018 billion USD, accounting for 66.76% of the total trade volume between China and Arab states. There was a slight increase compared with that of 2016, which was 112.4 billion USD. The proportion also increased by 1 percentage point.

Table 3.5 Condition of China's Main Trade Partners in Arab World in 2017

S/N	Country	Amount (100 million USD)			Year-on-year growth (%)		
		Import and export	Import	Export	Import and export	Import	Export
1	Saudi Arabia	501.37	183.75	317.62	18.59	-1.48	34.44
2	UAE	410.35	287.24	123.11	2.43	-4.47	23.18
3	Iraq	221.44	83.30	138.14	21.60	10.37	29.55
4	Oman	156.99	23.16	133.83	10.64	7.86	11.15
5	Kuwait	120.48	31.13	89.35	28.56	3.73	40.26
6	Egypt	108.28	94.86	13.42	-1.47	-9.11	142.57
7	Qatar	80.82	16.82	64.00	46.20	11.00	59.51

Continued

S/N	Country	Amount (100 million USD)			Year-on-year growth (%)		
		Import and export	Import	Export	Import and export	Import	Export
8	Algeria	72.33	67.85	4.48	-9.36	-11.29	35.08
9	Morocco	38.27	31.76	6.51	5.36	3.17	17.55
10	Jordan	30.83	28.04	2.79	-2.61	-5.10	32.21
11	Sudan	28.13	22.22	5.91	6.78	4.32	17.06
12	Yemen	23.03	16.43	6.60	23.93	-2.91	297.50
13	Djibouti	21.75	21.75	0.00	1.23	1.26	-88.44
14	Lebanon	20.34	20.11	0.23	-3.97	-4.27	30.37
15	Tunisia	15.26	13.28	1.98	6.36	2.48	42.72

Classification basis: HS3

Data source: Obtained by calculation and reorganization based on data in the International Trade Database of the United Nations

Note: Taking China as the reporting state.

3.2.3 Structure of China-Arab States Bilateral Trade

There has always been substantial trade complementarity between China and Arab States due to the resource endowment, industrial structure and industrial system of the two.

According to the United Nations Conference on Trade and Development, traded goods are divided into four categories, namely, raw materials, intermediate goods, consumer goods and capital goods. Such classification could specifically reflect the trade relations between countries, and their positions in international division of labor and industrial structure.

Statistical analysis of the bilateral trade structure between China and Arab states is then conducted based on the above classification. In 2017, the export of China to Arab states mainly involved consumer goods and capital goods, with export volume of 46.42 billion USD and 31.008 billion USD respectively. The two categories accounted for 78.46% of the total export. Both the export volume and proportion increased compared with those in 2009. In particular, the export volume increased by more than 2 times. However, the raw material export of China to Arab states was only 1.169 billion USD, accounting for 1.19%. This indicates that China's export to

Arab states focused on finished products. As for import, raw materials accounted for the largest proportion in imports of China from Arab states. In 2017, the import volume was 64.481 billion USD, increasing by over 1 time compared with that of 2009, accounting for 69.27% of the total imports of China from Arab states. Furthermore, the China's intermediate goods import from Arab states ranked the second place, with an import volume of 17.03 billion USD, accounting for 18.30%. The import of consumer goods and capital goods of China from Arab states accounted for 12.02% and 0.40% respectively of the total imports. The same trade pattern was seen in the bilateral trade between China and Arab states in 2016. There was little change in 2017. This indicates that the bilateral trade structure between China and Arab states has been comparatively stable in recent years.

Table 3.6 Trade Structure of Major Goods Categories between China and Arab States

UNCTAD Categories	Trade Volume and Proportion	2009	2016	2017
Raw material	Export Volume (100 million USD)	7.08	11.52	11.69
	Proportion (%)	1.31	1.14	1.19
	Import Volume (100 million USD)	387.97	494.82	644.81
	Proportion (%)	81.52	70.33	69.27
Intermediate products	Export Volume (100 million USD)	107.86	194.60	191.86
	Proportion (%)	19.88	19.33	19.44
	Import volume (100 million USD)	62.05	127.95	170.30
	Proportion (%)	13.04	18.19	18.30
Consumer products	Export Volume (100 million USD)	232.62	492.37	464.20
	Proportion (%)	42.87	48.91	47.04
	Import volume (100 million USD)	23.44	77.38	111.87
	Proportion (%)	4.93	11.00	12.02
Capital products	Export Volume (100 million USD)	191.30	299.58	310.08
	Proportion (%)	35.26	29.76	31.42
	Import Volume (100 million USD)	2.18	3.24	3.69
	Proportion (%)	0.46	0.46	0.40

Classification basis: HS3

Data source: Obtained by calculation and reorganization based on data in the International Trade Database of the United Nations

Goods classification: Based on the classification criteria of United Nations Conference on Trade and Development

Note: Taking China as the reporting state.

Based on more specific product classification, in 2017, the main products imported by China from Arab states were mechanical equipment and electrical products, textiles and clothing and metal products. Their export volume accounted for a large proportion in the total export volume, being respectively 32.35%, 18.22% and 11.94%. The proportion of the three major categories exceeded 60%. In addition, China also exported miscellaneous products, transportation equipment, plastics and rubber products, mineral and glass and chemical products to Arab states. Compared with the export structure of 2009, there was only a slight change in 2017, with only apparent change of the ranking of the transportation equipment, dropping from the 5th place in 2009 to the 7th place in 2017. Compared with that in 2016, the export structure remained basically the same in 2017, with only moderate increase or decrease of export volumes of the categories. Generally speaking, the structure of China's export to Arab states has been relatively stable.

Table 3.7 Structure of Goods Export from China to Arab States in 2017

Product code	Major product categories	Export volume of 2009 (100 million USD)	Export volume of 2016 (100 million USD)	Export volume of 2017 (100 million USD)	Proportion in the total export volume in 2017 (%)
84-85	Mechanical equipment and electrical products	183.06	312.02	319.16	32.35
50-63	Textiles and clothing	102.98	192.18	179.74	18.22
72-83	Metal products	63.37	122.61	117.85	11.94
90-99	Miscellaneous products	41.40	92.22	95.74	9.70
86-89	Transportation equipment	32.32	42.79	36.52	3.70
39-40	Plastics and rubber products	25.32	57.59	59.15	5.99
68-71	Minerals and glass	24.18	48.22	42.06	4.26
28-38	Chemical products	16.23	31.64	33.16	3.36
64-67	Shoes and boots	15.85	34.05	32.71	3.31

Continued

Product code	Major product categories	Export volume of 2009 (100 million USD)	Export volume of 2016 (100 million USD)	Export volume of 2017 (100 million USD)	Proportion in the total export volume in 2017 (%)
44-49	Wood and wood products	10.39	27.74	25.00	2.53
06-15	Vegetables	8.19	11.60	11.56	1.17
41-43	Leather and fur products	7.75	15.63	15.17	1.54
16-24	Food	5.02	7.88	8.50	0.86
27-27	Mineral fuel and oil	4.00	7.28	6.90	0.70
25-26	Mineral products	1.37	1.40	1.36	0.14
01-05	Animal products	1.14	1.89	2.14	0.22

Classification basis: HS3

Data source: Obtained by calculation and reorganization based on data in the International Trade Database of the United Nations

Note: Taking China as the reporting state.

In 2017, the structure of goods import of China from Arab states remained basically the same as that in 2016, and was relatively stable. Mineral fuel and oil still ranked the first place in terms of import volume, being 73.21 billion USD, accounting for 78.65% of the total import volume. Chemical products ranked the second place, with import volume of 8.127 billion USD, accounting for 8.73%. The third place was plastics and rubber products, with import volume of 7.54 billion USD, accounting for 8.10%. The import volume of other products was relatively low, and so were their proportions. Such a trade structure indicates that the industrial structure of Arab States is monotonous, with petroleum industry as the supporting industry. The manufacturing industry and agriculture are both weak and the industrial system is in need of improvement.

Table 3.8 Composition of Goods Imported by China from Arab States in 2017

Product code	Major product categories	Import volume of 2009 (100 million USD)	Import volume of 2016 (100 million USD)	Import volume of 2017 (100 million USD)	Proportion in the total import volume in 2017 (%)
27-27	Mineral fuel and oil	396.14	553.04	732.10	78.65
28-38	Chemical products	35.28	58.94	81.27	8.73
39-40	Plastics and rubber products	21.75	57.09	75.40	8.10
25-26	Mineral products	12.67	18.18	22.11	2.38
72-83	Metal products	5.65	4.19	4.82	0.52
84-85	Mechanical equipment and electrical products	2.16	3.33	3.92	0.42
06-15	Vegetables	0.27	1.99	3.53	0.38
50-63	Textiles and clothing	1.15	2.92	3.48	0.37
16-24	Food	0.01	0.49	1.47	0.16
68-71	Minerals and glass	0.40	2.24	1.24	0.13
41-43	Leather and fur products	0.20	0.30	0.44	0.05
44-49	Wood and wood products	0.04	0.06	0.32	0.03
90-99	Miscellaneous products	0.06	0.30	0.31	0.03
01-05	Animal products	0.10	0.28	0.23	0.02
86-89	Transportation equipment	0.01	0.10	0.16	0.02
64-67	Shoes and boots	0.04	0.11	0.04	0.00

Classification basis: HS3

Data source: Obtained by calculation and reorganization based on data in the International Trade Database of the United Nations

Note: Taking China as the reporting state.

Ever since the 21st Century, energy cooperation between China and Arab states has been a critical part of the trade cooperation between the two. Arab states have always been important exporters of crude oil to China. In 2007, the

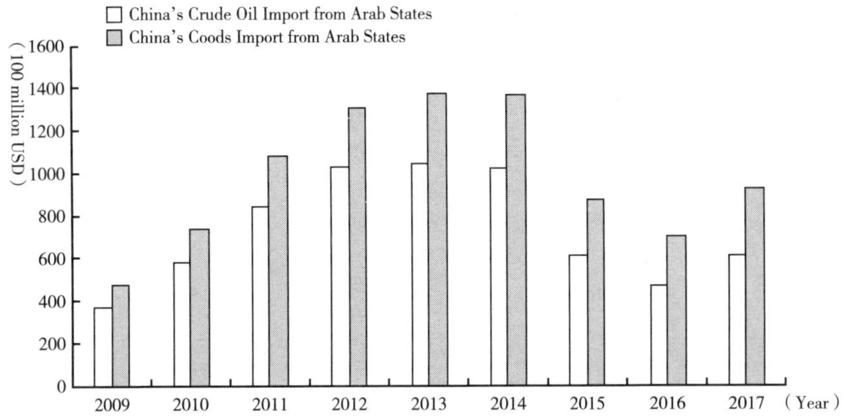

Figure 3.2 Trade Volume of China's Crude Oil Import from Arab States and Total Import Volume from 2009 to 2017

Classification basis: HS2003

Data source: WITS database

import volume of crude oil of China was 79.858 billion USD. Specifically, the import from Arab states was 28.666 billion USD, accounting for 35.90% of the total imports. The crude oil import of China in 2016 was 116.661 billion USD, including export from Arab States of 47.304 billion USD, accounting for 40.55% of the total import, a drastic increase compared with that in the previous year. China's crude oil import was 163.821 billion USD in 2017, including import of 61.611 billion USD from Arab States, accounting for 37.61%, showing a slight drop.

In 2009, in the ten largest crude oil exporters to China, there were 6 Arab states, including Saudi Arabia, Oman, Sudan, Iraq, Libya and Kuwait. In particular, Saudi Arabia ranked the first place in Arab states. In 2016, there was noticeable change of this import pattern, with Russia replacing Saudi Arabia as the No. 1 exporter of crude oil to China. Iraq also rose from the 7th place to the 5th place. The Largest ten Arab exporters of crude oil to China were Saudi Arabia, Oman, Iraq, Kuwait and UAE, respectively accounting for 13.35%, 9.56%, 9.14%, 4.14% and 3.31% of the total. In 2017 this pattern remained basically unchanged, with Saudi Arabia ranking the second place and Iraq rising from the 5th place to the 4th place.

Table 3.9 Condition of Main Exporters of Crude Oil to China (Category HS2709)

Ranking	Exporter	Import volume of 2016 (1 million USD)	Proportion in total import volume of 2016 (%)	Exporter	Import volume of 2017 (1 million USD)	Proportion in total import volume of 2017 (%)
1	Russia	168.90	14.48	Russia	238.84	14.58
2	Saudi Arabia	155.69	13.35	Saudi Arabia	205.15	12.52
3	Angola	138.66	11.89	Angola	201.23	12.28
4	Oman	111.48	9.56	Iraq	138.13	8.43
5	Iraq	106.60	9.14	Oman	123.75	7.55
6	Iran	93.57	8.02	Iran	119.29	7.28
7	Brazil	60.37	5.17	Brazil	91.77	5.60
8	Kuwait	48.29	4.14	Kuwait	70.83	4.32
9	Venezuela	45.87	3.93	Venezuela	65.66	4.01
10	UAE	38.62	3.31	UAE	41.57	2.54
—	World	1166.61	100	World	1638.21	100

Classification basis: HS3

Data source: Obtained by calculation and reorganization based on data in the International Trade Database of the United Nations. The ranking is based on data of 2016.

Note: Taking China as the reporting state.

On the whole, China's crude oil import is heavily reliant on Arab states. In particular, Gulf Cooperation Council states like Saudi Arabia, Oman and Kuwait are very important partners of China. Furthermore, Iraq is playing an increasingly important role as an exporter to China.

Table 3.10 China's Crude Oil Import from Arab States (Category HS2709)

Ranking	Exporter	Import volume of 2016 (100 million USD)	Proportion in total import volume of 2016 (%)	Import volume of 2017 (100 million USD)	Proportion in total import volume of 2017 (%)
1	Saudi Arabia	155.69	13.35	205.15	12.52
2	Oman	111.48	9.56	123.75	7.55
3	Iraq	106.60	9.14	138.13	8.43
4	Kuwait	48.29	4.14	70.83	4.32
5	UAE	38.62	3.31	41.57	2.54
6	Libya	3.45	0.30	13.62	0.83
7	Sudan	3.38	0.29	2.93	0.18
8	Egypt	2.53	0.22	8.80	0.54
9	Qatar	1.57	0.13	3.81	0.23
10	Yemen	1.43	0.12	6.33	0.39
—	Arab League	473.04	40.55	616.11	37.61

Classification basis: HS3

Data source: Obtained by calculation and reorganization based on data in the International Trade Database of the United Nations. The ranking is based on data of 2016.

Note: Taking China as the reporting state.

3.3 Service Trade between China and Arab States

3.3.1 Scale and Structure of China's Service Trade

According to data released by the Ministry of Commerce of China, the total import-export volume of China's service trade was 302.5 billion USD in 2009, with a slight drop as a result of influence of financial crisis in 2009, followed by constant increase of total import-export volume ever since. In 2017, the total service trade volume of China was 695.7 billion USD, with a year-on-year increase of 5.0%. As for export, in 2009, the export volume of China's service trade was 143.6 billion USD. In 2017, the export volume reached 228.1 billion USD, a historic high, with a year-on-year increase of 8.9%. As for import, the import volume in 2009 was 158.9 billion USD. In 2017, the import volume reached 467.6 billion USD, with a year-on-year increase of 3.4%.

Table 3.11 Import and Export Volume of China's Service Trade from 2009 to 2017

Year	Import and export of China		Export		Import		Balance (100 million USD)
	Amount (100 million USD)	Year-on-year increase (%)	Amount (100 million USD)	Year-on-year increase (%)	Amount (100 million USD)	Year-on-year increase (%)	
2009	3025	-6.1	1436	-12.1	1589	0	-153
2010	3717	22.9	1783	24.2	1934	21.7	-151
2011	4489	20.8	2010	12.7	2478	28.2	-468
2012	4829	7.6	2016	0.3	2813	13.5	-797
2013	5376	11.3	2070	2.7	3306	17.5	-1236
2014	6520	21.3	2191	5.9	4329	30.9	-2137
2015	6542	0.3	2186	-0.2	4355	0.6	-2169
2016	6616	1.1	2095	-4.2	4521	3.8	-2426
2017	6957	5.0	2281	8.9	4676	3.4	-2395

Data source: Website of the Ministry of Commerce of China

Proportion of China's service trade export in the world's total has been kept about 4% for a long time. In 2009, it was 3.58%. In 2012, it rose to 4.44%. In 2017, it dropped to 4.30%. In 2017, the export volume of China was lower than that of the United States, UK, Germany and France, all of which are developing countries. The export volume of China ranked the 5th place in the world in both 2017 and 2009. The proportion of China's service trade import in the world's total has been increasing continuously. In 2009, it was only 4.36%. In 2017, it reached 9.2%. China ranked the 6th place in the world in terms of import volume in 2009. In 2017, it went up to the second place, following the United States.

Generally, China's service trade is in deficit, and the deficit amount has been constantly growing. In 2009, the deficit was 15.3 billion USD and in 2017, it reached 239.5 billion USD. According to Table 3.13, the deficit amount of China was considerably large.

Table 3.12 Proportion of Major Economies' Service Trade Export and Import Volume in the World's Total (%)

Year / Countries and regions	2009		2012		2016		2017	
	Export proportion	Import proportion	Export proportion	Import proportion	Export proportion	Import proportion	Export proportion	Import proportion
Australia	1.29	1.40	1.29	1.67	1.17	1.28	1.22	1.33
Canada	2.00	2.48	1.97	2.53	1.66	2.06	1.64	2.09
China	3.58	4.36	4.44	6.35	4.23	9.34	4.30	9.20
France	5.66	5.26	5.17	4.57	4.75	4.86	4.70	4.73
Germany	6.50	7.47	5.56	6.65	5.68	6.30	5.73	6.37
India	2.71	2.40	3.21	2.93	3.27	2.76	3.47	3.03
Italy	2.84	3.27	2.39	2.45	2.03	2.14	2.09	2.26
Japan	3.53	4.65	3.02	4.17	3.51	3.81	3.48	3.76
South Korea	2.12	2.46	2.28	2.45	1.92	2.33	1.65	2.40
Russia	1.34	1.89	1.37	2.46	1.02	1.54	1.09	1.74
UK	7.75	5.47	6.94	4.42	6.69	4.27	6.61	4.23
USA	14.96	11.55	14.47	10.20	15.19	10.43	14.72	10.59
Arab States	0.03	6.32	0.03	6.26	0.04	6.27	0.04	5.78

Data source: Reorganization and calculation based on data provided by WTO website

Table 3.13 Trade Deficit between Service Trade Imports and Exports of Major Economies from 2009 to 2017

Year / Countries and regions	2009	2010	2011	2012	2013	2014	2015	2016	2017
Australia	-26.40	-58.10	-114.26	-156.30	-177.27	-119.28	-88.28	-42.75	-28.35
Brazil	-192.46	-300.27	-370.43	-398.49	-463.72	-481.07	-369.46	-304.47	-338.51
Canada	-143.23	-215.08	-220.25	-226.39	-224.32	-219.27	-199.94	-175.88	-192.97
China	-234.16	-150.63	-467.97	-797.24	-1236.02	-2137.42	-2169.07	-2425.68	-2394.99
Finland	4.96	5.22	-2.14	-23.83	-17.94	-33.27	-30.75	-30.62	-17.83
France	178.49	204.49	333.88	319.39	260.44	202.17	98.78	0.32	90.01
Germany	-274.09	-382.65	-451.39	-421.11	-549.37	-335.97	-206.31	-234.70	-195.89
Greece	161.97	171.10	199.73	191.81	209.14	242.41	187.79	169.37	199.16
India	123.37	21.40	132.39	156.06	222.73	288.34	327.11	282.87	299.67
Italy	-122.96	-121.54	-85.81	-1.58	5.89	-13.49	-29.70	-30.53	-41.52
Japan	-348.69	-302.90	-348.33	-477.62	-356.43	-286.33	-159.50	-105.52	-61.19
South Korea	-95.90	-142.38	-122.79	-52.14	-64.99	-36.79	-149.17	-177.37	-344.72
Russia	-176.01	-261.20	-334.56	-465.87	-582.59	-552.78	-369.20	-238.27	-308.18
UK	825.04	865.48	1115.26	1189.85	1319.70	1419.89	1317.80	1247.28	1357.42
USA	1259.21	1540.20	1920.20	2043.98	2403.68	2611.58	2614.10	2477.14	2427.65
Arab States	-976.44	-1064.07	-1343.20	-1466.65	-1571.52	-1684.00	-1404.39	-1208.46	-1025.46

Data source: Reorganization and calculation based on data provided by WTO website

Note: The data on service trade deficit of China in 2009 are in discrepancy with the data available on the website of the Ministry of Commerce of China.

Table 3.14 Import and Export Volumes of China's Service Trade in 2017

Service type	Import and export		Export		Import		Balance of trade (100 million USD)
	Amount (100 million USD)	Year-on-year increase (%)	Amount (100 million USD)	Year-on-year increase (%)	Amount (100 million USD)	Year-on-year increase (%)	
Total	6959.0	5.0	2281.0	9.0	4678.0	3.4	-2397.0
Processing service	183.0	-2.7	181.0	-3.0	2.0	12.3	179.0
Maintenance and repairing service	82.0	16.1	59.0	18.0	23.0	12.4	36.0
Transportation	1300.0	13.7	371.0	10.0	929.0	15.3	-558.0
Tourism	2935.0	-3.9	387.0	-13.0	2548.0	-2.4	-2161.0
Building	326.0	55.2	240.0	89.0	86.0	3.6	154.0
Insurance and pension service	144.0	-15.3	40.0	-3.0	104.0	-19.3	-64.0
Financial service	53.0	1.3	37.0	15.0	16.0	-20.5	21.0
Intellectual property loyalty	334.0	32.6	48.0	308.0	286.0	19.2	-238.0
Telecommunication, computer and information service	470.0	20.0	278.0	5.0	192.0	52.5	86.0
Other commercial services	1044.0	3.0	615.0	6.0	429.0	-1.3	186.0
Individual, cultural and entertainment services	36.0	21.8	8.0	2.0	28.0	28.6	-20.0
Government services unmentioned elsewhere	52.0	26.3	17.0	41.0	35.0	20.3	-18.0

Data source: Website of the Ministry of Commerce of China

As for China's service trade structure, tourism, transportation and other commercial services are all major components of service trade of China, with high trade volumes above 100 billion USD. Trade volume of the three categories accounted for 75.86% of the total service trade volume of China. Particularly, tourism accounted for 42.18%, being the largest part, followed by transportation, which accounted for 18.68%, and then other commercial services, accounting for 15.00%. As for export, other commercial services accounted for 26.96%, being the largest part, followed by tourism, which accounted for 16.97%, and then transportation, accounting for 16.26%. As for import, tourism accounted for 54.47%, being the largest part, followed by transportation, accounting for 19.86%, and then other commercial services, accounting for 9.17%. The import volume of intellectual property royalty was as high as 28.6 billion USD, accounting for 6.11%. Among the 12 service categories, processing service, maintenance and repairing service, building, financial service, telecommunication, computer and information service and other commercial services were seeing surplus. In particular, other commercial services had the highest surplus, being 18.6 billion USD, followed by that of processing service, being 17.9 billion USD. Transportation, tourism, insurance and pension service, intellectual property loyalty, individual, cultural and entertainment service and government services unmentioned elsewhere were all seeing trade deficit. In particular, tourism, transportation and intellectual property loyalty had the highest deficit amounts, being respectively 216.1 billion USD, 55.8 billion USD and 23.8 billion USD.

3.3.2 Scale and Structure of Arab States' Service Trade

According to data released by WTO, the service trade volume of Arab states in 2009 was 326.036 billion USD. In 2012, the service trade volume topped 400 billion USD. In 2014, it reached a historic high of 526.817 billion USD. Since 2015, there has been a downward trend of service trade volume of Arab states. In 2017, the service trade volume was 484.627 billion USD, dropping by 0.3% year on year. As for export, the service export volume of Arab States has been on the steady rise. In 2009, it was 114.196 billion USD; in 2015, it hit 181.273 billion USD. A further increase was observed in 2017, reaching 191.041 billion USD, with a year-on-year increase rate of 4.6%. The proportion of Arab State' service trade export in the world's total service trade export has been kept at around 3%. In 2016, the proportion was 3.6%. In 2017, it dropped to 2.74%. As for import, the service trade import of Arab states had been increasing constantly from 2009 to 2014. In 2014, it reached 347.609 billion USD. However, since 2015, the service trade import of Arab states has been seeing a downward trend. In 2017, it dropped to 293.587 billion USD, with a year-on-year decrease of 3.2%. Generally speaking, the service trade of Arab States has been seeing deficit. The highest amount of deficit was observed in 2014, being 168.4 billion USD. In 2017, the deficit was 102.546 billion USD, dropping by more than 10 billion USD compared with that of 2016.

Table 3.15 Service Trade Import and Export Volumes of Arab States from 2009 to 2017

Year	Import and export of Arab States		Export		Import		Balance (100 million USD)
	Amount (100 million USD)	Year-on-year increase (%)	Amount (100 million USD)	Year-on-year increase (%)	Amount (100 million USD)	Year-on-year increase (%)	
2009	3260.36	-5.2	1141.96	-4.7	2118.40	-5.5	-976.44
2010	3516.71	7.9	1226.32	7.4	2290.39	8.1	-1064.07
2011	3788.23	7.7	1222.52	-0.3	2565.72	12.0	-1343.20
2012	4077.73	7.6	1305.54	6.8	2772.19	8.0	-1466.65
2013	4220.32	3.5	1324.40	1.4	2895.92	4.5	-1571.52
2014	5268.17	24.8	1792.08	35.3	3476.09	20.0	-1684.00
2015	5029.84	-4.5	1812.73	1.2	3217.12	-7.5	-1404.39
2016	4859.74	-3.4	1825.64	0.7	3034.10	-5.7	-1208.46
2017	4846.27	-0.3	1910.41	4.6	2935.87	-3.2	-1025.46

Data source: Reorganization and calculation based on data provided by WTO website

In Arab states, Bahrain, Egypt, Lebanon, Morocco, Qatar, Saudi Arabia and UAE are major service trade exporters. In 2012, the top 5 countries in terms of export volume were respectively Egypt, UAE, Morocco, Lebanon and Saudi Arabia, with export volume of 21.767 billion USD, 16.065 billion USD, 15.347 billion USD, 15.125 billion USD and 11.05 billion USD respectively. In 2017, UAE was the largest exporter of service trade in the region, with export volume hitting 70.497 billion USD, followed by Egypt, with export volume of 20.033 billion USD. Saudi Arabia and Qatar respectively ranked the 3rd and 4th places, with export volume of 18.021 billion USD and 17.706 billion USD; the fifth place was Morocco, with export volume of 17.261 billion USD. In 2012, the service export volume of Comoros, Djibouti, Libya and Mauritania was low, being only 70 million USD, 339 million USD, 152 million USD and 145 million USD. The 2017 data were missing. In 2017, Somalia had the lowest export volume in the region, with export volume of only 393 million USD. Generally, Gulf Cooperation Council states led by UAE have been seeing rapid growth of service trade export in recent years, accounting for a large proportion. In 2017, total service export volume of those countries accounted for 64.13% of the Arab total. ①

Table 3.16 Service Trade Export Volume of Arab States from 2012 to 2017

Unit: 100 million USD

Year / Countries and regions	2012	2013	2014	2015	2016	2017
Algeria	37.49	37.73	35.44	34.55	34.33	32.61
Bahrain	83.32	85.01	85.71	91.13	109.98	111.30
Comoros	0.70	0.80	0.85	0.84	—	—
Djibouti	3.39	3.66	3.82	4.55	4.06	—
Egypt	217.67	182.62	218.98	185.39	136.06	200.33
Iraq	28.33	32.98	41.31	62.60	48.35	—
Jordan	64.21	63.15	71.40	62.69	60.35	67.20
Kuwait	88.37	61.80	62.68	60.56	55.29	51.63
Lebanon	151.25	157.20	147.51	159.10	151.93	160.80
Libya	1.52	1.80	0.79	4.83	0.86	—
Mauritania	1.45	1.86	2.79	2.46	2.70	—
Morocco	153.47	143.53	162.36	146.74	153.79	172.61
Oman	26.87	29.55	31.30	33.79	36.04	—
Qatar	99.22	111.75	135.26	149.97	151.76	177.06
Saudi Arabia	110.50	118.45	125.16	144.74	172.53	180.21

① The data on service export of Oman in 2017 are missing.

Continued

Year / Countries and regions	2012	2013	2014	2015	2016	2017
Somalia	—	1.99	3.37	3.55	3.73	3.93
Sudan	10.59	12.58	15.68	17.27	15.45	15.17
Syria	—	—	—	—	—	—
Tunisia	50.77	48.31	47.34	32.94	32.49	32.60
UAE	160.65	212.39	583.25	607.76	655.96	704.97
Yemen	15.77	17.26	17.07	7.28	—	—
Arab League	1305.54	1324.40	1792.08	1812.73	1825.64	1910.41
World	45376.57	48298.30	51900.42	49292.05	49533.86	53048.09
Proportion of Arab League	2.74%	3.45%	3.68%	3.68%	3.60%	2.74%

Data source: Reorganization and calculation based on data provided by WTO website

Note: "—" stands for data missing.

As for import, the top 5 countries in terms of service import were respectively Saudi Arabia, UAE, Qatar, Kuwait and Egypt in 2012, with import volume of 73.407 billion USD, 63.254 billion USD, 23.906 billion USD, 21.097 billion USD and 16.45 billion USD. In 2017, UAE surpassed Saudi Arabia and became No. 1. Saudi Arabia, Qatar, Kuwait and Egypt were respectively ranked the 2nd, 3rd, 4th and 5th places, with service trade import volume of 85.5 billion USD, 76.818 billion USD, 31.427 billion USD, 28.566 billion USD and 17.399 billion USD. Apparently, the service trade import volume of those countries had increased compared with that in 2012. In particular, the Gulf Cooperation Council still accounted for the largest part of total import volume of all Arab States, taking up 78.33%. ① In 2012, Comoros and Djibouti had the lowest import volume compared with other Arab States, being only 104 million USD and 160 million USD respectively. The import volume data of the two countries for 2017 are missing. In 2017, Somalia had the lowest import volume, which was only 1.452 billion USD.

① The data on service import of Oman in 2017 are missing.

Table 3.17 Service Trade Import Volume of Arab States from 2012 to 2017

Unit: 100 million USD

Year / Countries and regions	2012	2013	2014	2015	2016	2017
Algeria	108.73	107.95	118.03	110.77	108.81	115.99
Bahrain	60.45	70.51	67.64	65.92	75.30	76.42
Comoros	1.04	1.09	0.99	0.83	—	—
Djibouti	1.60	1.68	1.94	2.30	1.99	—
Egypt	164.50	164.08	175.50	175.19	170.32	173.99
Iraq	132.91	146.58	147.90	126.20	100.37	—
Jordan	45.44	46.12	46.34	45.28	45.65	46.70
Kuwait	210.97	210.04	237.87	237.96	263.48	285.66
Lebanon	115.06	130.02	132.16	136.93	132.80	138.53
Libya	69.96	84.72	74.56	46.58	28.83	—
Mauritania	10.17	9.99	9.00	6.41	6.05	—
Morocco	81.36	75.71	88.72	79.13	86.04	97.94
Oman	87.85	97.98	100.14	102.14	99.46	—
Qatar	239.06	274.79	328.59	307.75	315.41	314.27
Saudi Arabia	734.07	766.52	1005.45	880.36	702.67	768.18
Somalia	—	10.17	12.24	13.28	13.35	14.52
Sudan	21.09	20.30	20.75	17.79	15.07	19.06
Syria	—	—	—	—	—	—
Tunisia	31.96	33.04	34.00	30.76	30.11	29.62
UAE	632.54	621.92	846.83	818.79	838.39	855.00
Yemen	23.41	22.72	27.43	12.75	—	—
Arab League	2772.19	2895.92	3476.09	3217.12	3034.10	2935.87
World	44309.29	46960.67	51060.99	48230.43	48383.17	50803.23
Proportion of Arab League	6.26%	6.17%	6.81%	6.67%	6.27%	5.78%

Data source: Reorganization and calculation based on data provided by WTO website

Note: "—" stands for data missing.

As for the balance of service trade, most Arab states were seeing deficit in service trade. Only Bahrain, Djibouti, Egypt, Jordan, Lebanon, Morocco and Tunisia were seeing small surplus. Morocco had the largest amount of surplus, being 7.467 billion USD in 2017, increasing by more than 600 million USD compared with that of 2016, and by more than 200 million USD compared with that of 2012. Saudi Arabia, Kuwait, UAE, Qatar and Algeria were seeing heavy deficit, with deficit of respectively 58.797 billion USD, 23.403 billion USD, 15.003 billion USD, 13.721 billion USD and 8.338 billion USD in 2017. In particular, Saudi Arabia saw its largest deficit in 2014, and since then the deficit has been decreasing. The deficit of Kuwait has been on a steady rise since 2012, and reached the top in 2017. UAE saw its largest deficit in 2012, and since then, there has been a gradual decrease. Qatar saw its deficit peak in 2014, and then in 2017, the deficit dropped to 13.721 billion USD. The deficit of Algeria firstly increased, and then dropped and then rose again. The deficit of Algeria in 2017 was 1.214 billion USD more than that in 2012.

Table 3.18 Service Trade Balance of Arab States from 2012 to 2017

Unit: 100 million USD

Country \ Year	2012	2013	2014	2015	2016	2017
Algeria	-71.24	-70.22	-82.59	-76.22	-74.48	-83.38
Bahrain	22.87	14.5	18.07	25.21	34.68	34.88
Morocco	-0.34	-0.29	-0.14	0.01	—	—
Djibouti	1.79	1.98	1.88	2.25	2.07	—
Egypt	53.17	18.54	43.48	10.2	-34.26	26.34
Iraq	-104.58	-113.6	-106.59	-63.6	-52.02	—
Jordan	18.77	17.03	25.06	17.41	14.7	20.5
Kuwait	-122.6	-148.24	-175.19	-177.4	-208.19	-234.03
Lebanon	36.19	27.18	15.35	22.17	19.13	22.27

Continued

Year / Country	2012	2013	2014	2015	2016	2017
Libya	-68.44	-82.92	-73.77	-41.75	-27.97	—
Mauritania	-8.72	-8.13	-6.21	-3.95	-3.35	—
Morocco	72.11	67.82	73.64	67.61	67.75	74.67
Oman	-60.98	-68.43	-68.84	-68.35	-63.42	—
Qatar	-139.84	-163.04	-193.33	-157.78	-163.65	-137.21
Saudi Arabia	-623.57	-648.07	-880.29	-735.62	-530.14	-587.97
Somalia	—	-8.18	-8.87	-9.73	-9.62	-10.59
Sudan	-10.5	-7.72	-5.07	-0.52	0.38	-3.89
Syria	—	—	—	—	—	—
Tunisia	18.81	15.27	13.34	2.18	2.38	2.98
UAE	-471.89	-409.53	-263.58	-211.03	-182.43	-150.03
Yemen	-7.64	-5.46	-10.36	-5.47	—	—

Data source: Reorganization and calculation based on data provided by WTO website

Note: "—" stands for data missing.

The import and export of the Gulf Cooperation Council accounted for the vast majority of the Arab total. In the following part, the service import-export structure of the Gulf Cooperation Council states is taken as the example to explain the structure of Arab States' service trade.

As for export, among the four service categories, transportation of the Gulf Cooperation Council had the largest export volume, being 45.283 billion USD, followed by tourism, with export volume of 45.161 billion USD, and other commercial services (including building, insurance and pension service and financial service), with export volume of 33.26 billion USD. The export volume of those categories increased compared with that in 2016. Transportation had the highest growth rate, which was 12.68%. Other commercial services had the lowest growth rate, being only 2%.

Table 3.19 Export Volume of Service Trade of Gulf Cooperation Council States in 2017 by Categories

Unit: 100 million USD

Item \ Year	2012	2016	2017
Commercial services	539.71	1153.86	1241.38
Services related to goods	2.94	4.29	4.34
-Maintenance and repairing services	2.94	4.29	4.34
Transportation	171.88	401.86	452.83
-Air transportation	56.88	317.14	353.97
Tourism	237.89	421.74	451.61
Other commercial services	127.01	325.97	332.60
-Building	—	25.05	26.14
-Insurance and pension services	55.73	79.33	80.16
-Financial services	3.32	27.68	29.32
-Intellectual property loyalty	—	34.85	36.22
-"Telecommunication, computer and information service"	48.78	102.73	103.50
--Telecommunication service	46.32	52.92	51.66
Computer service	—	—	50.89
--Information service	—	—	0.94
-Other commercial services	16.22	52.54	54.35
--Research and development service	10.28	11.29	10.54
-"Individual, cultural and entertainment service"	8.89	3.79	2.91

Data source: Obtained by reorganization based on data available on WTO website.

Note: "—" stands for data missing.

According to the classification criteria of UNCTAD, services are divided into 4 major categories: services related to goods, transportation, tourism and other services. Other services are further divided into building, insurance and pension service, financial service, intellectual property loyalty, telecommunication, computer and information service, other commercial business, individual, cultural and entertainment service, government commodity, services unmentioned elsewhere and unclassified services.

As for import, other services of Gulf Cooperation Council had the largest service trade import volume in 2017, being 101.51 billion USD, accounting for 47.61% of the total import volume. Transportation and tourism were also major import categories of Gulf Cooperation Council states, accounting for more than 50% of the total import volume.

Generally speaking, Gulf Cooperation Council states boast certain advantages in transportation, resulting in a small deficit. However, a heavy deficit was seen in building, insurance and pension service, financial service and tourism. This indicates substantial import need of those categories in the market.

Table 3.20 Import Volume of Service Trade of Gulf Cooperation Council States in 2017 by Categories

Year	2012		2016		2017	
Item	Import volume (100 million USD)	Proportion (%)	Import volume (100 million USD)	Proportion (%)	Import volume (100 million USD)	Proportion (%)
Commercial services	1691.61	100	2054.81	100	2131.95	100
-Services related to goods	2.45	0.1	1.03	0.05	0.66	0.03
-Transportation	799.01	47.2	512.33	24.93	507.74	23.82
-Tourism	491.02	29.0	592.4	28.83	608.46	28.54
-Other commercial services	399.12	23.6	949.05	46.19	1015.10	47.61

Data source: Obtained by reorganizing data available on WTO website

Chapter 4 Special Report on China-Arab Science and Technology Cooperation Process

China-Arab cooperation in science and technology is an important part of China and Arab states cooperation. China-Arab cooperation has strongly supported the progress of China-Arab economic and trade relations. China and Arab states technology transfer is the main content of China-Arab cooperation. In recent years, China-Arab cooperation in science and technology, especially the technology transfer between China and Arab has made a rapid progress and has achieved significant results in cooperation mechanisms, cooperation content and cooperation prospects.

4.1 Cooperation Mechanism

China-Arab cooperation in science and technology is advancing with the development of China-Arab economic and trade cooperation. Subject to the special nature, long-term nature and intangibility of scientific and technological cooperation, the cooperation mechanism is very important. At present, China-Arab cooperation mechanism mainly includes two kinds which are official mechanisms and nongovernmental mechanisms.

4.1.1 Official Cooperation Mechanism

The official cooperation mechanism mainly includes the China-Arab States Cooperation Forum, the China-Arab States Expo, and the China-Arab States Technology Transfer Center.

The primary official body for China-Arab cooperation is the China-Arab States Cooperation Forum. On January 30, 2004, Chinese President Hu Jintao visited the headquarters of the League of Arab States and met with the Arab League Secretary General Amr Mahmoud Moussa and representatives of 22 Arab League member states. After the meeting, Foreign Minister Li Zhaoxing and Secretary General Moussa jointly announced the establishment of the "China-Arab States Cooperation Forum". China-Arab States Cooperation Forum organization includes ministerial conferences, senior officials' meetings, and other institutions ranging from China-Arab States Energy Cooperation Forum and the China-Arab States Cooperation Forum. All of the above meetings involve scientific and technological cooperation directly or indirectly. On June 5, 2014, at the Sixth Ministerial Meeting of the China-Arab States Cooperation Forum, Chinese President Xi Jinping proposed to build a "1+2+3" cooperation pattern between China and Arab states, that is, energy cooperation as the main axis, infrastructure construction and trade and the investment is facilitated into two wings. The three high-tech fields of nuclear energy, space satellite and new energy are new breakthroughs. The three high-tech fields have actually involved scientific and technological cooperation.

China-Arab States Expo (hereinafter referred to as the Expo) is another official institution of China-Arab cooperation. The Expo is a large-scale foreign trade, economic and trade exhibition which is organized by the Ministry of Commerce, the China Council for the Promotion of International Trade and the People's Government of Ningxia Hui Autonomous Region. Since 2010, it has successfully held three sessions of China-Arab States Economic and Trade Forum and three sessions of China-Arab States Expo. Since 2015, China-Arab States Expo has provided with the technology sector and technology cooperation. During the China-Arab States Expo 2015, the China-Arab States Technology Transfer and Innovation Cooperation Conference was held. The China-Arab States Technology Transfer Center was unveiled and a number of key scientific and technological cooperation projects between China and Arab states were signed. In 2017, The exhibition activities of the China-Arab States Expo include the China-Arab States Technology Transfer and Innovative and Advanced Technology and Equipment Exhibition.

China-Arab States Technology Transfer Center (hereinafter referred to as the Center) is a bilateral agency specializing in China-Arab technical cooperation.

China-Arab States Technology Transfer Center was proposed by Chinese President Xi Jinping at the Sixth Ministerial Conference of the China-Arab States Cooperation Forum in June 2014. It was jointly promoted and implemented by the Ministry of Science and Technology of the People's Republic of China and the People's Government of Ningxia Hui Autonomous Region. On January 5, 2015, the Ministry of Science and Technology officially approved that Ningxia would take the lead in integrating national scientific and technological innovation elements and technical resources to create an efficient and pragmatic platform for China's technology transfer and innovation cooperation in Arab States. The Party Committee and Government of Ningxia Hui Autonomous Region attaches great importance to it and requires that Ningxia try their best to construct in accordance with the needs of the state and ability of Ningxia, and on September 9, *the Notice of the General Office of the People's Government of the Ningxia Hui Autonomous Region on Printing and Issuing the Overall Plan for the Construction of China-Arab States Technology Transfer Center* (No. 133 [2015] of Office of People's Government of Ningxia Hui Autonomous Region). During the 2015 China-Arab States Expo, the Science and Technology Department of Ningxia Hui Autonomous Region invited the Assistant Secretary-General of the Arab League, Badr Ting Allari, in the name of the China-Arab States Technology Transfer Center, and 90 political dignitaries of the nine Arab states including Saudi Arabia, Egypt, Algeria, Oman and Morocco. The series activities of scientific and technological sector have achieved remarkable results. China and Arab states have reached 37 cooperation agreements, which have formed extensive influence at home and abroad, effectively enhancing Ningxia's position in China-Arab scientific and technological cooperation.

On January 13, 2016, the Chinese government issued the first *"China's Arab Policy Paper"*, which clearly stated that "Through the China-Arab technology transfer center, we will establish a China-Arab collaboration network of integrated technology transfer." On January 21, 2016, Xi Jinping visited Egypt at the headquarters of the League of Arab States and announced the formal establishment of the China-Arab States Technology Transfer Center, further establishing the status and role of the China-Arab States Technology Transfer Center in reflecting the pragmatic cooperation between China and Arab. On September 2, 2016, *the "Special Plan for Promoting the "The Belt and Road" to Build a Scientific and Technological Innovation Cooperation"* jointly issued by the Ministry of Science and Technology of the People's Republic of China, the National Development and Reform Commission, the Ministry of Foreign Affairs and the Ministry of Commerce, once again clarified the important mission of the China-Arab States Technology Transfer Center. On May 14th, 2017, Xi Jinping gave a speech on starting "The Belt and Road" Science and Technology Innovation Action Plan, and carrying out 4 actions include scientific and technological humanities communications, joint construction of joint laboratories, and cooperation in science and technology parks,technology transfer" at the opening ceremony of the "The Belt and Road" International Cooperation Summit Forum.

On July 10, 2018, the 8th Ministerial Conference of the China-Arab States Cooperation Forum was held in Beijing. The two sides reached and signed three important outcome documents include *the Beijing Declaration of the Eighth Ministerial Conference of the China-Arab States Cooperation Forum* and *the Execution Plan 2018-2020 of China-Arab States Cooperation Forum* and *the China-Arab Cooperation and Building "the Belt and Road"Action Declaration"*. The work of China-Arab States Technology Transfer Center, the China-Arab States Technology Transfer and Innovation Cooperation Conference has been included in the above-mentioned three documents, with clear requirements. and clearly stated the requirements. At the same time, the Department of International Cooperation of the Ministry of Science and Technology of the People's Republic of China is also an important driving force for China-Arab scientific and technological cooperation,its main tasks include building platforms, project matching, information release, organizing meetings or forums.

4.1.2 Nongovernmental Cooperation Mechanism

The nongovernmental mechanism of China-Arab science and technology (especially technology) cooperation: Firstly, Chinese companies and the relevant institutions of the Arab States carry out technology transfer, such as Huawei, China Railway Construction, China High-speed Railway and so on. Secondly, some market-oriented technology transfer institutions, such as the China-Arab International Science and Technology Industry Alliance. China-Arab International Science and Technology Industry Cooperation Alliance with 14 domestic and foreign companies and chambers of commerce including China Enterprise Park International Cooperation

Alliance, Ningxia Guochen Industrial Co., Ltd., China-Arab National Youth Entrepreneurship Management Committee, Beijing Shuimu Chunjin Capital Management Co., Ltd., China Agriculture and Science Industry Development Fund, Taihua Group, Beijing Jingpeng Global Technology Co., Ltd., are the core units, and nearly 100 companies are members of the alliance. The industry involves finance, intelligent manufacturing, intelligent and efficient agriculture, scientific and technological personnel exchange training base, and international trade service platform. Its members include large-scale enterprises in various fields in China, and have absorbed some powerful enterprises and chambers of commerce along the Silk Road Economic Belt. On October 19~20, 2017, the China-Arab International Science and Technology Industry Cooperation Alliance and the Oman Bahawan Group discussed cooperation in Beijing. The two parties intend to corporate in finance, new energy, high-efficiency technology and smart agriculture, and characteristic industrial parks (small towns),cooperative research and development of health industry, two-way international trade cooperation, smart technology, cold chain warehousing logistics, science and education culture, international cross-border e-commerce cooperation and other areas of cooperation, and signed a memorandum of cooperation.

4.2 Cooperation Content and Progress

4.2.1 Science and Technology Cooperation

Based on the tradition of China-Arab states friendly exchanges and the promotion of China-Arab States Cooperation Forum, China-Arab states cooperation has made rapid progress. The 8th Ministerial Conference of the China-Arab States Cooperation Forum has successively adopted the *"Beijing Declaration of the Eighth Ministerial Conference of the China-Arab States Cooperation Forum", "China-Arab Cooperation Declaration for the Belt and Road Initiative", "the Execution Plan 2018-2020 of China-Arab States Cooperation Forum"*. Meanwhile the contents of scientific and technological cooperation are mentioned in the three documents. The specific areas of cooperation and contents are as follows.

Table 4.1 Recent plans for China and Arab States Cooperation

Category	Content	Document
Continuously promote the "1+2+3" cooperation pattern between China and Arab	Taking energy cooperation as the main axis, infrastructure and trade, investment facilitation as the two wings to strengthen bilateral cooperation, enhance the level of pragmatic cooperation between the two sides in high-tech fields such as nuclear energy, space satellites and new energy, and implement the four major action plans about stability, innovation and cooperation, and capacity matching, and greater friendship; China and Arab states shall emphasize the implementation of relevant cooperation in accordance with the laws and regulations of both parties and relevant international obligations.	*"China-Arab Cooperation Declaration for the Belt and Road Initiative"*
Scientific and technological innovation and cooperation	Carry out scientific and cultural exchanges, co-build joint laboratories, scientific and technological parks and technology transfer; Jointly implement "the Belt and Road" Action Plan for Scientific and technological Innovation	*"Beijing Declaration of the Eighth Ministerial Conference of the China-Arab States Cooperation Forum"*
Satellite navigation system	China Satellite Navigation System Management Office and the Arab Information and Communication Technology Organization, based on the Memorandum of Understanding on the cooperation of Beidou Satellite Navigation, relying on the China-Arab Beidou/GNSS Center will strengthen cooperation in infrastructure construction, education and training, joint research and development and application industrialization in the Beidou Augmentation System. They will strengthen cooperation in the field of meteorological satellites	*"Beijing Declaration of the Eighth Ministerial Conference of the China-Arab States Cooperation Forum"*
Water resources	Both sides will strengthen cooperation in water technology, water resource utilization and conservation, rainwater harvesting, wastewater treatment and reuse, and water resources management in arid regions, and enhance the cooperation relationship between the two water resources research centers, especially holding training courses in the field of technology transfer.	*"The Execution Plan 2018-2020 of China-Arab States Cooperation Forum"*

Source: China-Arab States Cooperation Forum website, http://www.chinaarabcf.org/chn/.

4.2.2 Cooperation Progress

1. Overall Progress

Serving China-Arab cooperation strategy, China-Arab cooperation is progressing smoothly; the cooperation includes technology transfer, technical cooperation development, technical personnel exchange, scientific research cooperation, joint construction technology trading and R&D platform; cooperation areas include aerospace, information and communication, high-speed rail infrastructure, water resources utilization, modern agriculture, food production, health care, energy and environmental protection.

China-Arab States Technology Transfer Center was established, and the Arab Training Center for the Peaceful Use of Nuclear Energy and China-Arab Clean Energy Training Center made positive progress. Algerian No. 1 communication satellite was successfully launched, and the first China-Arab States BeiDou Cooperation Forum was successfully held. In April 2018, the Excellent Center of China-Arab Beidou Satellite Navigation System in Tunisia was launched. Chinese enterprises have won the bid for the Dubai Hassyan Clean Coal Power Station project.

On May 24, 2017, the first China-Arab States BeiDou Cooperation Forum was held in Shanghai. The forum was jointly held by the China Satellite Navigation System Management Office, the Chinese Secretariat of the China-Arab States Cooperation Forum, the Arab League Secretariat, and the Arab Information and Communication Technology Organization. It aimed to establish a multilateral platform and long-term mechanism for China-Arab satellite navigation cooperation and promote the Beidou system service Arabian countries. Representatives from 21 member states of Arab League and international organizations and relevant government departments and enterprises including the Ministry of Foreign Affairs, the Ministry of Commerce, the Ministry of Industry and Information Technology, the National Internet Information Office, and the China Satellite Navigation System Management Office attended the forum.

On October 17, Dubai Investment Forum 2017 & China-UAE Science and Technology Cooperation & Innovation Forum was jointly held by the Dubai Investment Promotion Agency, China High-Tech Industrialization Association, and co-organized by China-Arab International Science and Technology

Industry Alliance, China Financing & Investment Property Corporation combined with MERAAS. The Forum focused on the theme of "Technology Improves Industry· Innovation Shapes Future" and discussed in depth the "investment opportunities for infrastructure and energy Chinese enterprises in the background of the Belt and Road Policy", "mutually beneficial and win-win situation under the PPP Model", and "big data and development direction of cloud technology in the Middle East and North Africa, "The impact of artificial intelligence on future life and investment opportunities under new technologies" "How Chinese companies can increase their commercial influence in the Middle East and North Africa". For the first time, the Forum was aimed at Chinese enterprises. As an important communication platform for China-Arab technological innovation, it has invited well-known domestic and foreign business leaders, strategic experts and academic elites to jointly explore the development and cooperation opportunities in the field of science and technology innovation under the Belt and Road Initiative.

2. Platform Construction

China-Arab States Technology Transfer Center carries out major platform construction. Firstly, the network of China-Arab technology transfer and cooperation agencies was initially formed. With the goal of building a China-Arab states technology transfer and cooperation network covering the entire region, it has established a network of China-Arab technology transfer and cooperation agencies with relevant enterprises, scientific research institutions, institutions of higher learning, and intermediary service organizations to actively carry out various technology transfer and matching activities. At present, the number of members of the participating cooperation network has reached 4,264 including 2,778 in China and 1,486 in foreign countries. It has hosted or co-organized more than 10 high-level forums on technology transfer and cooperation networks, with more than 3,000 audiences. Secondly, the technology transfer integrated information service platform was officially launched. With the purpose of building a large network, applying big data, forming a large platform, and providing large services, it aims to provide data push, online matching, information retrieval and other services for the technology transfer between the both sides, and to build a "one stop, three libraries and the five systems" as the basic framework of the China-Arab technology transfer integrated information service system. Since the platform was put into trial operation, more than

700,000 technical supply and demand data have been collected, more than 80 times of supply and demand matching, more than 50 matching intentions, and realizing an agreement amount of 1.21 billion yuan. It has become a comprehensive information platform of technology transfer to Arab states with the richest, fastest updating and best docking effect of domestic technical data. Thirdly, the role of a number of bilateral technology transfer centers began to emerge. Eight bilateral technology transfer centers have been established which are successively built by Arab League, Saudi Arabia, Jordan, Oman, United Arab Emirates (Dubai), Egypt, Sudan, and Morocco. By integrating bilateral national science and technology resources, International Science and Technology Cooperation Base, such as joint research and development centers, joint key laboratories, and joint technology transfer, have been established, then carrying out a series of scientific and technological activities. For example, a technology transfer center was built with the support of the Arab League Secretariat; Arab Academy for Science, Technology and Maritime Transport carried out "foreign aid technical training in developing countries", technical matching and other work; the sub-centers, including "Ningxia (China-Arab) Key Laboratory for Resource Evaluation and Environmental Regulation in Arid Areas" and 100-mu Demonstration Base were jointly built by Oman National Commission for Science and Sultan Qaboos University; the Saudi King's Innovation and Development Center of Sci-tech City formed a sub-center to promote red palm weevil prevention, agricultural internet, and saving water and food production in technical cooperation; a bilateral technology transfer center was built with the help of Jordanian Middle East University to cooperate in information resource sharing, innovation platform cultivation, technology transfer, and university vocational training. Fourthly, the ability to host large international expositions has been enhanced. Technology group of China-Arab States Expo 2017 organized three activities including China-Arab States Technology Transfer and Innovation Cooperation Conference, High-tech and Equipment Exhibition, and Technology Matchmaking Promotion Conference. Thereinto, among the 580 participants in the China-Arab States Technology Transfer and Innovation Cooperation Conference, foreign guests accounted for half of them. The conference signed 19 scientific and technological cooperation projects covering the construction of China-Arab states technology transfer sub-centers, China-Arab states technology innovation platforms and China-Arab states technical cooperation. With the strong support of the Ministry of Science and Technology, the High-tech and Equipment Exhibition introduced the national "Twelfth Five-Year" Science and Technology Innovation Achievement Exhibition to Ningxia for the first time, with nearly 80,000 visitors. The exhibition also held 6 matchmaking meetings of special topics in China-Arab modern agriculture, semiconductor and smart cities, industrial fields, the Chinese Academy of Sciences, China-Arab joint scientific and technological cooperation platform, and Xihe system, and reached more than 30 cooperation intentions, signed 12 cooperation agreements or cooperation memorandums, with an intentional transaction amount of more than 300 million yuan.

3. Cooperation of Scientific and Technological Personnel

Thanks to the Arab League Secretariat, China-Arab States Technology Transfer Center was jointly built to actively cooperate with Arab Academy for Science, Technology and Maritime Transport, and to hold a technical matchmaking conference in Egypt, technical training courses for developing countries and innovation training courses for Arab states in China, cultivating the "seed" of technology transfer. China-Arab States Technology Transfer Center has worked closely with a number of agencies such as the International Cooperation Department of the Ministry of Science and Technology, the China Science and Technology Exchange Center, and the Shanghai Institute Science & Technology Management centering on special technology transformation and application and technology transfer professional manager training in Beidou Satellite, dry farming, water conservation, sand control and other special technologies. It has organized, hosted or co-organized 20 training courses such as the International Seminar on Science and Technology Policy and Management, and conducted special training for nearly 300 students from Egypt, Saudi Arabia, Morocco, Iraq, Iran, Thailand and other countries.

At the invitation of Arab agencies including Academy of Scientific Research and Technology of the Arab Republic of Egypt, the Africa City of Technology of Sudan, and the Abdullah Malik University of Morocco, China-Arab States Technology Transfer Center organized some agencies in the Ningxia Hui Autonomous Region or out of the Region including the Shanghai Jiaotong University and the Ningxia Remote Sensing, Surveying and Mapping Institute to hold four technical matchmaking conferences at abroad, hold 9 technical matchmaking conferences during the two sessions of the China-Arab States

Expo to promote face-to-face exchanges between Chinese and Arab technical representatives with remarkable result.A team of Chinese and Arab technology transfer talents have been gradually built. Training was carried out to solve the problem of serious shortage of technology transfer service talents. By doing this, a group of professionals have been trained to promote the transfer of technology between China and Arab states.

4. Technology Transfer

With the relevant China-Arab States Cooperation Forum, China-Arab States Expo, China-Arab States Technology Transfer Center and other institutions, China-Arab technology transfer has achieved phased achievements. More than 20 China-Arab technology innovation projects have been launched, and Ningxia (China-Arab) Dates Engineering Technology Research Center, Ningxia (China-Arab) Plant and Beverage Engineering Technology Research Center, Ningxia (China-Arab) Key Laboratory of Resource Evaluation and Environmental Regulation in Arid Areas and a number of China-Arab technology innovation platforms has been cultivated in the fields of date palm, halal food, agricultural internet, green smart water-saving equipment, satellite data service, and potato food development. The technologies have been demonstrated and promoted in Arab states for promoting red palm weevil prevention, agricultural interne, water conservation, potato cultivation and food production.[①]

In addition, with support of the Saudi King's Innovation and Development Center of Sci-tech City, a sub-center was set up to promote Huawei's joint innovation 4G-LTE laboratory in Saudi King's Innovation and Development Center of Sci-tech City. Guyuan Xinyue Halal Food Co., Ltd. and Saudi Abuljadayel Catering Co., Ltd. build a food production line in Saudi Arabia and export advanced food processing technology equipment. With support of Dubai Landscape Agriculture Bureau and the UAE National Agricultural Committee, a sub-center was formed to cooperate in the fields of date palm industry, agricultural internet, and water-saving technology applications. More than 700 agricultural intelligent management projects implemented by the Ningxia Agricultural Internet of Things Engineering Technology Research

① "Ningxia promotes China-Arab scientific and technological cooperation to achieve fruitful results", Ministry of Science and Technology of the People's Republic of China.http://www.most.gov.cn/dfkj/nx/zxdt/201801/t20180102_137328.htm,3 Jan,2018.

Center and the UAE farmer have produced positive demonstration effects. Relying on the sub-center established by the Middle East University of Jordan, two sides have conducted mutual cooperation in information resource sharing, innovation platform cultivation, technology transfer, and college vocational training. Established industrial technology transfer cooperation with Jordanian enterprises and universities, China established a 1,500-mu demonstration base of seed potato and commercial potato in Jordan. Thanks to a bilateral technology transfer sub-center built with the support of Oman National Commission for Science and Sultan Qaboos University, both sides jointly build a "Ningxia (China-Arab) Key Laboratory for Environmental Assessment and Environmental Regulation of Arid Areas" and a demonstration base to carry out applied basic research, new technologies and equipment developing. It has realized the export of 110 million yuan of water-saving technology and equipment to Oman. Based on the Academy of Scientific Research and Technology of the Arab Republic of Egypt to establish the bilateral technology transfer sub-center, the universities and research institutes and enterprises in the Region or out of the Region participated in the 4th and 5th Cairo International Innovation Exhibition. There are many cooperation in the international talent training, co-hosting technical matching activities, and jointly building a joint laboratory and other areas. With support of the Africa City of Technology of Sudan and the Department of International Cooperation and Partners of the Ministry of Higher Education of Morocco, bilateral technology transfer sub-centers in Sudan and Morocco respectively were built. China have mastered the technical needs of the Arab and cooperated with them in the China-Arab States Expo, international talent training, and joint technical promotion matching and other aspects.

4.3 Prospects

4.3.1 Prospects Planning

In accordance with the spirit of the Eighth Ministerial Conference of the China-Arab States Cooperation Forum, especially the contents of the documents adopted by the meeting, the two sides have planned a broad, pragmatic and complementary strategic cooperation prospect, including the following aspects.

We will strengthen scientific and cultural exchanges and cooperation, enhance mutual understanding and exchanges between politics, productions, universities and researching of China and Arab states, and encourage the two sides to carry out various forms of scientific and technological cooperation in areas of common interest. Seminars and training courses in the field of intellectual property will be organized to promote cultural construction that respects intellectual property, patents, trademarks, copyrights and neighboring rights. On international occasions, China and the League of Arab States shall coordinate on issues of common concern in the field of intellectual property and competitiveness, and explore the cooperation on intellectual property rights and the comparative study of the intellectual property system between China and the Arab states. China and the Arab states have already explored and cooperated on intellectual property rights to promote the conservation and development of genetic resources, traditional knowledge and folklore.

China welcomes young Arabian researchers to conduct short-term research work in China through the "Outstanding Young Scientists Work Plan in China", and invites Arabian technology management and technical personnel to participate in the "Advanced Applicable Technology and Technology Management Training Class" held by the Ministry of Science and Technology of China every year.

Joint labs will be built in key areas of common interest to support long-term and stable cooperative relations of both sides in production, university and research institutes. In terms of mutual cooperation in science and technology parks, China is willing to share with Chinese experience in the construction and development of Chinese science and technology parks, and carry out pragmatic cooperation in planning and construction, policy consultation, personnel training, and industrial matching with Arab states. China will continue to support the "China-Arab States Technology Transfer Center" and the construction of bilateral technology transfer sub-centers, and to build an integrated technology transfer network covering China and Arab states. According to the technical needs of both parties, through the training of professional and technical personnel, both sides shall arrange technical experts to visit each other, organize more various forms of exchange activities, carry out technical demonstrations and training, promote the transfer and promotion of advanced and practical technologies, and conduct training and exchange experience with Arab youth on China Aerospace Program. It is hoped that the Tunisian Ministry of Higher Education and Scientific Research could hold the second China-Arab States BeiDou Cooperation Forum in Tunis in 2019 under the framework of the Forum; launch the China-Arab Beidou/GNSS Excellent Center in Tunisia, construct the China-Saudi Arabia Beidou/GNSS Center, and strengthen cooperation in infrastructure construction, education training, joint research and development and application industrialization in the Beidou augmentation system, according to the memorandum of understanding signed between China Satellite Navigation System Management Office and the Saudi Kingdom Abdul Aziz on King Abdulaziz City for Science and Technology and Arabia ICT Organization. It is also hoped that China Satellite Navigation System Management Office and Arab Academy for Science, Technology & Maritime Transport could sign a memorandum of understanding on Beidou satellite navigation cooperation and carry out cooperation in training, application and promotion of Beidou in the fields of sea transportation and inland water transportation. A Beidou User Experience Evaluation Program in the Arab Region shall be jointly launched China Satellite Navigation System Management Office, Arab ICT Organization,Institute of Marine Engineering, Science & Technology and other units.①

4.3.2 Market Prospects

In today's economic globalization, developing countries actively connect with the world, integrate into the world, and develop an open economy. Both China and Arab states conform to the new world trends and continue to promote all-round cooperation including science and technology and deep cooperation for politics, economy, trade, energy, science, technology and humanities. It is very urgent to carry out financial, technological and humanity cooperation. At present, the Arab states have become China's largest crude oil supplier and the seventh largest trading partner. Such initiatives as jointly establishing the Belt and Road with Arab states proposed by China, "1+2 +3" cooperation pattern which means taking energy cooperation as the main axis, infrastructure construction and trade and investment as the two wings, and the three high-tech fields of nuclear energy, space satellite and new energy as the breakthrough point, and strengthening capacity cooperation have been positively responded by the Arab states.

Scientific and technological cooperation is an important part of China-Arab

① *Action Plan for China-Arab Cooperation Forum 2018-2020.*

cooperation. In contrast with the general transfer of science and technology in the world — from developed countries to developing countries, China and Arab states technology transfer is just between developing countries. China-Arab cooperation is driven by the government and dominated by the market. Chinese high-tech and equipment with international competition such as high-speed railways, aerospace communications, nuclear energy, new energy, modern agriculture are all needed by Arab states, while the Arab states are rich in energy and face opportunities and impetus for economic and social development. In particular, the GCC countries have their own revitalization plans to develop a "knowledge economy" led by information technology. Oman clearly listed the information technology industry as a key development industry for the new five-year plan. Bahrain planed to spend 3.5 billion USD to build a high-tech city. In 2008, Saudi Arabia invested a total of 40 billion USD in the development of the information and communication technology industry, becoming the world's largest investment in this field. At the same time, the Chinese government attaches great importance to accelerate the construction of a China-Arab government's science and technology innovation cooperation mechanism, implement the China-Arab technology partnership program, and continuously improve the technological capabilities of the Arab states.

Based on the traditional friendship, development stage and technical energy demand of the two sides, China and Arab states have optimistic prospects in science and technology cooperation.

Chapter 5 Special Report on China-Arab Financial Investment Cooperation

5.1 Indirect Investment in the Arab States[①]

According to the statistics of the International Monetary Fund (IMF), the portfolio investment of Arab states as of December 2017, although it is not the mainstream in the international capital market with small-scale, it showed a rapid growth trend. In addition, it is showed that the portfolio investment still focused on such five the Arab states as Saudi Arabia (156.967 billion USD), Bahrain (39.501 billion USD), Kuwait (16.924 billion USD), Lebanon (3.963 billion USD), and Egypt (1.557 billion USD) (see Table 5.1). The main targets of investment really aim at European and the American related markets. The United States accounted for about 40%, which was more than one-third of the sum of relevant European markets investments of Arab states (see Figure 5.1). Overall, Saudi Arabia's total investment declined in 2017 due to changes in the Crown Prince. As for the market of China's mainland, it enjoys a steady rise while Hong Kong market has shrunk. Saudi Arabia was still the largest investment country to China, which was equivalent to 10% of the amount of investment in the United States. In addition, the Taiwan (China) market has also attracted investment from Arab States. At the same time, Meanwhile, other countries had also absorbed the portfolio investment from the Arab states in varying degrees. The investment entities in the Arab states were mainly concentrated in the Gulf countries, with the United Arab Emirates as the head, Bahrain and Qatar ranking the second and third positions (see Table 5.2 and Table 5.3). According

① This section only considers portfolio investment and the data is limited to 2016 and 2017.

to report of the International Department of the People's Bank of China, on December 27, 2017, Zhou Xiaochuan, the president of the People's Bank of China, met with Saudi Finance Minister Mohammed Al-Jadaan in China. The two parties exchanged views on strengthening China-Saudi Arabia financial cooperation.①

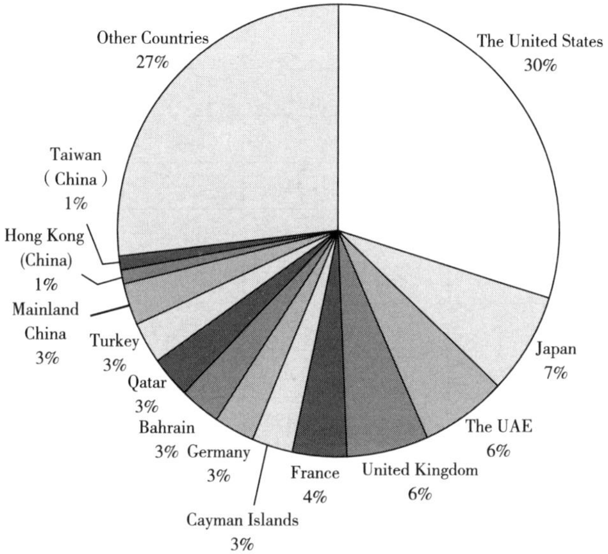

Figure 5.1 Main Countries Status of Portfolio Investment of Foreign Assets in Arab States in 2017

Data Source: International Monetary Fund (IMF), till for March 18, 2018.

Fig 5.1 Main Countries Status of Portfolio Investment of Foreign Assets in Arab States in 2017

(Unit: Million USD)

Target Investor	Bahrain	Egypt	Kuwait	Lebanon	Saudi Arabia	Total
Algeria	—	—	—	0	0	0
Bahrain	0	12	4168	226	2042	6448

① Http://www.pbc.gov.cn/goujisi/144449/144464/3449938/index.html.

Continued

Target Investor	Bahrain	Egypt	Kuwait	Lebanon	Saudi Arabia	Total
Palestine	—	—	—	—	—	—
Comoros	—	—	—	0	0	0
Djibouti	—	—	—	0	0	0
Egypt	418	—	108	9	2300	2835
Iraq	16	—	11	1	0	28
Jordan	878	2	37	113	61	1091
Kuwait	354	15	—	20	668	1057
Lebanon	—	13	44	—	88	145
Libya	25	—	—	0	0	25
Mauritania	—	—	—	0	0	0
Morocco	95	—	5	0	5	105
Oman	270	—	541	7	382	1200
Qatar	2795	9	1045	32	2416	6297
Saudi Arabia	1841	394	2059	38	—	4332
Somalia	—	—	—	0	0	0
Sudan	2	2	14	4	0	22
Syria	—	1	80	1	28	110
Tunisia	117	2	8	0	34	161
The UAE	5502	45	2483	112	5787	13929
Yemen	3	—	1	0	0	4
Hong Kong (China)	1040	4	13	8	1837	2902
Macao (China)	—	—	—	0	0	0
Taiwan (China)	4	—	—	0	2177	2181
Mainland China	61	52	75	12	5598	5798
Brazil	1534	0	—	16	1389	2939

Continued

Target Investor	Bahrain	Egypt	Kuwait	Lebanon	Saudi Arabia	Total
Cayman Islands	3253	—	944	139	2745	7081
France	668	442	32	392	6119	7672
German	510	92	28	82	5690	6402
India	1421	0	23	2	877	2323
Japan	194	9	3	3	15730	15939
South Korea	513	—	67	1	3572	4153
Luxembourg	347	1	21	228	511	1108
Malaysia	487	25	835	4	1484	2779
Holland	405	2	17	62	2211	2753
Pakistan	259	—	2	10	548	829
Russia	225	—	—	1	960	1186
South Africa	206	—	—	59	1271	1536
Spain	136	2	2	18	2453	2611
Sweden	109	3	98	8	1283	1501
Switzerland	168	6	80	179	2735	3168
Turkey	4090	0	401	49	2045	6585
United Kingdom	1636	56	737	388	9934	12751
the United States	5145	251	1768	1327	55449	63940
Total	39501	1557	16924	3963	156967	218912

Data Source: International Monetary Fund, Coordinated Portfolio Investment Survey.

Note: the total investment amount is not exactly equal to the breakdown amount due to rounding; 0 means the amount is less than $ 500,000 or zero, "—" means no data.

5.2 Indirect Investment of Arab States from Foreign Countries

In view of the state of foreign investment in the world, compared with 2016 (scc Table 5.5), the total amount of portfolio investment attracted by Arab states in 2016 has increased, but the Arab states are still not hot areas for international capital inflows, accounting for about 0.4% of the world's total investment (See Table 5.2, Table 5.3, Table 5.4). Judging from the composition of capital inflows in 2016, the sources of funding for Arab States are becoming increasingly diverse, and the main investing entity was bonds (see Table 5.3) and mainly from Europe and the United States (see Table 5.4). Compared with 2016 (see Table 5.5), the total of the world's portfolio investment in Arab States was 168.9 billion USD, and in 2017 it was about 226.5 billion USD, an overall increase of 7.5%. In addition, Table 5.2 shows that the UAE is a hot spot for investment with a year-on-year growth of 7.4%. Egypt, Iraq and Qatar increased by 3.4%, 7.1% and 10% respectively; but Lebanon decreased by 7.2% (14.422 billion USD in 2016). Except Djibouti, Palestine and Somalia, at the same time, Libya, Sudan and Yemen are the lowest relevant investment countries. In 2017, funds from the United States, Luxembourg, the United Kingdom, Ireland, Switzerland, Germany, the Cayman Islands, France and Netherlands accounted for 22%, 12%, 7%, 6%, 5%, 4%, 3%, 2%, and 2% of the market share respectively (see Figure 5.2). As of the end of 2017, the United States, Japan, Luxembourg, the United Kingdom, South Korea, Germany, Switzerland, France, Ireland, the Cayman Islands, and the Netherlands had individually invested 49.485 billion USD, 5.418 billion USD, 25.966 billion USD, 14.861 billion USD, 2.054 billion USD, 9.493 billion USD, 8.759 billion USD, 5.214 billion USD, 14.528 billion USD, 6.824 billion USD, 3.606 billion USD, accounting for 65% of the total portfolio investment in the Arab states. Mainland China, Hong Kong of China and Macao of China had invested 2.682 billion USD, 2.157 billion USD and 737 million USD respectively, accounting for 2.5% of total portfolio investment (see Table 5.4). It can be seen that Europe is still the largest investment source of Arab states. Finally, capital flows in the Arab states were still very active in 2016, and Bahrain, Kuwait and Saudi Arabia remain the main investors, thus demonstrating a further strengthening of economic cooperation within Arab states. In short, although the volume of foreign investment of the Arab states is higher than the foreign investment to Arab States, the new trend is the two-way capital inflow, and the inflow rate is still on the rise.

Table 5.2 Total Financial Investment of Bahrain, Egypt and Kuwait to the Arab States and China in 2017

Unit: Million USD

Investing Project / Investor	Bahrain					Egypt					Kuwait				
	Total Equity Investment and Investment Funds	Total Bond Investment	Long-term Bond	Short-term Bond	Total Portfolio Investment	Total Equity Investment and Investment Funds	Total Bond Investment	Long-term Bond	Short-term Bond	Total Portfolio Investment	Total Equity Investment and Investment Funds	Total Bond Investment	Long-term Bond	Short-term Bond	Total Portfolio Investment
Algeria	..	..	..	..	..	..	..	..	..	..	..	..	..	..	..
Palestine	..	..	..	..	..	..	..	..	..	..	..	..	..	..	..
Bahrain	..	..	..	..	..	12	..	..	..	12	3663	504	486	18	3867
Comoros	..	..	..	..	..	..	..	..	..	..	..	..	..	..	..
Djibouti	..	..	..	..	..	..	..	..	..	..	..	..	..	..	..
Egypt	8	410	399	12	418	..	..	..	..	..	107	0	0	0	107
Iraq	..	16	16	..	16	..	..	..	..	..	11	..	..	..	..
Jordan	299	578	578	..	977	..	..	..	..	..	37	0	..	..	37
Kuwait	182	172	169	3	354	..	15	15	..	15	..	..	..	..	..
Lebanon	..	..	..	..	..	6	8	..	8	14	44	0	0	0	44
Libya	25	..	..	..	25	..	..	..	..	..	..	..	..	..	..
Mauritania	..	..	..	..	..	..	..	..	..	..	..	..	..	..	..
Morocco	..	95	95	..	95	..	..	..	..	..	4	0	0	0	4
Oman	72	197	197	..	269	..	..	..	..	..	218	323	311	12	541
Qatar	374	2421	2326	95	1506	..	9	9	..	9	220	825	649	176	1045
Saudi Arabia	709	1132	1070	62	1841	318	80	51	29	398	1542	517	502	16	2059
Somalia	..	..	..	..	..	..	..	..	..	..	..	..	..	..	..

Continued

Investing Project / Investor	Bahrain					Egypt					Kuwait				
	Total Equity Investment and Investment Funds	Total Bond Investment	Long-term Bond	Short-term Bond	Total Portfolio Investment	Total Equity Investment and Investment Funds	Total Bond Investment	Long-term Bond	Short-term Bond	Total Portfolio Investment	Total Equity Investment and Investment Funds	Total Bond Investment	Long-term Bond	Short-term Bond	Total Portfolio Investment
Sudan	2	..	..	..	..	2	..	..	..	..	14	..	..	..	14
Syria	..	..	..	..	..	1	..	..	..	..	80	..	..	..	80
Tunisia	38	79	79	..	..	2	1	..	1	1	8	..	..	..	8
The UAE	565	4937	4628	309	5502	10	47	46	1	57	1263	1220	1181	39	2483
Yemen	3	..	..	..	3	..	..	..	..	..	1	..	..	..	1
Hong Kong (China)	52	988	988	..	1040	..	4	..	4	4	2	10	10	0	12
Macao (China)	..	..	..	..	..	..	..	..	..		..	..	..	..	..
Taiwan (China)	4	..	..	..	..	..	..	..	..		..	..	..	..	..
Mainland China	61	..	..	..	..	1	51	..	51	52	11	64	64	0	75
World Total	8262	37239	29627	1613	45501	1074	483	353	130	1557	11169	5754	4802	952	16923

Data Source: International Monetary Fund, Coordinated Portfolio Investment Survey.

Note: the total investment amount is not exactly equal to the breakdown amount due to rounding; 0 means the amount is less than $ 500,000 or zero, ".."means data is not available.

Table 5.3 Total Financial Investment of Lebanon and Saudi Arabia to the Arab States and China in 2017

Unit: Million USD

	Lebanon					Egypt				
Investing Project / Investor	Total Equity Investment and Investment Funds	Total Bond Investment	Long-term Bond	Short-term Bond	Total Portfolio Investment	Total Equity Investment and Investment Funds	Total Bond Investment	Long-term Bond	Short-term Bond	Total Portfolio Investment
Algeria	0	0	0	0	0	0	0	0	0	0
Palestine	..	..	..	..	..	..	..	..	..	0
Bahrain	214	12	12	0	226	336	1706	1657	49	2042
Comoros	0	0	0	0	0	0	0	0	0	0
Djibouti	0	0	0	0	0	0	0	0	0	0
Egypt	3	6	6	0	9	25	2275	72	2204	2300
Iraq	0	1	1	0	1	1	0	0	0	0
Jordan	112	1	1	0	113	0	61	61	0	61
Kuwait	14	5	5	0	19	23	645	377	269	668
Lebanon	..	..	..	..	..	26	62	62	0	88
Libya	0	0	0	0	0	0	0	0	0	0
Mauritania	0	0	0	0	0	0	0	0	0	0
Morocco	0	0	0	0	0	0	5	5	0	5
Oman	0	7	7	0	7	1	381	363	18	382
Qatar	2	30	30	0	32	20	2396	1930	466	2416

Continued

Investing Project / Investor	Lebanon					Egypt				
	Total Equity Investment and Investment Funds	Total Bond Investment	Long-term Bond	Short-term Bond	Total Portfolio Investment	Total Equity Investment and Investment Funds	Total Bond Investment	Long-term Bond	Short-term Bond	Total Portfolio Investment
Saudi Arabia	37	0	0	0	37	..	..	..	..	..
Somalia	0	0	0	0	0	0	0	0	0	0
Sudan	4	0	0	0	4	0	0	0	0	0
Syria	1	0	0	0	1	28	0	0	0	28
Tunisia	0	0	0	0	0	0	34	34	0	34
The UAE	33	79	79	0	102	265	5522	4435	1086	5787
Yemen	0	0	0	0	0	0	0	0	0	0
Hong Kong (China)	4	4	0	0	8	1579	258	258	0	1837
Macao (China)	0	0	0	0	0	0	0	0	0	0
Taiwan (China)	0	0	0	0	0	2177	0	0	0	2177
Mainland China	10	3	3	0	0	5401	197	197	0	5607
World Total	2004	1959	1926	34	3963	95897	61069	41820	19249	156966

Data Source: International Monetary Fund, Coordinated Portfolio Investment Survey.

Note: the total investment amount is not exactly equal to the breakdown amount due to rounding; 0 means the amount is less than $ 500,000 or zero, "..''means data is not available.

Table 5.4 Main Countries of Portfolio Investment Inflow of the Arab States in 2017

(Unit: Million USD)

Source of Investment / Target of Investment	The United States	Japan	Luxembourg	UK	South Korea	Germany	Switzerland	France	Ireland	Cayman Islands	Holland	Hong Kong (China)	Macao (China)	Taiwan (China)	Mainland China	Total
Algeria	..	0	0	29	0	0	15	254	0	0	0	9	..	..	0	539
Palestine	..	..	..	..	..		..	..	..	..	..	..	..		..	..
Bahrain	967	32	1037	245	4	215	131	346	150	0	16	259	..	..	10	10442
Comoros	..	0	0	0	0	0	0	..	0	0	0	0	..	..	0	0
Djibouti	..	0	0	0	0	0	0	..	0	0	0	0	..	..	0	0
Egypt	8418	167	5296	6223	29	798	194	85	1831	539	884	30	..	..	133	29908
Iraq	..	15	753	12	318	83	34	30	279	119	55	0	..	..	35	2006
Jordan	4630	20	580	247	3	164	51	1	211	56	76	0	..	..	18	8367
Kuwait	..	113	1070	315	111	277	28	46	541	174	15	17	5	..	12	4901
Lebanon	4124	52	2421	650	6	342	152	53	552	373	426	7	..	..	65	10376
Libya	..	0	1	16	0	0	0	..	0	0	0	0	..	..	0	96
Mauritania	..	0	28	53	0	0	5	..	0	5	0	0	..	..	0	91
Morocco	2249	56	1540	200	19	973	279	1142	258	24	165	285	..	..	81	8492
Oman	1791	82	1190	109	47	788	275	57	520	52	316	20	..	..	19	7141

Continued

Source of Investment / Target of Investment	The United States	Japan	Luxembourg	UK	South Korea	Germany	Switzerland	France	Ireland	Cayman Islands	Holland	Hong Kong (China)	Macao (China)	Taiwan (China)	Mainland China	Total
Qatar	7541	1254	1221	1692	385	907	699	70	1015	966	422	996	422	..	42	29444
Saudi Arabia	..	809	1039	1237	389	793	214	1523	1028	495	19	132	94	..	55	17001
Somalia	..	0	0	0	0	0	0	..	0	0	0	0	..	..	0	0
Sudan	..	0	0	0	0	0	0	..	0	0	0	0	..	..	0	26
Syria	..	0	0	0	19	0	0	..	0	0	0	0	..	..	0	130
Tunisia	1934	1038	417	25	0	416	56	308	324	45	145	6	..	..	10	5495
The UAE	17822	1780	9391	3783	724	3737	6901	1209	7819	3976	1067	4012	396	..	2240	92073
Yemen	..	0	0	0	0	0	0	..	0	0	0	0	..	..	0	4
Total	49485	5418	25966	14836	2054	9493	8759	5214	14528	6824	3606	2157	737	..	2682	226532

Data Source: International Monetary Fund, Coordinated Portfolio Investment Survey.

Note: the total investment amount is not exactly equal to the breakdown amount due to rounding; 0 means the amount is less than $ 500,000 or zero, “..”means data is not available.

Table 5.5 Overall Situation of Foreign Investment in Arab States in 2016

(Unit: Million USD)

Investor / Year	2016	Investor / Year	2016
Algeria	612	Oman	3202
Bahrain	8014	Palestine	—
Comoros	1018	Qatar	29142
Djibouti	0	Saudi Arabia	11933
Egypt	10165	Somalia	0
Iraq	1433	Sudan	29
Jordan	6287	Syria	108
Kuwait	1324	Tunisia	4400
Lebanon	14422	The UAE	68134
Libya	51	Yemen	47
Mauritania	73	Total Arab States	168877
Morocco	8483	Total countries and regions of the world	52088314

Data Source: International Monetary Fund, Coordinated Portfolio Investment Survey.

Note: the total investment amount is not exactly equal to the breakdown amount due to rounding; 0 means the amount is less than $ 500,000 or zero, "..''means data is not available.

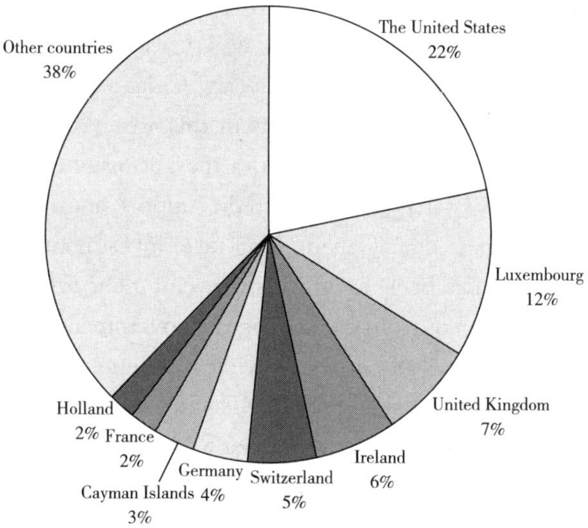

Figure 5.2 Main Countries of the Portfolio Investment in Arab States in 2017

Data Source: International Monetary Fund (IMF), till March 18, 2018.

5.3 "The Belt and Road" China-Arab Financial Cooperation①

According to the report of the People's Bank of China, Zhou Xiaochuan said at the Belt and Road Forum for International Cooperation & "Financing Promotion" Conference that the core of the Belt and Road is consultation, contribution and shared benefits, which means that the countries along the Belt and Road shall work together to enhance investment and financing cooperation. As the government has limited resources, it is necessary to strengthen the cooperation between the government and the market, and insist on taking the enterprise as the main body and market-oriented operation to ensure the sustainability of investment and financing. In accordance with the principles of openness, tolerance, equality and mutual benefit, China will work with relevant countries to strengthen mutual cooperation in the field of investment and financing of the "The Belt and Road", mainly in the following aspects.

China is willing to support the Belt and Road Financing through development finance. The construction of the Belt and Road is characterized by long cycle of project recovery and huge scale of capital demand; therefor development finance can play an important role in it. For a long time, institutions of development finance such as the World Bank, the European Bank for Reconstruction and Development and the Pan American Bank & Trust have raised a large sum of money to developing countries. In recent years, China's development financial institutions have also made active attempts in this area. According to Chinese experience, development finance refers to a market-oriented financial model that serves the national strategy, relies on credit support, and refuse government subsidies, featuring in self-management, long-term investment, low profits, and sustainable finance. It has been found that development finance business has multiple advantages, ranging from connecting the government and the market, to integrating the resources of all parties, providing medium and long-term credit support for specific demand-side, and also leading the demonstration role of commercial funds in a market-oriented manner to support.

China is committed to making commercial banks carry out network layouts for better financial services in trade and investment. "The Belt and Road" construction

① http://www.pbc.gov.cn/goutongjiaoliu/113456/113469/3307453/index.html.

not only requires investment and financing cooperation, but also involves a large number of supporting financial services, including agency relationships, syndicated loans, fund settlement and liquidation, project loans, account management, and risk management. In terms of trade financing promotion or better foreign investment service, it is necessary to accelerate the network layouts of financial institutions and financial services and improve the financial service in trade in order to form a virtuous circle of mutual promotion of finance and economy.

China is working with financial supervisory authorities of various countries to strengthen exchanges and cooperation on jointly eliminating various unreasonable barriers in entry and restrictions and providing an open, fair and orderly regulatory environment. By doing this, the network layouts of financial institutions and financial services can be better promoted to make a contribution the construction of the Belt and Road.

China focuses on the interconnection of financial infrastructure and promotes the development of inclusive finance represented by community banks and Internet/telecom online payments. The financial infrastructure of the countries along the Belt and Road will ensure the efficient operation and overall stability of the financial market. In recent years, China has made some progress in this fields, for example, China Union Pay's cross-border payment network has expanded in over 160 countries and regions, including many countries along the Belt and Road, providing payment service with high quality, safety and efficiency for enterprises and residents of various countries.

At last, China actively makes the local currency play its role in the construction of the Belt and Road. In the construction of "The Belt and Road", the active use of the national currency will help to effectively mobilize local savings, reduce the cost of exchanges, and maintain financial stability, which can be proved in the past experience. China has made some useful attempts in signing local currency swap agreements, direct transactions of currency, RMB clearing banks and RMB cross-border payment systems. China is willing to share relevant experience with countries along the route to jointly explore the expansion of local currency in the Belt and Road cooperation to better meet market demand and economic development needs. In addition, China seems to want to further promote the development of capital markets such as stocks and bond markets, and expand the connectivity of stock equity and bond financing markets.

5.4 Degree of Freedom of China-Arab States Finance

According to the "Financial Freedom Index"①, (See Table 5.6), among 185 global countries and regions, 4 Arab countries rank in Top 10 Financial Freedom List, of which, Bahrain ranks first in the world, the UAE snaps at its heels, Saudi Arabia ranks fifth, Oman ranks eighth, and Hong Kong China ranks ninth. Ranking in Top Ten List indicates that their financial market enjoys

---

① Based on the published data from different international financial organizations, analysis was conducted by the "*Index of Financial Freedom*", such as, the World Bank, the International Monetary Fund (IMF), Ernst & Young (EY), PricewaterhouseCoopers (PWC), Deloitte & Touche and other institutions. In this section, the author conducted induction and analogy on the financial freedom of China and the Arab countries in accordance with the 2014 Edition and 2015 Edition of "*Index of Financial Freedom*". Inside the "*Index of Financial Freedom*", an integral analysis on the financial freedom of different countries was conducted through 15 indexes and sub-indexes. Among them, 6 indexes of "tax rates" include the Maximum Income Tax Rate, Corporate Tax Rate, Value Added Tax (VAT), Capital Gains Tax Rate, Inheritance Tax Rate and Most-Favored-Nation (MFN) Treatment Tariff (the higher the overall "tax score" of a country is, the lower the occurrence of overall tax rate of the country will be); 3 international taxation indexes include income tax payable respectively by the citizens and residents, foreign residents and non-residents in the world, meanwhile, the above mentioned 6 indexes and 3 international taxation indexes are incorporated into one "overall taxation point"; 1 index of "investor protection intensity" is composed of 3 measurable indexes, namely, the extent index of disclosure, the director's liability range index and the shareholder's lawsuit mitigation index; 1 index "legal right intensity" is the protection of the rights of the borrower and the lender by the World Bank through a country's Mortgage and Bankruptcy Law; 1 index "currency exchange" refers to countries that can freely exchange currencies to make it easier for their citizens and external investors to be engaged in international trade, investment and capital circulation; 1 index "real estate ownership" refers to the ability of foreign investors to acquire permanent (referred to non-lease) property rights in a country without citizenship, which refers to ownership of buildings and land; 1 index "cost of living" refers that the World Bank adjusts the GDP figures to global price level differences to better compare national output of different countries, however, the adjustment of GDP to local prices requires the use of the so-called "PPP conversion factor and market exchange rate", so the cost of all manufactured goods and services in a certain economic entity is measured by PPP conversion factor, then the cost of living of a certain country will be measured; the last index "inflation" applies the world economic outlook database of the Monetary Fund to estimate the average figure of annual inflation rate from 2011 to 2018. Meanwhile, owing to the lack of data in some countries, not all countries are enrolled into the ranking list. Each index is graded evenly according to the relevant detailed classification and description of financial organizations in different countries, eventually a score between 0 and 1 will be obtained as the final rating index.

higher degree of openness and relative freedom of capital flows. Among 22 Arab countries, a total of 17 countries whose financial freedom degree is above the average, of which, 14 countries rank Top 100 in the world. In addition to the above GCC countries and regions, Kuwait and Qatar rank 12th and 38th respectively. And Algeria ranks 162. Libya has no rank, but according to the data, Libya is the world's penultimate. At the same time, Mauritania and Djibouti rank 150th and 182nd respectively, and Somalia is the last one. Although China's Macao is not ranked, according to the data, its ranking is between Syria (59) and Egypt (65), while China's Taiwan ranks after Egypt (67), China's Mainland ranks 159th. Secondly, it can be seen from Table 7.5 that the legal level of national financial openness in the Arab region is widely fluctuating, and the open level is differentiated, among which only the "legal power intensity" index of the Comoros exceeds 0.5, however, the legal freedom and openness of the GCC countries and other Arab countries are at a low level. As for the "investor protection intensity" indicator, only three countries reach the level above the average, namely, Saudi Arabia (0.69), Kuwait (0.61) and Tunisia (0.57). These countries put a lot of money into the U.S. derivatives market before the financial crisis, and regulatory departments set more restrictions on cross-border capital flows under capital projects for the sake of capital outflows at that time. After the outbreak of the financial crisis, these countries opened the regulation and control on relevant cross-border capital flow to avoid losses, especially for capital inflows. Excluding the special period of financial crisis, these countries maintained a higher degree of freedom of financial legal freedom, because they maintained a more stable internal and external environment, as well as more perfect financial legal system and market. In addition, among these countries, Bahrain, Kuwait, Qatar, Saudi Arabia and the United Arab Emirates are member states of OAPEC; they maintain free currency convertibility and a higher degree of freedom of capital flows due to oil trade, meanwhile, maintain a higher statutory degree of freedom for private asset transfer and bank cross-border business. Due to long-term chaos and wars and social unrest in such countries as Iraq, Libya, Syria and Somalia and others, resulted in the lack of relevant systems and laws in these countries, thus a significant drop in the legal financial freedom could be seen, but with the accelerated pace of reconstruction in the past two years, these countries (except Syria) have also developed cross-border capital management systems, and their legal financial freedom also improved.

According to the "Index of Economic Freedom"①, Hong Kong of China and Bahrain have maintained a relatively high degree of financial freedom, and the degree of financial freedom of Morocco, Qatar, Kuwait and the Sudan rise in 2017. In addition, China's Taiwan and Macao's financial freedom remains unchanged, while China's Mainland declines. Second, it is shown from Table 5.7 that China's Hong Kong scores 90 points, indicating that government intervention is minimal, and that the regulation from financial institutions is minimal, but might exceed the enforcement of contractual obligations and prevent from fraud. Bahrain scores 80 points, reflecting nominal government intervention. The government's ownership towards financial institutions in the overall assets of the share is very small, and almost no restrictions on financial institutions' ability to provide financial services to the government; China's Macao remains at a level of 70 points, which is a limited government intervention.

---

① In this section, the author analyzed the financial freedom of China and the Arab countries through the "*Index of Economic Freedom*" published by American "Heritage Foundation" over the years. Inside the "*Index of Economic Freedom*", the index of financial freedom is put under the category of "open market", which is an index to measure the efficiency of banking, as well as an index to measure the government control and intervention towards the financial departments. According to the interpretation of the "*Index of Economic Freedom*", the state reduces competition on ownership towards banks and other financial institutions (such as, insurance companies and capital markets), and generally lowers the level of access to credit. In the ideal bank and financing environment characterized by the minimum level of government intervention, the central bank's regulation towards financial institutions is restricted to the enforcement of contractual obligations and the prevention of fraud. Credit is allocated by market, and the government doesn't own financial institutions. All financial institutions provide various types of financial services to individuals and companies. Banks can freely extend credit business, accept deposits and operate in foreign currency. Foreign financial institutions are free to operate and are treated like domestic institutions. The "*Index of Economic Freedom*" assesses the financial freedom of a country by assessing five wide areas, namely, the degree of the government's supervision on financial services, the degree of intervention by states through direct and indirect ownership towards banks and other financial companies, the degree of government's impact on the distribution of credit, the degree of development of financial and capital markets, and the degree of openness to foreign competition. The five areas are considered to be the assessment on the overall level of financial freedom in a country. Moreover, "*Index of Economic Freedom*" is centesimal system; the financial freedom will be reflected from 0 point to 100 points for Mainland China, Hong Kong, Macao and Taiwan, as well as Arab countries. The data sources of the financial freedom for the "*Index of Economic Freedom*" are as following: "*The Economist*", the International Monetary Fund (IMF), economic surveys from Organization for Economic Cooperation and Development (OECD), The United States Department of Commerce, The World Bank, etc.

Credit allocation is affected by the government, while private credit allocation is almost unrestrained. The government has considerable ownership towards financial institutions, and foreign financial institutions receive less restriction, meanwhile, Morocco also rises to this level. China's Taiwan, Jordan and Oman are respectively at a level of 60 points, which indicates government intervention, banking and financial regulations have a burden, and the government manages the ownership and control right of financial institutions, accounts for a considerable share of the overall assets, as well as receives certain restrictions on the ability of financial institutions to provide financial services.At the same time, the UAE, Qatar and Kuwait have also reached and maintained this level. Both Saudi Arabia and Djibouti have maintained a level of 50 points in recent years, indicating that the degree of government intervention is considerable, that the credit allocation is significantly affected by the government, that private credit allocation is faced with major obstacles, that the ability of financial institutions to provide financial services is severely constrained, and that foreign financial institutions have received certain restrictions, meanwhile, Lebanon has also fallen to that level; two countries maintain at a level of 40 points, namely, Egypt and Mauritania, reflecting strong government intervention. The central bank is affected by the government, and the financial institutions are heavily regulated. Their ability to enforce contracts and prevent fraud is greater. The government has ownership and control rights of financial institutions, accounting for a small share of the overall assets; three countries maintain at a level of 30 points, namely, Tunisia, Comoros and Algeria, indicating that government intervention is widespread, and credit allocation is widely affected by the government who owns or controls most financial institutions or possesses a dominant place. Financial institutions are severely restricted, and also foreign financial institutions are subjected to significant restrictions. In addition, the formation of banks is faced with major obstacles. China's mainland is at a level of 20 points, reflecting severe government intervention. Non-independent central bank and financial institutions receives mandatory regulation, while foreign financial institutions are subjected to significant restrictions. Meanwhile, Sudan rises to that level (see Table 5.8).

According to the contents in 2017 Edition "World Development Indicators"①

---

① In this section, the author analyzed the financial freedom in China and Arab countries through financial status in different countries reflected from 11 indexes in 2017 Edition "World Development Indexes: Financial Access, Stability and Efficiency" published by the World Bank. In the first place, the credit acquisition is reflected through the strength of legal rights and the depth of credit information; in the second place, financial access and external connectivity are reflected through depositors, borrowers, branches and ATMs of commercial banks; other indexes are as following: the ratio of bank capital and asset, non-performing loans of the bank, lending margin from domestic banks to private sector, loan risk premiums and so on. In particular, illustration will be made through 11 points. 1. The index "strength of legal rights index" is used to measure the extent to which Mortgages and Insolvency Laws protects the rights of borrowers and lenders, thus to facilitate loans. The index ranges from 0 to 12, and the higher score indicates that the well-designed laws are to expand the acquisition of the credit; 2. The depth of credit information index is used to measure and affect the range, accessibility and quality rules of credit information provided through public or private credit registration systems. The index ranges from 0 to 8, where the higher value represents the availability of more credit information from the public or private registries in order to determine the loan; 3. The depositors of commercial banks refer to the report quantity of commercial banks and other non-financial corporation (public and private) and household deposit account holders. For many countries, this data only covers the total number of deposit accounts due to lack of account holder information. The main types of deposits include check accounts, savings accounts and fixed time deposits; 4. The borrower of a commercial bank refers to non-financial companies (public and private) and the number of resident clients obtaining loans from commercial banks and other banks. For many countries, the data only covers the total number of loan accounts owing to the lack of information on the holders of loan accounts; 5. The branch of a commercial bank refers to the place of retail of resident commercial banks and other resident banks. As a commercial bank, it will provide financial services for the clients, separated from the main office, but not as a legal divided subsidiary organization; 6. ATM refers to provide clients of financial institutions with equipment for financial transactions in public places; 7. Bank capital and assets refers to the ratio of bank capital and reserves to total assets. Capital and reserves include funds provided by the owner, retained earnings, general and special reserve fund, as well as reserves and valuation adjustments and so on. Capital included tier one capital (fully paid shares and common shares), which is a common feature of banking systems of all countries; in addition, the total regulatory capital includes several specific types of subordinated bonds, and if the funds is insufficient, there is no need to repay, but need to maintain a minimum level of capital (including secondary and tertiary capital), moreover, the total assets include all non-financial and financial assets; 8. The ratio of non-performing loans (NPL) to total loans refers to the value of non-performing loans divided by the total value of the loan portfolio (including non-performing loans before deducting specific Loan Loss Provision). The amount of loans recorded as non-performing loans should be the sum of the loans recorded on the balance sheet, not just overdue amounts; 9. Domestic credit provided by banks to the private sector refers to financial resources provided to the private sector by other depository companies (depository companies except for the central bank), such as the establishment of claims through loans, the (turn the note)

(see Table 5.7), compared to 2016, among all Arab countries, the Comoros still maintains a relatively high degree of legal rights freedom, indicating that the number of international capital flows bypassing legislation is relatively low; however, Bahrain, Egypt, Saudi Arabia and the United Arab Emirates maintain a high level of credit, reflecting that their financial industries have maintained a fast momentum of development. Their laws on financial market and international capital flow are comparatively perfect, and there are relatively few control measures. In particular, Bahrain and the United Arab Emirates are the financial centers in the Gulf region, and they own not only skilled bilingual talents, but also a management framework passed repeated examinations; their operating costs is not high and the geographical location is interconnected and convenient, especially they are adjoining neighbors of Saudi Arabia which is the first economic entity of its kind in the region. Therefore, its legal freedom and factual financial freedom maintain a relative consistency. However, a certain difference is demonstrated between the legal financial freedom and the factual degree of freedom in Egypt. The reason for this difference is that strict control measures on derivatives, real estate and financial institutions' external financial activities are imposed by the Egyptian government, which allows international capital to enter Egypt, bypassing the provisions and restrictions of laws, through such channels as investment, trade and others. In addition, Kuwait, Lebanon, Morocco, Oman and Qatar have maintained a relatively high level of credit information in recent years and outwardly their capital markets are more active. As for financial access and public relation, bank assets and non-performing loans, compared with 2016, the Arab countries as a whole have improved in 2017. At the same time, China's Hong Kong is at a very high degree of legal freedom

---

(take the page) purchase of non-material securities and trade credit and other accounts receivable. For some countries, the claim includes credit to public enterprises; 10. The interest rate spread refers to the interest rate charged by the bank for demand, time or savings deposits in commercial banks or similar banks towards those private sectors; the charged rate for the above-mentioned payment is subtracted from the loan rate. The terms and conditions attached to the interest rate varies from country to country, thus the comparability is restricted; 11. Loan risk premium refers to a value that the "risk-free" Treasury bill rate issued or traded on the market by short-term government securities, which is deducted from the interest rate of bank loans for private sector clients. In some countries, this interest rate might be negative, indicating that the risk of its best customer is lower than the government by market validation. However, the terms and conditions attached to the loan interest rate varies from country to country, thus the comparability is restricted.

and high level of credit information, thus indicating integrity and activity of its financial market, however, China's Mainland maintains a relatively high level, outwardly its capital market still has a great potential for development. In recent years, China has gradually determined the general direction of opening financial markets and actively participates in international financial activities, and begins to gradually reduce the restrictions on international capital flows and foreign investment. In contrast, China is not in the front rank, but shows a steady escalating trend, indicating that the level of China's real financial openness is also gradually improved, and has more active capital flows outside the scope of legal restrictions. As seen from the data, although the trend of real financial openness is deepening in China, legal restrictions are gradually opening up. Seen from the absolute data of the utilization of foreign capital, there is still a declining trend in recent three years, indicating that China has a slowdown in attracting foreign investment. As for the capital flows outside the legal restrictions, in general, when the legal limit is relatively loose, the real financial integration of the country will rise steadily under a favorable legal system conditions; conversely, when the legal limit is stricter, it is stated that other countries may have more options to circumvent restrictions on the country's legal regime, thereby allowing capital injections or other financial activities(see Table 5.6).

Table 5.6 China and Arab States Financial Freedom Index in 2017

Countries and Regions	Ranking	Average Score	Overall Tax Points	Legal Rights Tension	Investor Protection	Currency Exchange	Real Estate Ownership	Living Cost	Inflation
Bahrain	1	0.856	0.992	0.22	0.49	Yes	Yes	0.78	1.00
The UAE	2	0.830	0.992	0.33	0.38	Yes	Yes	0.65	1.00
Saudi Arabia	5	0.796	0.753	0.44	0.69	Yes	Yes	0.84	0.85
Oman	8	0.769	0.956	0.33	0.46	No	Yes	0.83	0.86
Hong Kong (China)	9	0.756	0.819	1.00	0.92	Yes	No	0.65	0.81
Kuwait	12	0.737	0.947	0.22	0.61	Yes	No	0.70	0.80

Continued

Countries and Regions	Ranking	Average Score	Overall Tax Points	Legal Rights Tension	Investor Protection	Currency Exchange	Real Estate Ownership	Living Cost	Inflation
Lebanon	25	0.671	0.696	0.22	0.46	Part	Yes	0.76	0.78
Qatar	38	0.651	0.962	0.22	0.46	No	No	0.69	0.82
Jordan	53	0.631	0.636	0.11	0.38	No	Yes	0.89	0.87
Yemen	55	0.628	0.679	0.11	0.34	No	Yes	0.93	0.30
Syria	59	0.622	0.703	0.00	0.43	No	Yes	0.76	0.78
Macao (China)	N/A	0.621	0.856	N/A	N/A	No	Part	0.74	0.61
Egypt	65	0.615	0.563	0.22	0.49	No	Yes	0.99	0.34
Taiwan (China)	67	0.604	0.588	N/A	0.61	No	Yes	0.78	1.00
Tunisia	92	0.571	0.432	0.22	0.57	No	Yes	0.91	0.71
Iraq	93	0.570	0.693	0.22	0.38	No	No	0.87	0.62
Morocco	102	0.559	0.398	0.22	0.46	No	Yes	0.89	1.00
Sudan	108	0.533	0.537	0.33	0.26	No	Yes	0.86	0.05
Comoros	146	0.513	0.526	0.56	0.34	No	No	0.79	0.76
Mauritania	150	0.507	0.507	0.22	0.31	No	No	0.93	0.64
Mainland China	159	0.494	0.461	0.44	0.46	No	No	0.78	0.92
Algeria	162	0.484	0.432	0.22	0.49	No	No	0.90	0.67
Djibouti	182	0.429	0.407	0.11	0.15	No	No	0.80	0.92
Libya	N/A	0.410	0.830	0.00	N/A	No	Part	N/A	0.57
Somalia	N/A	0.116	0.289	N/A	N/A	No	No	N/A	N/A
Palestine	…	…	…	…	…	…	…	…	…

Data Source: Financial Freedom Index. Note: The Financial Freedom Index is based on 15 indicators and sub-indicators. For an overview of the entire index, six tax rates and three international tax indicators are combined into one "tax score"; the other six main indicatorsappears on the index page. N/A means no data; ... means that data is not available; 1.00 is divided into the best, that is, 1.00 means low tax, because 1.00 "living cost" translates into low cost of living.

Table 5.7 China-Arab States Financial Freedom Index for 2014-2017

Degree of Freedom of China-Arab States Finance					Comprehensive Ranking 2017	
Countries and Regions / Year	2014	2015	2016	2017	World Ranking	Regional Ranking
Hong Kong (China)	90	90	90	90	1	1
Bahrain	80	80	80	80	44	4
Macao (China)	70	70	70	70	N/A	N/A
Taiwan (China)	60	60	60	60	11	5
Jordan	60	60	60	60	53	5
Oman	60	60	60	60	82	8
Morocco	60	60	60	70	86	9
Lebanon	60	60	50	50	137	11
The UAE	50	50	60	60	8	1
Qatar	50	50	60	60	29	2
Kuwait	50	50	50	60	61	6
Saudi Arabia	50	50	50	50	64	7
Djibouti	50	50	50	50	171	43
Egypt	40	40	40	40	144	12
Mauritania	40	40	40	40	131	25
Tunisia	30	30	30	30	123	10
Yemen	30	30	30	N/A	N/A	N/A
Mainland China	30	30	30	20	111	24
Comoros	30	30	30	30	121	22
Algeria	30	30	30	30	172	14
Libya	20	20	N/A	N/A	N/A	N/A
Syria	20	20	20	N/A	N/A	N/A
Sudan	N/A	N/A	N/A	20	164	40
Iraq	N/A	N/A	N/A	N/A	N/A	N/A
Somalia	N/A	N/A	N/A	N/A	N/A	N/A
Palestine	...	...	...	...	...	...

Note: N/A means no data; ... means that data is not available.

.Table 5.8 Financial Access, Stability and Efficiency Matrix in 2017

	Credit		Financial Access and Outreach				Bank Capital and Asset Ratio	Percentage of Bank Non-performing Loans to Total Loans	Loans of Domestic Banks to Private Sectors	Interest Rate Difference	Loan Risk Premium
	Legal Power Index	Credit Information Index	Commercial Bank Depositor	Commercial Bank Borrower	Commercial Bank Branch	ATM				Loan interest rate minus deposit interest rate	Main lending rate minus treasury bill rate
	0-12 (weak to strong)	0-8 (low to high)	Every 1,000 Adults	Every 1,000 Adults	Every 100,000 Adults	Every 100,000 Adults	Percentage	Percentage	Percentage of GDP	Percentage Point	Percentage Point
Algeria	2	0	544	39	5.2	8.67	9.8	11.4	23	6.3	6.8
Bahrain	1	8	..	..	..	..	..	..	73.7	4.2	5.1
Comoros	6	2	136	11	3.1	5.03	..	20.5	26.2	8.8	..
Djibouti	1	0	167	35	5.9	9.61	..	..	30.5	9.6	..
Egypt	2	8	440	100	4.5	13.45	..	..	34.1	5.7	5.4
Iraq	0	0	..	..	4.1	1.88	..	..	9.2	7.4	..
Jordan	0	5	534	..	15.1	27.12	..	..	75	5.1	..
Kuwait	1	6	..	211	14.3	62.17	..	..	103.6	2.9	..
Lebanon	2	6	1046	234	24.1	39.05	..	4.9	102.9	2.4	3.9
Libya	0	0	..	..	..	..	..	..	..	3.5	..
Mauritania	2	3	147	67	8.3	9.7	..	..	..	..	..
Morocco	2	7	933	..	24.7	26.7	..	..	64	..	..
Oman	1	6	1105	..	13.6	34.23	..	..	75.5	1.9	..
Qatar	1	6	..	252	11.7	60.73	..	..	79.3	1.6	..
Saudi Arabia	2	8	1141	166	8.6	74.42	14.8	1.4	58	..	..
Somalia	0	0	..	..	..	..	..	..	..	..	..

Continued

	Credit		Financial Access and Outreach				Bank Capital and Asset Ratio	Percentage of Bank Non-performing Loans to Total Loans	Loans of Domestic Banks to Private Sectors	Interest Rate Difference	Loan Risk Premium
	Legal Power Index	Credit Information Index	Commercial Bank Depositor	Commercial Bank Borrower	Commercial Bank Branch	ATM				Loan interest rate minus deposit interest rate	Main lending rate minus treasury bill rate
	0-12 (weak to strong)	0-8 (low to high)	Every 1,000 Adults	Every 1,000 Adults	Every 100,000 Adults	Every 100,000 Adults	Percentage	Percentage	Percentage of GDP	Percentage Point	Percentage Point
Sudan	..	..	..	..	..	..	..	..	..	..	..
Syria	3	0	..	..	3.4	4.75	..	..	8.9	..	..
Tunisia	1	2	..	..	..	..	..	..	..	..	..
The UAE	3	6	..	218	20.5	27.44	..	..	77	..	..
Yemen	2	8	1222	266	12.4	65.68	..	5.3	85.9	..	..
Saudi Arabia	0	0	124	13	1.6	6.28	..	..	..	..	..
Mainland China	0	0	34	384	8.8	81.45	8.4	1.7	156.7	2.9	..
Hong Kong (China)	8	8	..	..	21.4	50.59	9.8	0.9	203.8	..	4.3
Macao (China)	..	7	..	..	37.5	282.32	4.6	0.2	118.1	5.2	..
Taiwan (China)	..	..	..	..	..	..	..	..	..	..	..

Data Source: World Bank

Note: ".." means no data

Chapter 6 Special Report on China-Arab States Tourism Cooperation in the Context of the Belt and Road

In 2015, China National Tourism Administration first proposed the concept of "tourism diplomacy" ① and the goal of "exploiting tourism diplomacy and building a new pattern of tourism opening up" ②. As a leading industry to promote the "Silk Road Economic Belt", the tourism has a great significance to promote successful trade and people-to-people ties among the countries along the Belt and Road. The development of tourism drives information and capital flows through people, which will help eliminate ideological, economic, trade, administrative and industrial barriers between countries and promote the trade development in depth .

6.1 Dynamic Mechanism of China-Arab States Tourism Cooperation

6.1.1 China-Arab Tourism Cooperation as Internal Demand for Tourism Development in Arab States

In the past 20 years, the tourism industry in the Arab states has experienced a gradual process of "moving from the west to the east". The "911" attack was

① "Heated Discussion Work Report of Representatives of the 2015 National Tourism Work Conference", *China National Tourism Administration,* January 16, 2015, http://dj.cnta.gov.cn/html/2015-01/1712.shtml.

② "515 Strategy" - 52 Measures, China National Tourism Administration, May 13, 2015, http://www.cnta.gov.cn/ztwz/515zl/52xjc/201505/t20150513_644.html.

a turning point; prior to the "911" attack, the preferred targets for Arabians to travel abroad were the European countries such as the United Kingdom, France, Italy, and Spain. These countries favored by Arab tourists have a large number of Arab immigrants, and the geographical distance is relatively close. From the perspective of the source of inbound tourists, European and American tourists were also the main force of inbound tourism in the Arab region.

Since the "911" attack happened, the global wave of anti-terrorism and the resulting "Islamophobia" has led to a growing political conflict between Western and Arab States. It has a direct negative impact on tourism in the Arab region. On the one hand, the number of Western tourists visiting the Arab States has fallen sharply, and the local tourism industry has been hit hard. Among them, the losses are most serious in countries such as Tunisia, Morocco and Egypt. These countries have to take down the tourist prices and reduce the construction funds for tourism projects to deal with the crisis; on the other hand, Western countries represented by Europe and the United States continue to tighten visa policies, resulting in a decline in the number of Arab tourists traveling to Western countries.

Without going out or inviting in, Egypt, Jordan and other countries gradually shift the target country of inbound tourists from the West to the surrounding Arab states, especially the Gulf Arab States with higher per capita income. In just a few months, the number of inbound tourists in these countries has returned to the level before 911 attack. In 2002, the number of inbound tourists in Europe and the United States fell by 30% and 50%, while the number of tourists in the Middle East reached an all-time high of 16.7%. That is to say, from this period, the structure of the source countries of the inbound tourists in the Arab region has gradually shifted from the European and American countries to the Arab States, especially the Gulf Arab States. The regional tourism mobility has shown a sharp upward trend and many scholars call this phenomenon "the paradox of tourism development in the Middle East".[①]

In the early 1990s, Dubai took the lead in establishing a diversified economic development strategy based on the four major industries of finance, trade, real

① Ala Al-Hamarneh and Christian Steiner, "Islamic Tourism: Rethinking the Strategies of Tourism Development in the Arab World After September 11: Comparative Studies of South Asia," Africa and the Middle East, Vol. 24, No. 1, 2004, pp.18-27.

estate and tourism, and successfully established itself as a world-famous tourist destination. The "911" attack in 2001 and the "Arab Spring" that broke out at the end of 2010 not only did not impact the tourism industry in Dubai, but helped the industry to grow against the trend. By 2017, the total contribution rate of Dubai tourism to GDP has reached 12%.① Perhaps inspired by the Dubai model, almost all of the Gulf Arab States have made their determination to develop tourism in the recent five years. Saudi Arabia's "Vision 2030" has positioned the tourism industry as a new pillar of the sunrise industry and the future development of Saudi Arabia's economy. It has established a goal that Tourism will contribute 18% of Saudi GDP by 2020 with tourism revenue of 31.68 billion USD, making tourism the second largest source of revenue after oil②; Qatar's "2030 National Tourism Development Strategy" indicates that Qatar will attract 7 million international tourists by 2030; Oman's Ministry of Tourism says its international visitors will reach 5 million by 2040.

In order to achieve the above goals as scheduled, the Arab states face large challenges. Except the turbulent regional security situation, some factors such as backward infrastructure construction, violent fluctuations in international oil prices, and insufficient investment in tourism have all restricted the development of tourism in the region. In recent years, the scale of China's overseas travel market has grown rapidly, and the bilateral relations between China and Arab states have continued to improve in the context of the Belt and Road, which has brought rare opportunities for the development of tourism in the Arab States.

6.1.2 China-Arab States Tourism Cooperation as an Important Method to Deepen China-Arab States Economic and Trade Cooperation

In recent years, the Arab states' "looking east" and China's "westward strate. gy" have common interests, which provides favorable conditions for deepening China and Arab states economic and trade cooperation. From 2004 to 2014, the bilateral trade volume between China and Arab increased from 36.7 billion

① Travel & Tourism Economic Impact 2017:UAE, World Travel&Tourism Council,https://www.wttc.org/-/media/files/reports/economic-impact-research/countries-2017/unitedarabemirates2017.pdf.

② Saudi Arabia 2030 Vision, Saudi Government Official Websi, http://vision2030.gov.sa/.

USD to 251.2 billion USD,① an increase of nearly 6 times. At present, China has become the largest trading partner of nine Arab states including Saudi Arabia.

While China-Arab economic and trade relations continue to deepen, the deep-seated structural problems in bilateral trade have also become increasingly prominent. At present, China-Arab economic and trade cooperation is mainly concentrated in the four major fields of energy, import and export trade, engineering contracting and labor cooperation. The main body of cooperation is mainly between the states and local governments, because of lacking of mature market mechanism,which has led to a relatively simple cooperation field and a relatively low level of cooperation. It has seen the structural imbalance of trade for a long time, and the growth of two-way investment is weak.② China-Arab tourism cooperation is conducive to fostering a new growth point for China-Arab economic and trade cooperation. Through tourism, it will drive aviation, transportation, infrastructure, catering, accommodation, cultural and creative industries, and guide economic and trade cooperation from the government to enterprises and the private sectors.

The tourism market in the Arab States has great potential for development. Judging from the growth rate of the world, the future Middle East tourism market, especially the Gulf Arab States, will become the fastest growing area of Arab tourism worldwide. In 2015, the total overseas tourism consumption of GCC visitors exceeded 60% of the total overseas tourism consumption of Arab along the Belt and Road.③ Tourists from the Gulf Arab States have become a high-quality tourist source for all countries because of their long stay, high per capital consumption and high demand for tourism services. Strengthening China-Arab tourism cooperation has important practical significance for promoting the upgrading of China's existing tourism industry, optimizing the structure of inbound tourists, promoting the diversified development of China's tourism industry and further enhancing the internationalization level of China's tourism industry.

---

① Li Boya, "The Belt and Road Boosting China-Arab trade and Hopefully Reach 600 billion USD in a Decade" ,*21st Century Economic Report*, September 11, 2015, 9th edition.

② Wang Meng, "The Development and Problems of China-Arab Economy and Trade", Ningxia Social Science, No. 5, 2012, pp. 74-80.

③ Data from the State of the Global Islamic Economy Report 2016-2017 jointly issued by Dubai Islamic Economic Center and the Dinar Standards Corporation.

6.1.3 China-Arab tourism cooperation is conducive to enhancing China's soft power in the Middle East

The tourism industry is China's leading industry in promoting the construction of the Belt and Road and it plays a unique role in promoting successful trade and people-to-people ties among countries along the route. It is precisely because of this that China's "13th Five-Year Plan for Tourism Development" proposed the tourism diplomacy strategy for the first time, with a purpose to deepen the cultural exchanges and cooperation with countries along the Belt and Road and enhance China's soft power and external influence.

"The Arabian", the well-known media in the Arab region, commented: "The growing number of Chinese tourists in the Middle East can be seen as a symbol of their soft power. Compared with the efforts of United States to expand its presence in the Middle East by sending fleets and building military bases, tourism cooperation between China and the Gulf Arab States is a more cost-effective strategy."[①]

6.2 Current Status of Bilateral Exchanges of China and Arab States in Tourism

6.2.1 Construction of China-Arab Tourism Cooperation Mechanism

Although China and Arab states have established mutual exchanges in tourism for a long time, the government-level tourism cooperation mechanism was not established until 2010. In 2010, the China-Arab States Culture and Tourism Industry Cooperation Matchmaking Conference was held in Yinchuan, Ningxia, later renamed as the China-Arab States Tour Operators Conference. At present, the governments of both sides mainly rely on this mechanism to carry out bilateral tourism cooperation.

In recent years, the Ningxia government has taken advantage of the Belt and Road to focus on creating tourist destinations for Arab States. In 2015, the China-Arab States Tour Operators Conference was held in Ningxia. The guest of

① "The Arabian" news website: Tourism - China's Plan to Expand Its Influence in the Middle East, April 15, 2018,Http://alarab.uk/السياحة -خطة-الصين-لتوسيع-نفوذها-في-منطقة-الشرق-الأوسط.

honor issued the "Ningxia Declaration" with the establishment of The Belt and Road Tourism Development Alliance. With theme of "going into the beautiful China, feeling the charm of the Silk Road and magical Ningxia", the conference, adhering to the purpose of "friendship, cooperation, and development", strengthened tourism cooperation between China and Arab States in the areas of tourism resources promotion, aviation route development, and tourism platform construction.①

6.2.2 Source Countries of Tourists between China and Arab States

1. Tourists from Arab States to China

"Annual Report of China Inbound Tourism Development 2018" shows that in 2017, source countries of inbound tourist to China (except Hong Kong, Macao and Taiwan) were still dominated by short-distance source markets. Besides the United States, the top 10 source countries were all China's neighboring countries or southeast Asian countries close to China.② The number of visitors from the Arab states is small, and even no detailed and reliable official statistics can be found. According to relevant surveys, the reasons why Arab states, especially Gulf tourists, are unwilling to travel to China are mainly because of low awareness of China and low cultural exchanges. This is directly related to China's lack of publicity in the Arab region and its neglect of the development of the tourist source market in the Middle East.

2. Tourists from China to the Arab States

Since the 21st century, China's outbound travel has entered a period of rapid development. The destinations of Chinese outbound tourists continue to expand from neighboring countries to long-distance travel countries such as Europe and the United States. Since the Belt and Road Initiative proposed, the destinations of outbound travel have shown new changes, and the unknown tourist destinations along the Belt and Road have gradually been favored. In this context, the number of Chinese citizens traveling to the Arab states has also increased significantly. Among them, the United Arab Emirates (Dubai) is the most representative place. In the past five years, the number of Chinese tourists

① Li Hui: "China-Arab States Tour Operators Conference will Market Ningxia to the world", *Ningxia Daily,* July 1, 2015, the second edition.

② China Tourism Academy, *Annual Report of China Inbound Tourism Development 2018*, Tourism Education Press, 2018. Page 19.

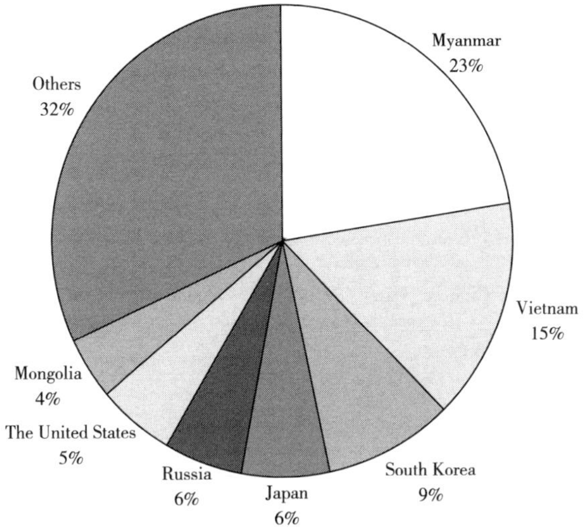

Figure 6.1 Main Source Structure of China's Inbound Tourism in 2017

Data Source: China Tourism Academy.

visiting Dubai has doubled (see Table 6.1). As of the first half of 2018, China became the fourth largest tourist source of Dubai.

Despite the increasing number of Chinese tourists visiting Dubai, the "Chinese Luxury Traveler" published annually by Rupert Hoogewerf and ILTM Asia, Dubai's ranking as the most popular destination for wealthy Chinese overseas has fallen from third in 2014 to ninth in 2017①, indicating that the structure of the Chinese source of tourists visiting Dubai in recent years is changing, and Dubai is gradually shifting from elite tourism destination to popular one. In the future, if Arab states want to better attract Chinese tourists, especially high-end tourists, they should constantly strive to optimize tourism routes, enhance the image of tourist destinations and improve the quality of tourism services.

① "Dubai Ranks in Top 3 Preferred Destinations for Rich Chinese Travelers," Emirates 24|7, June 17, 2014, http://www.emirates247.com/news/emirates/dubai-ranks-in-top-3-preferred-destinations-for-rich-chinese-travellers-2014-06-17-1.553290, accessed November 20, 2015.2017 data from:http://www.hurun.net/cn/article/details?num=dd1b436cb86e.

Table 6.1 Chinese Tourists to Dubai and Egypt from 2014 to 2017

Country\ Year		2014	2015	2016	2017
Dubai	Number of Chinese Tourists (10,000)	35	45	54	76.4
	Percentage of total Inbound Visitors (%)	2.7	3.2	3.6	4.8
	Ranking of Inbound Tourist country	9	9	7	5
Egypt	Number of Chinese Tourists (10,000)	6.5	13.5	17.9	28.7

Data sources: Dubai Statistics Centre

Egypt is second only to the United Arab Emirates which receives the largest number of Chinese tourists. In recent years, the development of tourism in Egypt is not ideal. Due to the influence of the "Arab Spring", the number of inbound tourists continued to decline during the shock, but the number of Chinese tourists to Egypt has maintained an annual increase of more than 30% from 65,000 in 2014 to 287,000 in 2017, an increase of more than four times. By 2017, China became Egypt's seventh largest tourist source country.

Except Dubai and Egypt, among the Arab States that have seen rapid growth in recent years includes Morocco, Tunisia and Oman. Since Oman signed a tourism memorandum of understanding with China in 2006, the number of Chinese tourists

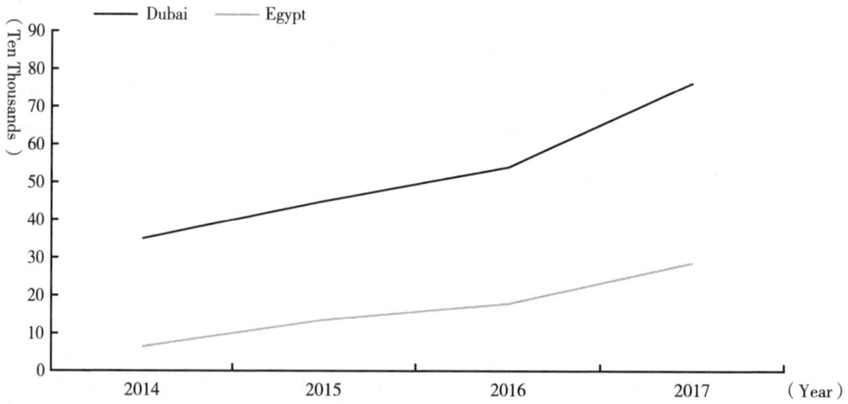

Figure 6.2 Growth Curve of Chinese Tourists to Dubai and Egypt from 2014 to 2017

visiting Oman has increased by more than 30% every year.① Since Morocco opened its landing visa to Chinese tourists in June 2016, the number of Chinese tourists to Morocco has been skyrocketed from 43,000 in 2016.to 107,000 in 2017; Tunisia implemented a visa-free policy for Chinese tourists in February 2017. At that year, the number of inbound tourists increased by more than 150% year-on-year, and China became the fastest growing source② of tourists in Tunisia.

Up to now, ten Arab States have implemented visa-free or landing visa policies for China. ③ More and more Arab States are aware of the new opportunities brought about by the development of China's tourism industry in the context of the Belt and Road.

6.3 Constraints on China-Arab Sates Tourism Cooperation

6.3.1 Regional Turmoil in Arab Region

Regional turmoil in the Arab region is the primary factor affecting the development of tourism in the countries of the region. The "Arab Spring" has led to a general decline in tourism sources in the region. According to the statistics of the World Tourism Organization, the number of visitors to the Middle East in 2011 decreased by 8.4% compared with 2010. The tourism industry in Egypt, Lebanon and Tunisia, which experienced political turmoil during the Arab Spring, was seriously damaged, and the number of inbound tourists showed a sharp decline. In 2010, the number of inbound tourists in Egypt was 14 million, and tourism revenue accounted for 13% of GDP; in 2011, the number of inbound tourists in Egypt fell to 9.5 million. In the same year, the occupancy rate of domestic hotels in Bahrain fell by 40%, the revenue of Jordan's tourism industry shrank by about 1 billion USD, the number of Lebanese tourists dropped by about 25% year-on-year, and the number of international tourists in Tunisia fell by about 1/3.④

① Liu Gang: "China's rapid growth in tourists to Oman", *Beijing Times*, August 12, 2010, No 02 version.

② The surge in the number of Chinese tourists to Tunisia", *People's Daily*, September 28, 2018, http://travel.people.com.cn/n1/2018/0928/c41570-30317828.html.

③ Including the United Arab Emirates, Morocco, Tunisia, Lebanon, Bahrain, Qatar, Jordan, Egypt, Comoros and Mauritania.

④ "Tourism in Egypt: Arab Spring Break", *The Economist*, May 4, 2013, http://www.economist.com/news/business/21577089-turmoil-has-scared-all-rugged-and-russians-arab-spring-breakaccessed December 2, 2015.

After the "Arab Spring" broke out, the polarization of tourism development in the Arab States has become increasingly apparent, and the tourism industry in the Middle East has undergone profound adjustment. The number of inbound tourists in Syria, Egypt, Lebanon, Jordan and other countries decreased by 41%, 32%, 24% and 13% respectively in 2011; the number of tourists in stable countries such as Morocco, UAE and Saudi Arabia continued to rise: the number of inbound tourists in Morocco increased in 2011 4%,① UAE tourists increased by 9%; Saudi Arabian inbound tourists increased by 60%.② The development of tourism in the Arab states in the future is still largely determined by the direction of the political security situation in the region.

6.3.2 Incomplete Bilateral Tourism Cooperation Mechanism

At present, China and Arab states tourism cooperation is still dominated by the construction of administrative means, lacking the guarantee of multiple cooperation mechanisms such as market regulation, negotiation, humanities integration and legal norms. The construction of the three-dimensional cooperation mechanism is still not perfect. The main body of cooperation is mainly the central government and local governments with weak influence of tourism enterprises and incomplete industry associations. The level of cooperation is relatively simple and there is no sub-regional tourism cooperation strategy. In the future, cooperation mechanisms should be improved mainly from the following three aspects.

1. Division of Responsibilities between the States and Local Governments

As the leading partner of bilateral tourism cooperation between China and Arab states, the countries mainly undertake the work of formulating framework agreements for tourism cooperation, eliminating barriers to tourist visas for various countries, setting up tourism cooperation platforms, and strengthening investment in foreign tourism infrastructure construction. Local governments mainly work on formulating tourism development plans and policies in line with the actual situation of local tourism development, protecting and developing local tourism resources, promoting the development cooperation of tourism

① Mark Johanson, "Post-Arab Spring Travel And Tourism In The Middle East: A Country-By-Country Look", *International Business Times,* June 1, 2012, accessed December 2, 2015.

② Gordana Kovjanic,"Islamic tourism as a factor of the middle east regional development",*Turizam,*Vol.18, No.1,2014, pp.33-43.

within the region, improving the construction of regional basic tourism facilities, and cultivating regional tourism talents. Therefore, it is helpful for China's tourism cooperation with Arab states to clarify the division of responsibilities between the states and local governments.

2. Major Role of Tourism Enterprises

Tourism enterprises and tourism agencies are mainly responsible for the development of tourism products and tourism routes, joint tourism marketing and upgrading of tourism services. In the future, they could try to accelerate the process of tourism cooperation between China and Arab states through the establishment of China and Arab transnational tourism enterprises or strengthening cooperation with Arab states' tourism enterprises, especially those large-scale multinational tourism enterprises with regional and international influences. These enterprises have an important voice in the formulation of local tourism industry standards and norms.

3. Sub-regional Tourism Cooperation

Judging from the practice of China's international tourism cooperation in the past decade, sub-regional tourism cooperation is one of the main modes of cross-border tourism cooperation, such as tourism development in the Lancang River-Mekong region, tourism cooperation in Tumen River, and China-Russian tourism border cooperation, which is commonly characterized by that the economies of both parties are at the level of developing countries, and it is still difficult to carry out an all-round integrated mode of tourism cooperation. Both China and Arab states have vast territory, diverse regional tourism resources, and diverse regional tourism development. The sub-regional tourism cooperation model is the best choice for the initial stage of cooperation. In the future, two sides should give full play to the main role of local governments at all levels in China, and hierarchically promote the "one-on-one" sub-regional tourism with the Arab states in the tourism circles and tourism sectors of relevant regions in China according to the characteristics of local tourism resources, development planning and development level to improve the pertinence of bilateral tourism cooperation.

The tourist areas of the Arab States are mainly divided into the Maghreb region of North Africa, the Nile Valley region, the Sham region and the Gulf region. China's tourism regions are mainly divided into three major regional tourism cooperation circles (the Yangtze River Delta, the Pearl River Delta and the Regional Tourism Cooperation Circle around Bohai Rim) and five regional tourism cooperation plates

(Southwest, Northwest, Northeast, Central Plains and Central China). From the current level of China's tourism development, the Arab states should focus on exploring sub-regional tourism cooperation between the Yangtze River Delta, the Pearl River Delta and the Northwest Region with the Gulf region. The Yangtze River Delta and the Pearl River Delta region have a relatively high overall economic level, relatively complete infrastructure construction, and the advantages of a tourism economic superior area, ① and close economic and trade relations with Arab States. The northwestern region, represented by Ningxia, has a natural advantage in developing tourism to Arab, and it is also a key area for China to implement the strategy of "opening to the west". The Gulf region has a high level of economic development and per capita income, and its politics is relatively stable. It has the foundation for foreign tourism cooperation. China-Arab tourism cooperation should first consider sub-regional tourism cooperation between the Yangtze River Delta, the Pearl River Delta with the the Gulf region of Arab States. After accumulating experience, it will be promoted in depth.

6.3.3 China's Weak Tourism Foundation to Arab States

The Global Arab Tourism Index (GMTI), co-published by Mastercard and the Crescent Rating Agency, is the current authoritative indicator of the attractiveness of destinations around the world to tourists of this area, consisting of four dimensions: destination transportation convenience, tourism ecosystem, and tourism development consciousness and the impact of tourism on local society.② In general, the GMTI index summarizes the potential of developing a Middle East tourism market in a region into two major factors: one is the developing basis of local tourism, that is, whether it is a tourism economic superior area; the other is the eco-environment and development consciousness of developing Middle East tourism market in this area.

① The tourism economic superior area refers to a specific area where the tourism economy is relatively developed and the tourism industry has a high income.

② Among the four indicators, the destination transportation convenience refers to providing driver services for inbound Arab tourists; the Arab tourism ecological environment refers to the tourism services and facilities; Arab tourism development awareness refers to news reports and the number of incidents related to Arab tourism; social impact refers to the number of jobs created by tourism for tourist destinations.

Compared with index system that the main disadvantages of China's current development of the tourist source market in the Arab States are shown as the following aspects.

Firstly, there is a lack of development awareness of the tourist source market in Arab states (mainly the Gulf Arab States), lack of tourism products and tourist route design specifically for tourists in the region, and lack of targeted marketing strategies and channels.

Secondly, the level of infrastructure construction and services for Arab tourists is low. The weak construction of tourism infrastructure mainly refers to catering, hotels, tourist attractions and activity facilities suitable for Arab tourists, and inadequate construction of relevant measures in public areas such as airports, scenic spots and shopping malls. The low level of tourism services mainly refers to lack of the channels for obtaining relevant tourism information, lack of personnel with the quality of the Arab tourism-related industry.

Among the many constraints, "food" and "tourism information acquisition" are two core issues. Arab tourists have to comply with relevant regulations in terms of diet. It is very important for Arab tourists to find a suitable restaurant at a convenient destination.

The importance of destination tourism information acquisition is that the tourists from the Gulf Arab States do not use the group tour method, but the family-based self-help tour mode. However, at present, most of the cities and scenic spots in China do not provide Arab tourists tourism-related information services, and there is no tourism website or APP developed specifically for Arab tourists.

Although the tourism sector in the northwest region has the awareness of exploring the tourist source market in the Middle East States, the overall development level of regional tourism is low, the tourism industry is weak, and infrastructure construction is insufficient. Although the southeast coastal areas are the tourism economic superior regions, they have lacked the awareness of developing the Arab tourist source market for a long time. Thus,China can draw from its own strengths to complement its weaknesses based on their current tourism development status and characteristics. For example, the southeast coastal areas should actively change their concepts and learn from the experiences of Singapore, Japan and other countries, as well as the Taiwan region of China to explore Southeast Asian tourists and GCC countries to promotes the construction of China's "Silk Road Cultural Tourism Economic Belt".

6.4 Fields of China-Arab States Tourism Cooperation

6.4.1 Tourist Source Market

Tourism market cooperation is a common form of international tourism cooperation. The advancement of global economic integration has made the tourism market undergo a process of development from domestic to foreign market, from local to global market. Tourism market cooperation mainly refers to cooperation in the field of tourist source market, including the joint development of tourism market and mutual tourism destination and source of tourists. China and the Arab states are not geographically adjacent. The tourism resources of the two parties are different, so as to the characteristics of tourism. Therefore, it is advisable to adopt a cooperative approach for mutual tourism destinations and tourist sources.

Both China and the Arab states have enormous potential for tourism development. The Belt and Road Initiative provides new opportunities for China to carry out tourism cooperation. In March 2015, the National Development and Reform Commission, the Ministry of Foreign Affairs and the Ministry of Commerce issued the "Vision and Actions on Jointly Building Silk Road Economic Belt and 21st-Century Maritime Silk Road" during the Boao Forum for Asia, with an aim to promoting the rapid development of tourism in countries and cities along the Belt and Road. As estimated by China National Tourism Administration, during the 13th Five-Year Plan period, China will transport 150 million Chinese tourists and 200 billion USD in tourism consumption for the countries along the Belt and Road. China's huge outbound travel consumption will inject a motive force into the overall development of tourism in the Arab States.[①] Many Arab states have realized that the historic opportunity offered by the Belt and Road initiative to the local region and has responded positively. Beginning in 2015, Morocco, Egypt, Tunisia, Lebanon, Qatar and other countries have adopted measures such as relaxing visa policies, opening direct routes, and conducting tourism promotion activities in China to explore the Chinese source market. Although the volume of outbound tourists in the Middle East is not

① How to Realize the Tourism Vision of the Belt and Road Initiative, China National Tourism Administration, April 7, 2015, http://dj.cnta.gov.cn/html/2015-04/1824.shtml.

large, the growth rate ranks first in the world.

The deepened tourism cooperation with Arab states will help China further explore the Arab tourist source market in other countries along the Belt and Road. In 2016, the total tourism consumption of Arab tourists worldwide exceeded 196 billion USD, accounting for 11.8% of the global tourism market share. It is predicted that by 2022, tourism consumption will reach 283 billion USD, accounting for 14% of tourism market.①

In the future, China and Arab states should jointly define tourism promotion principles and promotion plans by actively promoting tourism routes and developing tourism products through mutual promotion, and work together to build regional tourism publicity platforms. The mutual tourists source and destination should be promoted by such policies as visa and currency exchange.

6.4.2 Related Industries of Arab Tourism

Influenced by religious beliefs and customs, Arab tourists have different characteristics from other tourists in terms of destination choice, travel mode and consumption preferences. In order to meet these special needs of Arab tourists, the related hotel industry, catering industry, aviation industry and tourism information industry have sprung up and developed rapidly around the world. Relying on the huge Arab tourist source market, these industries are committed to providing travel services for Arab tourists around the world.

In recent years, the development of Arab tourism-related industries has shown a trend of branding, standardization and globalization. For example, in hotel industry that welcomes Arab tourists, after several years of development, it has formed several world-leading industry-leading brands, such as the Almulla Hotel Group in the United Arab Emirates. In October 2007, the group launched its first hotel construction project specifically for Arab tourists, carefully building its three famous brands. By 2013, the Group invested 2 billion USD in global construction of 150 hotels for Arab tourists, located in Saudi Arabia, UAE, Jordan, Egypt and Malaysia, and it will continue to open 35 hotels in European cities for Arab tourists such as London and Paris. In addition, the UAE also owns

① Data source: Thomson Reuters, State of the Global Islamic Economy Report 2016/2017, *Halal Focus*, https://ceif.iba.edu.pk/pdf/ThomsonReuters-stateoftheGlobalIslamicEconomyReport201617.pdf.

Kempinshi's Shaza brand, Rezidor, Rotana and Tamani from the KM group.①

Besides the Arab states, other internationally renowned tourist destinations are gradually turning their attention to the Arab tourist source market. As of 2011, Singapore issued industry certificates to 366 hotels and resorts in the country, recognizing that it had the qualifications to host Arab tourists, 289 of which are directly recognized by the Singapore Religious Department, including Pullman and Thistle and other well-known hotel brands. In 2009, the total tourist consumption of Arab tourists in the UK exceeded 1.3 billion USD. Such countries with most Arab tourist countries as the United Kingdom, Russia, France are paying more and more attention to the development of the relevant hotel industry.②

By strengthening cooperation with transnational tourism groups of Arab states, China is conducive to steadily improving the tourism infrastructure and service levels of receiving Arab tourists in China and increasing the visibility of China as a new destination for Arab tourism as well as the diversity and internationalization level of Chinese cultural tourism.

6.4.3 Cooperation of Information technology in Tourism

The cooperation of information technology in tourism between China and Arab states mainly includes two areas: internet tourism industry cooperation and the construction and sharing of tourism data information.

Internet information technology has an important impact on tourism. The Internet-based tourism information service has become an important means of global tourism business development and tourism marketing. In 2014, China National Tourism Administration formally proposed the concept of "smart tourism" to accelerate the promotion of smart tourism services such as online travel services, online marketing, online booking, and online payment.

As early as 2004, the Arab states formulated the "three-step" development plan for the regional e-tourism industry: the first step is to coordinate the tourism authorities of the Arab states for the disclosure and sharing of tourism-related data and tourism enterprise information resources; the second step is

① Mohamed M. Battour et al., "Toward a Halal Tourism Market," *Tourism Analysis*,Vol, 15, No. 4, 2010, pp. 461-470.

② Marcus L. Stephenson, "Deciphering 'Islamic Hospitality': Developments, Challenges and Opportunities," *Tourism Management*,Vol. 40, 2014, pp. 155-164.

to realize online transactions and financial settlement of tourism enterprises in various countries, online purchase and payment of tourism products through the establishment of a network information platform; and the third step is to realize the comprehensive integration of regional electronic tourism industry and other financial industries. Since 2008, the Arab States have held an International Federation for IT and Travel & Tourism (IFITT) every year to promote the online development of regional tourism.[①]

It can be the goal and direction of developing tourism cooperation between China and Arab states with the help of Internet information technology in the future through the Internet to carry out tourism joint promotion and marketing, the integration of bilateral tourism resources and industrial chain, and the cultivation of tourists' Internet habits, so as to realize the organic integration of traditional tourism marketing model and network marketing, .

Singapore is worthy of China's reference in exploring the Arab tourist source market by using the Internet. Its experience can be summarized as the use of the Internet to integrate domestic tourism resources and provide packaged travel services for Arab tourists. The Singapore-based Arab travel company, Crescent Rating, launched the "Arab Tourism" [②] online Travel Reservation website in December 2013, which sorts restaurants, resorts and tourist attractions according to industry standards, provides tourist information and reservation services for hotels, air tickets, travel agencies, etc., and provides great convenience for Arab tourists from Arab States and other regions. In 2014, Crescent Rating and Mastercard signed an agreement to provide professional financial advice and services to Arab tourism investors worldwide through data joint analysis. In recent years, the number of Arab tourists visiting Singapore has grown rapidly. According to Arab Travel Index released in 2014, Singapore ranked third, becoming the third largest destination of Arab tourism after Malaysia and the United Arab Emirates.

The co-construction and sharing of tourism data information between China and Arab states means that the two sides, under the leadership of the states and local governments, establish a tourism data statistics system and a tourism public opinion monitoring website. As a socialized service industry, the tourism

① Hasan Emir: "International Federation for IT and Travel & Tourism will be held recently at the Sharm el-Sheikh Resort" (Arabic), *Riyadh,* October 13, 2008, http://www.alriyadh.com /380553.

② Website http://www.halatrip.com/.

industry has effectively promoted the design, planning of tourism products and improvement of tourism service based on relevant statistical data. Through the establishment of hardware platforms, tourism statistics could be used by China and Arab states through multiple channels and models to enhance bilateral tourism cooperation through big data.

6.4.4 Talent Cultivation and Joint Research Fields

Joint talent training is the basic condition for promoting China-Arab tourism cooperation. On the one hand, the tourism industry involves a wide range of knowledge, and requires higher comprehensive quality of employees; On the other hand, China and the Arab states have great differences in culture, language and folk customs. he development of China-Arab tourism cooperation urgently needs to develop a group of tourism practitioners who master both Chinese and Arab languages and are familiar with both cultures, including foreign language translation, tourism marketing and management personnel, information technology personnel and other talents.

Thus, China and Arab states can establish a college through cooperation, set professional direction according to market demand, recruit students from all countries in the region, conduct cross-teaching and practice between China and Arab states, and realize training and exchange of high-quality tourism management talents in the short term.

And also, China and Arab states should also attach importance to joint research in the field of tourism. At present, China's theoretical research on tourism cooperation between China and Arab states cannot meet the needs of China-Arab tourism practice in every single level. The concept of "theoretical research first" is helpful to promote the rapid, orderly and healthy development of tourism between China and Arab states.

Chapter 7 Special Report on Building China-Arab States Industrial Parks

The economic and trade cooperation zones (including industrial parks) are the main platform and starting point to promote industrial capacity cooperation between China and the Arab states. In January 2016, the "China's Arab Policy Paper" promulgated by the Chinese government stated: "Following the principle of market-oriented business operation in which enterprises serve as the main player and government as the facilitator, we will combine China's advantage of production capacity with demands of Arab states, carry out with Arab states advanced, suitable, effective, employment-oriented and environment-friendly production capacity cooperation, supporting Arab states in their efforts to realize industrialization." On July 10, 2018, the 8th Ministerial Meeting of the China-Arab States Cooperation Forum was held in Beijing. The meeting discussed and adopted "the Execution Plan 2018-2020 of China-Arab States Cooperation Forum", emphasizes in the third economic cooperation that " it should give full play to the role of economic and trade cooperation zones and other areas in deepening cooperation between the two sides in terms of capacity and investment, and support more cooperation between China and Arab enterprises in the construction of the cooperation zone".

In order to respond positively to national policies, the National Development and Reform Commission, the Ministry of Commerce and other national ministries, as well as local governments such as the Ningxia Hui Autonomous Region, attaching great importance to international capacity cooperation with Arab states, successively corporate with government department and related agencies of countries along the Belt and Road such as Oman, Saudi Arabia and Egypt to establish a number of industrial parks. After years of unremitting efforts, China-Oman (Duqm) Industrial Park and China-Saudi Arabia (Jizan) Industrial Park have made positive progress. The construction of the China-UAE (Dubai) Food Industrial Park and China-Egypt Mankai Textile Industrial Park is steadily moving forward.

7.1 China-Oman (Duqm) Industrial Park

7.1.1 Basic Situation

1. Project Background

On September 10, 2015, the Ningxia government and Special Economic Zone Authority of Duqm in Oman signed a framework agreement for investment cooperation at the China-Arab States Expo in Yinchuan of Ningxia. On May 23, 2016, holding the signing and unveiling ceremony of the China-Oman (Duqm) Industrial Park. The National Development and Reform Commission listed the China-Oman (Duqm) Industrial Park as the one of the 20 capacity cooperation demonstration parks that will be promoted in 2016. The Ministry of Commerce also listed the China-Oman (Duqm) Industrial Park as one of the 16 key overseas economic and trade cooperation zones to promote international capacity cooperation. In 2018, it was included in the key projects of "Building the Silk Road Pearl".

2. Planning and Industrial Positioning

China-Oman (Duqm) Industrial Park is mainly operated by the enterprise. China-Arab Wanfang Investment Management Co., Ltd. was established by some of the investment companies in the Industrial Park to carry out planning, building and operating work. China-Oman (Duqm) Industrial Park covers an area of 11.72 square kilometers. The planned investment of the proposed project is 67 billion yuan, including 9 fields such as petrochemicals, building materials and e-commerce. It will be divided into heavy industrial area, light industrial comprehensive area and five-star hotel tourist area. It is expected to be put into operation in 35 projects, including heavy industry projects such as crude oil smelting and building materials production, as well as light industrial projects such as solar photovoltaic projects, logistics and automobile assembly and also with training centers, schools, hospitals and other ancillary services.

3. Preferential Policies

The Park has a land use right of 50 years and can be renewed for 50 years.

It can enjoy a tax exemption period of 30 years and establish 100% foreign-owned company. The goods imported into the special zone will enjoy tax-free treatment. Profits and funds can be remitted freely, without minimum investment requirements. There is no currency restrictions in the Park. EIA indicators for settled enterprises are equivalent to those of China. The commodities that account for more than 33% of local output value can issue certificates of origin.

As one of the six countries in the Gulf, Oman enjoys the relevant rights to export to the GCC countries and other countries that have signed free trade agreements. The Gulf countries signed a free trade agreement with Australia in 2007; Oman and the United States signed a free trade agreement in 2009; and the GCC countries and Singapore signed a free trade agreement in 2013; the GCC countries and the European Free Trade Association (Norway , Iceland, Switzerland and Liechtenstein) signed a free trade agreement in 2014.

In addition, the investors are available to enjoy the convenient and fast "one-stop" service that is popular in the world for registration, business license and environmental permit, and the work visa required for the project is not limited.

7.1.2 Progress

1. Complete The Park Planning and Feasibility Study Report and Launched Infrastructure Construction

Three reports of "China-Oman (Duqm) Industrial Park Feasibility Study", "China-Oman (Duqm) Industrial Park General Plan" and "China-Oman (Duqm) Industrial Park Municipal Detailed Planning" was finished separately by China International Engineering Consulting Corporation. It was planned to invest more than 30 projects in nine industries including petrochemicals, natural gas chemicals, building materials, renewable energy, oilfield equipment, modern agriculture, cross-border e-commerce, life services and seafood processing in about 10 years, with a total investment of about 67 billion yuan, 12,000 mu of land and 10,000 workers. At present, the feasibility study report has been completed in major projects, and a number of professionals have gone to the site for investigation and research. Other projects have also issued project proposals. Eighteen sets of Ningxia construction machinery have been delivered to the Park with 3 registered Ningxia companies and more than 50 employees. It has built 3 kilometers of roads and completed temporary water, electricity and road projects in the Park. The construction of the main road base and foreign labor camps of the Industrial Park are currently underway.

2. Signing Development Agreement for a Number of Preferential Policies

On May 23, 2016, the agreement on the construction of China's industrial park between the Ningxia government and the Special Economic Zone Authority in Duqm was officially signed in Muscat, the capital of Oman. According to the agreement, China has obtained a number of preferential policies: (1) exemption from all taxes for 30 years; (2) possessing 12 square kilometers of land with 50-years and can be renewal; (3) canceling any financial control; (4) work visas are unrestricted on the basis of work requirements; (5) 12 industries including energy, metallurgy, chemical industry and building materials involved in the international capacity cooperation document can be put to the ground; (6) self-provided power plants and self-owned water plants can be constructed; (7) allowing the Chinese to establish a 100% sole proprietorship enterprise, with Oman citizens accounting for 10% of the total number of employees, and other policies.

3. Holding a Groundbreaking Ceremony with a Number of Investment Projects

On April 19, 2017, a groundbreaking ceremony for the China Industrial Park was held in the Duqm Special Economic Zone in Oman. More than 60 guests from the Ningxia Hui Autonomous Region attended the ceremony. The event was highly valued by the Sultanate of Oman, and five ministerial officials including Royal Highness Prince of Oman, chairman of the Duqm Special Economic Zone, Minister of Urban Development and Water Resources of Oman, Vice Minister of Commerce Department and Governor of the Central Province attended the ceremony. Ten Chinese companies signed an admission agreement with Wanfang Co., Ltd., with a total investment of more than 22 billion yuan. At present, the first phase of the infrastructure construction project of the Industrial Park Light Industry Zone has completed land leveling. A total of 13 contracted projects included natural gas chemical, thermal power generation, photovoltaic modules, building materials market, talent training. In terms of project progress, at present, the first batch of of 37 foreign students from Oman has been trained for the vocational education program; the second batch of 30 Oman students have entered the Ningxia Vocational and Technical College for training in September 2018. In addition, on April 15, 2018, the comprehensive commercial and residential building project invested by Oman Wanfang Co., Ltd.

was started. The project has a total investment of 200 million yuan and is built by Ningxia Housing Construction Development (Group) Co., Ltd. It is expected to be completed in July 2019. On April 23, 2018, the shareholder agreement of Building Materials Wholesales project was formally signed. The project will be developed and operated by Duqm Material Market SAOC jointly established by Oman Wanfang Co., Ltd. and Al Thabat Holding (100% owned subsidiary of Oman Internal Pension Fund) and Tatweer (subordinate investment company of Special Economic Zone Authority in Duqm.). At present, the project has entered the tendering stage.

4. Preparing a Special Fund for the Park to Promote Key Projects in the Construction of the Park

Firstly, the Ningxia government has agreed that the government industry guidance fund will invest 100 million yuan in the sub-funds of the foreign cooperative industry, adopting market-oriented operations and fund-guided methods to ensure that the proportion of social funds is not less than 1:3. At present, it has been initially determined that Dongyuan (Tianjin) Equity Investment Fund Management Co., Ltd., Taicang Ruosen Investment Management Co., Ltd., Ningxia China-Oman Wanfang Investment Management Co., Ltd. and other units will allocate 335 million yuan to jointly establish China-Oman (Duqm) Industrial Park Special Fund for further promoting the construction of the Industrial Park. Secondly, 10 million yuan pre-work expenses supported by the National Development and Reform Commission for the development of the China-Oman (Duqm) Industrial Park has been allocated to the financial account of the Ningxia Hui Autonomous Region. Currently, according to relevant regulations, the enterprises in the China-Oman (Duqm) Industrial Park are given subsidy in the preliminary work .

5. Increasing the Industrial Park Publicity and Actively Engage in Second Batch of Enterprises Entering the Park

Firstly, at the invitation of the People's Government of Ningxia Hui Autonomous Region, Yahya Jabiri, Chairman of the Duqm Special Economic Zone in Oman, visited Ningxia and attended the China-Arab States Expo from September 5 to 9, 2017. In the meantime, Wanfang Company signed 13 cooperation agreements with domestic related enterprises, involving natural gas processing, thermal power generation, desalination, new energy and building materials. Secondly, it should continuously hold investment marketing activities for the China-Oman (Duqm) Industrial Park. From September 9 to 12, 2017, Yahya Jabiri, Chairman of the Oman Duqm Special Economic Zone, and his delegation went to Dalian and Shanghai to attend the investment marketing activities of the China-Oman (Duqm) Industrial Park, focusing on cooperative projects such as petrochemicals and natural gas, chemical industry, port, power plant, dry dock, and park supporting projects with fruitful achievements.

In late September 2018, the Expo Bureau of Ningxia Hui Autonomous Region (CCPIT) worked with relevant units to organize a number of promotional activities in Jinan, Hangzhou and Guangzhou, and to reach a basic consensus with the the Duqm Special Economic Zone of Authority in Oman on the allocation of oil and gas resources, water and electricity supply, policy support, financing channels, project advancement and other important issues. The projects was matched with Jingneng Group, Sinopec Ningbo Company, Zhejiang Oceanic Fisheries Co., Ltd., Guangzhou Automobile Group, Shandong Petrochemical Association, etc. They work with financial institutions such as China Import and Export Bank Shaanxi Branch, Dianshi Financial Holding Group, and Silk Road (China) Group Co., Ltd. to provide a new path for industrial park financing.

7.2 China-Saudi Arabia (Jizan) Industrial Park

7.2.1 Basic Situation

1. Project Background

On January 19, 2016, with the witness of President Xi Jinping's visit to Saudi Arabia and King Shatmanman, Yinchuan Yucheng Investment Co., Ltd. (referred to as Yinchuan Yucheng) belonged to Yinchuan Development Zone, Guangzhou Gaoxin District Investment Group and Saudi Aramco Oil Company. (referred to as Saudi Aramco) jointly signed a memorandum of cooperation to agree on the establishment of a joint venture company.

In April 2016, the Saudi government announced the "Vision of the Kingdom of Saudi Arabia 2030", proposing to establish special development zones in places with conditions and implementing special preferential policies different from other economic cities and industrial cities to attract more investment and accelerate the development of the Jizan Economic City. Based on this Vision, in accordance with the consensus reached by the high-level partners of the China-Saudi Arabia capacity cooperation, the Saudi side proposed to set up a special enterprise development zone for Chinese enterprises in Jizan Basic Industrial City and implement a more preferential investment policy for Chinese-funded enterprises.

On August 31, 2016, during the first meeting of the China-Saudi High-Level Committee, Yinchuan Yucheng, Guangzhou Gaoxin District Investment Group, The Royal Commission for Jizan and Yanbu (referred to as the Royal Commission) and Saudi Aramco signed in Beijing a framework agreement for the establishment of a joint venture company in Jizan Basic Industrial City.

Jizan Basic Industrial City is one of the four economic cities built by the Saudi government to accelerate the development of the domestic non-oil industry. It was formally laid on the foundation on November 5, 2005. The basic industrial city is 81 kilometers away from Jizan City,with an area of 106 square kilometers; the total planned investment in infrastructure is 30 billion US D, and the construction will be completed in 2025. As of the end of 2017, Saudi Aramco has completed an investment of approximately18 billion USD, of which infrastructure such as road network, port, water supply, power supply and sewage treatment was scheduled to be completed in early 2018. And then it would be handed over from Saudi Aramco to Yanbu and the Royal Commission to manage and operate.

2. Planning and Industrial Positioning

The China Enterprise Special Development Zone (China-Saudi (Jizan) Industrial Park of) has a total planned area of 32 square kilometers, including a 30 square kilometer industrial zone with no fixed physical boundaries and a 2 square kilometer living zone with closed management. According to the industrial layout plan of Jizan Basic Industrial City, there are heavy industrial, manufacturing, light industry, residential area and commercial area from south to north. In terms of heavy industry, we will focus on the development of energy stations, seawater purification stations, fuel storage plants, power stations, etc.; for light industry, we will focus on the development of raw materials, electronic products, modern services, garbage disposal, industrial components, biotechnology and agricultural technology. From 2018 to 2020, we will focus on the introduction of steel industry, petrochemical industry, silicon industry and ship service industry; from 2020 to 2025, we will put an eye on the introduction of food industry, packaging industry, home appliance assembly, mechanical and electrical equipment assembly, and building materials. The Park was listed by the National Development and

Reform Commission as one of the 20 key international capacity demonstration parks in 2016, and as an important industrial park supported by the Ministry of Commerce.

3. Preferential Policies

Firstly, the Saudi Investment Administration provides one-stop assistance for projects invested in the economic city in the areas of project data collation, approval, building permits, commercial registration, industrial licensing and environmental compliance. Secondly, in terms of financial assistance, it provides discount loans and grants for industrial projects, mainly including loans from the Saudi Industrial Development Fund to the project with 50% to 75% of total investment and a term of 15 to 20 years. Among them, the maximum loan amount of a wholly foreign-owned enterprise is 400 million riyals (about 107 million USD), and the joint venture has a maximum of 1.2 billion riyals (about 321 million USD). Thirdly, in terms of exemption of import tariffs, the Saudi Ministry of Finance exempts imported raw materials, machinery and equipment and spare parts used for production by 5% to 12% of import duties. At the same time, Jizan Economic City is located in the less developed provinces of Saudi Arabia. It can also enjoy the preferential policies of the Ministry of Finance for the reduction and exemption of the Zakat and income tax in the less developed areas. For example, it is subsidized by 50% of the cost of training Saudi staff, and granted at 50% of the employee's annual salary. Fourthly, in terms of human resources support, the Saudi Human Resources Development Foundation subsidizes enterprises to train Saudi labors. The main contents are: training subsidies of 500 riyals per month and 75% of salary for per student per month (up to 1500 riyals), 50% of monthly salary after training induction (up to 2000 riyals, 12 months).

7.2.2 Progress

1. Two-way Matchmaking

On April 25, 2018, China-Saudi Rubber Industry Development Forum, jointly organized the Saudi Industrial Cluster Development Program, the Royal Commission for Yanbu (RCY), the Saudi Arabia General Investment Administration (SAGIA), the Saudi Arabia Basic Industries Corporation (SABIC) and the China National Development and Reform Commission International Cooperation Center, was held at the Shanghai International Convention and

Exhibition Center. The purpose of the Forum lies in strengthening the strategic cooperation of the rubber and plastics industry with China, and attracting Chinese enterprises to invest in the rubber processing industry in Saudi Arabia. More than 70 enterprises and financial institutions from all over the country participated in the event. At the invitation of the Saudi Arabia, delegation from Yinchuan Development Zone and Guangzhou Development Zone respectively attended the forum. During the Forum, several companies recommended by the China-Saudi Office actively cooperated with Saudi Arabia. Among them, Shandong Linyi Mall Overseas Investment Co., Ltd. clearly expressed its interest in investing in Saudi Jizan Basic Industrial City and intended to promote Shandong New Energy Automobile Assembly Project to build in Jizan; Jiangsu Zhonghao Yinhe Rubber Co., Ltd. inspected Daman of Saudi Arabia and other cities in early 2018, hoping to establish cooperation with Saudi Aramco, using EPDM downstream product EPDM as its raw material, investing in EPDM Glue mixing plant project. The two companies exchanged views with the Saudi Arabian Investment Authority, the Industrial Cluster Development Program and Saudi Aramco respectively, and all indicated that they would continue to communicate further.

On August 11-18, 2018, at the invitation of the Saudi National Energy and Minerals Industry Cluster UNDP, a group of 8 people from the Office of the Leading Group for China and Saudi Arabia Industrial Capacity Cooperation, Yinchuan Yucheng Investment Co., Ltd. and Longi Clean Energy Co., Ltd. who were willing to invest in Saudi Arabia, visited to Saudi Arabia and the United Arab Emirates to promote Longi's investment in the new energy photovoltaic industrial project in Saudi Arabia, to investigate the investment environment and accelerate the construction of the China-Saudi Arabia capacity cooperation project. With the high attention and active cooperation of the Saudi Arabian, the visit had pragmatic, efficient and fruitful results, and achieved the goal of understanding, enhancing friendship and promoting cooperation with the Saudi Arabia.

On September 8-11, 2018, The 20th China International Fair for Investment and Trade hosted by the Ministry of Commerce was held in Xiamen, Fujian Province. The Economic Development Zone of Yinchuan City held the"China (Ningxia)-Arab Overseas Industrial Park Promotion Conference" at the Xiamen Convention Center. CEO of Royal Committee for Yanbu and Jizan, Nassif, represented all partners of China-Saudi Arabia capacity cooperation to introduce the planning of the Jizan Economic City.

On September 10th and 11th, 2018, the representative of Saudi Arabia for production capacity cooperation, Ala Nassif, the CEO of Jizan Royal Commission, forming a four-member delegation visited Yinchuan. The delegation visited the leaders of Yinchuan City and inspected the investment environment of Yinchuan City and the development zone. The two parties discussed the promotion of China and Saudi Arabia capacity cooperation, further promoted the integration of China's "The Belt and Road Initiative" and Saudi Arabia's "2030 Vision", and enhanced mutual trust for win-win development.

2. Progress of Park Construction

Currently, the completed and basically completed projects include: Aramco's refineries, power plants, ports and a steel mill with an annual output of 2 million tons. The first Chinese-funded enterprise entering the park project – Guangzhou Fanya Polyester Petrochemical Chemical Fiber Integration Project has been approved by the Saudi Arabia Investment Administration. The project is the first investment attraction project of Saudi Jizan Basic Industrial City and the first foreign-owned petrochemical project since the founding of the Kingdom of Saudi Arabia. The project construction is a large-scale chemical enterprise with an annual output of 2.5 million tons of PTA and 1 million tons of PET as the core of production. Through rolling development, the entire polyester industry chain is gradually covered. The project covers an area of about 1 million square meters, with a total investment of 3.2 billion USD. After the completion of the project, the annual output value is about 4.8 billion USD. The project was listed as an important investment promotion demonstration project by the Saudi government, and it is the first time to adopt Chinese technology, standards and equipment in Saudi Arabia, which will provide a model for future Chinese companies.

With the in-depth implementation of Saudi Arabia's "Vision 2030", the Saudi government aims to create an investment environment with local and international attractiveness to enhance investor confidence in Saudi Arabia. Its main objectives are: firstly, improving the administrative examination and approval environment for major investment; secondly, improving the necessary infrastructure and optimizing the investment environment; thirdly, developing a unified national investment vision to promote direct investment and support the national economy; fourthly, highlighting investment services and improving service satisfaction. These reforms will have a great significance to attract and serve Chinese investors in the future.

7.3 China-UAE (Dubai) Food Industrial Park

7.3.1 Project Background

China-UAE (Dubai) Food Industrial Park is located in Dubai Whole Sale City, Dubai, United Arab Emirates. It is planned to cover an area of 400,000 square meters and a building area of 300,000 square meters. It is located next to the entrance to Dubai Markum airport, 3 km from the Dubai 2020 Expo Park, adjacent to the Jebel Ali Free Zone across the highway. After completion, the industrial park will become the main supplier of airport meals and air food for the world's largest airport, the main supplier of tourist fast food and hotel meals in the world's largest theme park, and will also be an important supplier of humanitarian relief food in the Middle East.

7.3.2 Planning and Industrial Positioning

The industrial park is divided into a meal processing area, a convenient food processing area, a snack food processing area, a pastry processing area, a beef and mutton processing area, a frozen food processing area, a beef and mutton processing area, a frozen food area, equipped with a centralized cold chain storage and logistics district, central energy station, central cold station and central business district. Taking advantage of centralized energy supply stations and cold chain storage and logistics district, it will make the full use of energy, resources and land, and reduce operating and management costs for enterprises entering the Park.

The food industry park adopts an innovative fund model to initiate construction. After the completion of the project, the whole factory will be leased to the food production enterprise funded by the equipment; the fund company are responsible for the food enterprise equipment relocation, the industrial park plant construction, and the bottoming liquidity; the food production enterprise is responsible for the project operation; the fund and the entering enterprise jointly confirm the business target, and ensure that the industrial capacity can achieve the agreed gross profit index. The income source of the food enterprises entering the park is divided into two parts: firstly, the food enterprise as a partner to participate in the fund income distribution; secondly, the income from the food enterprises. In addition to the necessary expenses such as rents paid to the industrial park management company, all other incomes are owned by the food enterprises. The industrial park management companies and funds do not participate in the profit distribution of the food enterprises. Upon expiration of the fund, the food company may choose to repurchase the factory or renew the contract to continue the operation.

Through working with the Dubai Royal Family and major distributors in the UAE (including major suppliers of Emirates), the fund will used to establish a joint sales company and cross-border e-commerce platform for the enterprises to sell and export. Among them: meal processing products, pastry confectionery products, tea processing products, etc. are mainly sold to the Middle East and North Africa market; beef and mutton processing products, seafood products, and date palm processing products are mainly exported to the Chinese market.

7.3.3 Preferential Policies

After the enterprises entering the Park use the equipment and technology to convert cash into the "China-Arab Food Industry Cooperation Fund", the fund will be used to design and construct the factory according to the scale and requirements of the company's production capacity, and also provide capital for equipment relocation and ground floor operation, move-in service for enterprises, and services to solve corporate financing difficulties. It may retain the fund share or be operated it by others, if the enterprise entering the park is unable to continue to operate due to various reasons, and continue to enjoy the annual income distribution of the fund and withdraw from the investment after the expiration.

1. Tax policy

Value-added tax and other taxes: In 2018, Dubai, United Arab Emirates began to impose uniformly 5% fixed value-added tax on all industries, estates and services. In addition to this tax, Dubai does not impose other taxes. Tariff: the tariff is 5% for ordinary goods in Dubai, UAE, and the basic food and food ingredients enjoy tax exemption policy. At the same time, goods exported by the Food Industry Park are exempt from customs duties.

2. Insurer System Policy

According to Dubai law, foreign investment in Dubai requires a local legal person or natural person to be the legal representative hold a 51% stake in the legal level. The joint venture needs to invite the local insurer who act as the legal person at the legal level and hold 51% of the shares to establish a new company (a private agreement guarantees that the foreign capital holding 100% of the company's shares and it has legal effect in the local area). The Food Industry Park has reached an agreement with the Dubai government. The enterprises in the park are guaranteed by the Dubai government and can own 100% of the company. The local government only charges a small service fee.

3. Sales Policy

The park works with local major distributors to establish a joint sales company, providing ready-made sales channels and orders for enterprises in the Park.

7.4 China-Egypt Mankai Textile Industrial Park

7.4.1 Basic Situation

1. Project Background

In November 2016, Mankai Investment noted that Egypt encouraged domestic manufacturing and foreign investors to invest in Egypt. It then went to Egypt to inspect the textile industry and the domestic textile province and decided to invest in Egypt. In December 2016, Mankai Investment attended the Ningxia-Guangdong Economic and Technological Cooperation & Communication Symposium. Worked with several leading enterprises in the textile industry, it decided to invest in Egypt. During the China-Arab States Expo 2017, under the witness of the relevant leaders of China and Egypt, Mankai Investment and Egypt signed a cooperation framework agreement in Yinchuan.

2. Planning and Industrial Positioning

China-Egypt Mankai Textile Industrial Park is located in the industrial city of Sadat City, Monufia Province, Egypt. It covers an area of 3.1 million square meters and plans to attract 568 enterprises with a total investment of 2 billion USD. It mainly divided into five major areas including industrial land, training schools, supporting commerce, supporting business, and supporting residential, and functional zones such as production and processing base, raw and auxiliary materials base, training center, technology research and development center, warehouse logistics center, brand cultivation center, financial cultivation center, business service center, network information service centers, and five-star hotels. A industrial pattern, with production and trade of spinning, weaving, printing and dyeing, washing, garment manufacturing, embroidery, printing, accessories, shoes, hats, bags and suitcases, and integration of the development of warehousing, logistics, and e-commerce and other related industries (education, health care, finance, convention and exhibition, hotel, office, research and development, etc.), will be formed, aiming at creating a new modern industrial park with industrial cluster and linkage.

3. Preferential Policies

The Egyptian stipulates that the investment projects established after the "New Investment Law in Egypt" (May 2017) entry into force will enjoy the investment incentives for tax reduction according to the investment area as follows.

Class A area: Investment cost is reduced by 70%, including the areas mostly needed to be developed according to the statistical report of the Central Information and Statistics Center and the investment distribution of implementation regulations of the"New Investment Law in Egypt".

Class B area: Investment cost is reduced by 50%, including the areas needed to be developed except for Class A area according to the statistical report of the Central Information and Statistics Center and the investment distribution of implementation regulations of the"New Investment Law in Egypt".

Class C area: Investment cost is reduced by 30%, including, according to the distribution of investment activities, a large number of employment projects in the remaining areas of the Republic; small and micro projects; projects using new energy, renewable energy and energy production projects; national and strategic projects identified by the Supreme Investment Committee; travel projects identified by the Supreme Investment Committee, etc.

7.4.2 Progress of Park Construction

In March 2017, Ningxia Mankai Investment Co., Ltd. was registered.

From May to August 2017, the "Feasibility Study Report of China's Egypt Mankai Textile Industrial Park"was officially compiled and completed.

In October 2017, Mankai Investment organized 25 Chinese textile companies to to Egypt, and finally selected the "Sadat" Industrial City as the address of the Park. Conducted formal negotiations with the Egyptian Industrial Development

Administration and the Minister of Trade and Industry, Tarik Kabir, it signed a land use framework agreement with the Egyptian Ministry of Trade and Industry.

In December 2017, Egypt Mankai Textile Manufacturing Co., Ltd. formally registered, paid 5% land transfer fees to relevant government departments. After the Egyptian cabinet meeting and the approval of the Congress, the Egyptian Minister of Trade and Industry Tarik Kabir personally issued a formal approval for Mankai Investment,witnessed by the Chinese Ambassador to Egypt, Song Aiguo.

In January 2018, when Egyptian President Sisi visited the Sadat Industrial City, Minister of Trade and Industry Tarik Kabir personally introduced the Mankai Textile Industrial Park project to the President, which was highly valued by President Sisi. President Sisi spoke highly of the project, saying that the Egyptian government will fully cooperate with Mankai Investment, simplify all procedures for project, which make the implementation period of the project be reduced from 7 years to 4 years, and the implementation period of the first phase will be reduced to one and a half years.

From March to April 2018, Mankai Investment signed a land property sale and purchase agreement (permanent property rights) with the Industrial Development Administration, and successively signed the construction agreement for the first phase of the industrial park with the Egyptian Armed Engineering Administration.

In April 2018, it signed a general contract of construction contract with China Metallurgical International Engineering Group Co., Ltd. in Beijing.

Since June 2018, Mankai Investment has launched special promotion activities in textile provinces such as Guangdong, Fujian, Zhejiang, Jiangsu and Hunan, with remarkable results. At present, more than 70 domestic enterprises have signed the intention letter to invest in the Park.

In October 2018, Mankai Investment accepted the proposal made by the Egyptian government department, and Ningxia Mankai Investment Co., Ltd. to re-establish the investment entity in Egypt — Changjiang Investment Co., Ltd. (Mankai Investment wholly-owned). All land ownership belongs to the Changjiang Investment Co., Ltd.

CA

中阿经贸关系发展进程 2018年度报告

金忠杰　主编

Development Process of
China-Arab States Economic and Trade
Relations Annual Report

2018

社会科学文献出版社
SOCIAL SCIENCES ACADEMIC PRESS(CHINA)

图书在版编目(CIP)数据

中阿经贸关系发展进程2018年度报告 / 金忠杰主编
. -- 北京：社会科学文献出版社，2019.9
ISBN 978-7-5201-4835-1

Ⅰ. ①中… Ⅱ. ①金… Ⅲ. ①对外经济关系-研究报告-中国、阿拉伯半岛地区-2018 Ⅳ. ①F125.537.1

中国版本图书馆CIP数据核字（2019）第089057号

中阿经贸关系发展进程2018年度报告

主　　编 / 金忠杰

出 版 人 / 谢寿光
组稿编辑 / 宋月华　周志静
责任编辑 / 周志静

出　　版 / 社会科学文献出版社・人文分社（010）59367215
地址：北京市北三环中路甲29号院华龙大厦　邮编：100029
网址：www.ssap.com.cn
发　　行 / 市场营销中心（010）59367081　59367083
印　　装 / 三河市龙林印务有限公司

规　　格 / 开 本：787mm×1092mm 1/16
印 张：18.25　字 数：350千字
版　　次 / 2019年9月第1版　2019年9月第1次印刷
书　　号 / ISBN 978-7-5201-4835-1
定　　价 / 198.00元

本书如有印装质量问题，请与读者服务中心（010-59367028）联系

版权所有 翻印必究

编写说明

本报告是在中阿博览会秘书处指导下，金忠杰担任主编，由宁夏大学中国阿拉伯国家研究院组织编写完成（参加编写成员见下列作者名单）。编写成员依托其在中阿经贸关系方面长期的知识积累，运用适当的分析工具描绘了中阿经贸关系的进程、特征和发展趋势。

本报告中文版由金忠杰主编。丁丽萍对中文本进行了审校。由陈玉香、路建刚负责协调，马博颖、张娟、金杰秀、宁姣等将中文版翻译为英文，马博颖对报告的英文版进行了高质量的校对。

对所有人员在编写本报告过程中所付出的努力和所体现的专业精神，表示衷心的感谢。同时感谢中阿博览会秘书处对本报告给予的支持和帮助。

本报告中所表述的观点仅属作者本人，不代表中阿博览会秘书处的观点及其政策。

《中阿经贸关系发展进程 2018 年度报告》编写组成员

主编

金忠杰（宁夏大学中国阿拉伯国家研究院教授）

审校

丁丽萍（宁夏人民出版社编辑）

编写组成员

孙德刚 / 余泳（上海外国语大学中东研究所研究员 / 副研究员）

夏淑琴（宁夏大学经济管理学院教授）

杨韶艳（宁夏大学经济管理学院教授）

马鑫（中共银川市委党校副教授）

王永宝（西安外国语大学经济金融学院教授、宁夏大学中国阿拉伯国家研究院特聘研究员）

曹笑笑（浙江外国语学院东方语学院副教授）

杨子实（宁夏大学博士研究生）

目　录

第 1 章　中阿共建“一带一路”与中阿经贸合作专题报告

阿拉伯世界地域广阔，从印度洋经红海、地中海一直延伸到大西洋，面积 1313 万平方千米，人口约 4 亿，包括西亚 12 国和非洲 10 国。这些国家均有出海口，海上贸易便利，且大多数国家拥有漫长的海岸线和丰富的海洋资源，成为陆上与海上丝绸之路的交会地带，也是中阿合作论坛建设和中非合作论坛建设的重要参与方。

过去六年，中阿在共建“一带一路”过程中，双边和多边合作关系不断升级：2014 年，国家主席习近平出席中阿合作论坛第六届部长级会议，提议中阿共建“一带一路”和“1+2+3”合作范式；[①]2016 年 1 月，中国政府公布首份《中国对阿拉伯国家政策文件》，同月，习近平成功对沙特阿拉伯和埃及进行国事访问；2018 年 7 月，习近平出席中阿合作论坛第八届部长级会议，中阿双方一致同意打造升级版中阿合作——“战略伙伴关系”，同月，习近平访问阿联酋，成为中共十九大后国家元首国际访问的第一站，对“一带一路”在中东的推进以及中阿经贸合作产生了积极影响。

1.1　中阿共建“一带一路”：方向、路径、成果

中阿既是古丝绸之路的缔造者，也是新时代“一带一路”的建设者。

① 丁俊：《中国与阿拉伯国家合作之路越走越宽》，《新民晚报》2018 年 7 月 12 日，第 23 版。

近六年来，中阿围绕“一带一路”开展务实合作，顶层设计不断完善，目标制订日益明确，战略合作稳步推进。基于“共商、共建、共享”原则，中国支持阿拉伯国家在“一带一路”建设中发挥桥梁和纽带作用，支持阿拉伯国家之间的互联互通。阿拉伯世界是中国与中东和非洲等广大发展中国家开展战略合作的重要伙伴。中阿同属发展中世界，都面临改革、发展、稳定的任务，都在推动工业化、信息化和智能化，都在发展科技、改善民生，也都在紧紧抓住“一带一路”带来的改革与发展机遇。2016 年 1 月，中国政府发布《中国对阿拉伯国家政策文件》，以“一带一路”建设为主轴，全面规划了“中阿全方位、多层次、宽领域合作格局”。文件还围绕产能合作、投资合作、贸易、能源合作、基础设施建设、航天合作、民用核领域合作、金融合作、经贸合作机制和平台建设提出了一系列可操作性强的方案和举措。①2018 年 7 月，国家主席习近平在出席中阿合作论坛第八届部长级会议上指出：“中方愿参与阿拉伯国家有关港口和未来阿拉伯铁路网建设，支持阿方构建连接中亚和东非、沟通印度洋和地中海的黄金枢纽物流网。”②

2004 年成立的中阿合作论坛（以下简称“论坛”）是中国与阿拉伯国家整体合作的最重要平台。论坛成立 14 年来，中阿关系大致经历了 7 年的平稳发展期和 7 年多的动荡期（“阿拉伯之春”以来），阿拉伯世界分化为三大类：第一类是相对稳定国家，如沙特、阿联酋、卡塔尔、摩洛哥、约旦、阿曼、科威特等君主制国家；第二类是转型国家，如埃及、苏丹、吉布提、伊拉克、阿尔及利亚、黎巴嫩、突尼斯等共和制国家；第三类是由乱而治的国家，如也门、叙利亚、索马里、利比亚等。③

“阿拉伯之春”爆发初期，受西方主流媒体的影响，不少阿拉伯国家

---

① 刘中民：《在中东推进“一带一路”建设的政治和安全风险及应对》，《国际观察》2018 年第 2 期，第 43 页。

② 习近平：《携手推进新时代中阿战略伙伴关系——在中阿合作论坛第八届部长级会议开幕式上的讲话》，《人民日报》2018 年 7 月 11 日，第 1 版。

③ 孙德刚等：《冷战后中国参与中东地区治理的理论与案例研究》，社会科学文献出版社，2018，第 30 页。

忙于国内政治事务，对国际经济合作关注度不够。然而，经过几年的发展，阿拉伯国家不仅未能实现民主转型，而且国家认同下降，分裂主义、恐怖主义和极端主义肆虐，经济停滞不前，就业不景气，通货膨胀加剧。阿拉伯国家尽管政治制度、发展阶段不同，但均努力实现经济转型，将升级基础设施、扩大就业和改善民生作为首要任务，越来越认可中国的“一带一路”倡议。

中阿共建“一带一路”是互利共赢、平等合作、共同发展的必然结果。中阿同属发展中世界，人口之和占世界的 1/4，是“亚非合作、南南合作”的典范。① 在中长期发展规划中，中阿倡导经济多元化，均把基础设施建设和民生改善放在显要位置。新时代，中国正朝着“两个一百年奋斗目标”前进，与沙特、苏丹、伊拉克、阿曼、卡塔尔、科威特、黎巴嫩、埃及、摩洛哥等 9 个阿拉伯国家签署了“一带一路”协议；同阿联酋、阿尔及利亚、沙特、苏丹和埃及等 5 个阿拉伯国家签署了产能合作文件；阿联酋、沙特、约旦、阿曼、卡塔尔、科威特和埃及等 7 个阿拉伯国家成为亚投行的创始成员国。② 中阿经贸合作的密切程度超过了历史上的任何时候。

“一带一路”倡议与阿拉伯国家发展战略高度契合，如埃及的“经济振兴计划”，沙特、阿联酋、卡塔尔和巴林等国的“2030 愿景”，约旦的“2025 愿景”，阿尔及利亚的“2035 愿景”，摩洛哥的“2020 工业加速发展计划”，伊拉克的“157 个重建重点计划”等。“一带一路”有力地促进了中阿政策沟通、设施联通、贸易畅通、资金融通和民心相通，丰富了中阿“1+2+3”合作的内涵。

中阿双方基于相似的发展诉求，积极围绕“一带一路”倡议开展政策和项目对接。“论坛”成立 14 年来，中阿贸易额增加 4 倍多，中国对阿投资增加 6 倍，中国在阿新签承包工程合同额增加 7 倍，阿拉伯国家孔子学

---

① 刘宝莱:《中阿合作论坛正在新的历史起点上》，环球网，http://opinion.huanqiu.com/opinion_world/2018-07/12431973.html。

② 《中国和阿拉伯国家合作共建“一带一路”行动宣言》，中阿合作论坛网，http://www.cascf.org/chn/zagx/gjydyl/t1577010.htm，2018 年 7 月 10 日。

院和孔子课堂增加到16家，中阿友好城市达26对。[①] 除中阿合作外，中国与各阿拉伯国家也建立了密切合作关系。目前，中国已同11个阿拉伯国家建立了不同形式的战略关系，包括与阿尔及利亚（2014年）、埃及（2014年）、沙特（2016年）和阿联酋（2018年）建立全面战略伙伴关系；同卡塔尔（2014年）、约旦（2015年）、伊拉克（2015年）、摩洛哥（2016年）、苏丹（2016年）、吉布提（2017年）、阿曼（2018年）建立战略伙伴关系。[②] 在共建“一带一路”过程中，中阿合作从2010年的战略合作关系提升为2018年的“全面合作、共同发展、面向未来的中阿战略伙伴关系”，阿拉伯国家成为“一带一路”建设的重要合作伙伴。

中阿共建“一带一路”促进了双方治国理政经验交流。改革开放40多年来，中国人民在中国特色社会主义道路上不断探索，积累了丰富的治国理政经验，值得其他发展中国家互学互鉴，如提高执政党执政能力与建立广泛统一战线的关系，正确处理改革、发展和稳定的关系，民主与民生的关系，独立自主与借鉴外部模式的关系，传承民族文化与应对西方文化渗透的关系等。[③] 阿拉伯国家从各自国情出发，也有可贵的成功案例。中阿双方平等对话，在“一带一路”建设过程中相互借鉴成功经验，有利于实现联合国2030年可持续发展议程。中国政府在扶贫脱贫、防沙治沙、对口支援、经济特区、招商引资、义务教育、民族区域自治、粮食安全、青年发展等问题上取得的成就值得阿拉伯国家借鉴；阿拉伯国家的成功经验，如迪拜自贸区建设对中国港口城市的自贸区建设也有重要借鉴意义。中国在“一带一路”推进过程中，向阿拉伯国家提供力所能及的帮助，以促进中阿经济与社会共同进步。2018年7月，习近平宣布，中方将再向叙利亚、也门、

---

① 上海外国语大学中东研究所、中阿合作论坛研究中心:《共建“一带一路”，推动中阿集体合作站上新起点——“中国—阿拉伯国家合作论坛”成就与展望》，2018，第22页，中阿合作论坛网，http://www.chinaarabcf.org/chn/zagx/ltdt/P020180614580301500634.pdf。

② 李伟建:《中阿战略伙伴关系：基础、现状与趋势》,《西亚非洲》2018年第4期，第5~6页。

③ 张建卫:《加强治国理政经验交流　深化中阿合作关系》,《当代世界》2014年第12期，第44~45页。

约旦、黎巴嫩提供 6 亿元援助，用于当地人道主义重建；再向巴勒斯坦提供 1 亿元无偿援助，用于改善巴勒斯坦民生；设立 10 亿元专项资金，支持阿拉伯国家维稳能力建设。① 中国和国际社会一道对阿拉伯国家的援助，有助于阿拉伯国家在经济和社会建设过程中由“输血”式发展转变为“造血”。

1.2　近年来中阿经贸合作进展情况

虽然中阿政治制度、意识形态和文化传统不同，但在改善民生、发展经济、扩大就业等方面有共同诉求。阿拉伯国家人口自然增长率高，尤其是青年人口比例高，30 岁以下年轻人占总人口的 65%~70%，民生改善压力大。“一带一路”倡议为阿拉伯国家产业升级提供了机遇，“互联互通”是中阿共建“一带一路”的重要特征，积极推动“五通”（政策沟通、设施联通、贸易畅通、资金融通、民心相通）是实现双方合作目标的重要手段。

截至 2017 年，中国已成为阿拉伯国家第二大贸易伙伴；中国是巴林、阿联酋、卡塔尔、埃及、约旦、科威特、黎巴嫩、摩洛哥、阿曼、沙特等 10 个阿拉伯国家第一大贸易伙伴，阿盟成为中国全球第七大贸易伙伴。中阿经济总量占世界经济总量的 1/8。在国际货币基金组织、世界银行、二十国集团、亚投行和国际能源组织中，中阿拥有相似的诉求——积极维护发展中国家在国际多边合作组织中的话语权。

中阿贸易互补性强，互利共赢是中阿战略伙伴关系的保障。正如习主席所指出的：“中国欢迎阿拉伯国家参加今年（2018 年——编者注）11 月在上海举办的首届中国国际进口博览会，将在今后 5 年实现阿拉伯国家参加博览会及贸易和投资综合展全覆盖。”② 中国积极与阿拉伯国家分享发展成果，得到广泛好评。

---

① 习近平：《携手推进新时代中阿战略伙伴关系——在中阿合作论坛第八届部长级会议开幕式上的讲话》，《人民日报》2018 年 7 月 11 日，第 1 版。

② 习近平：《携手推进新时代中阿战略伙伴关系——在中阿合作论坛第八届部长级会议开幕式上的讲话》，《人民日报》2018 年 7 月 11 日，第 1 版。

长期以来，中阿贸易领域单一，中国超过40%的能源进口来自阿拉伯国家。21世纪以来，中阿经贸合作经历了三个阶段：第一阶段是2000~2013年，主要以能源合作为主；第二阶段是2014年中阿合作论坛第六届部长级会议以后，中阿双方合作围绕“1+2+3”展开，即以能源合作为“主轴”，以基础设施建设、贸易和投资便利化为“两翼”，以核能、航天卫星、新能源三大高新领域为新的突破口①；第三阶段是2018年以来，中阿合作更具复合立体的全方位特征，既有经贸合作，又有产能合作，既有双边合作，又有多边合作。

为促进中阿贸易便利化，中国已同22个阿拉伯国家和海合会建有经贸联委会机制，同所有阿拉伯国家签署了双边政府经济、贸易和技术合作协定。中阿合作论坛成立以来，中阿贸易额、中国对阿拉伯国家直接投资流量和在阿拉伯国家新签承包工程合同额等方面都取得了令人瞩目的大幅增长。2004年，中阿贸易额为367亿美元，2008年突破1000亿美元，2012年突破2000亿美元，2014年达2512亿美元，同比增长5.2%，占中国外贸总额的5.8%，2017年，中阿贸易额达1913.52亿美元，同比增长11.9%。②

能源合作成为中阿贸易合作的重中之重。2016年，中国从海合会6国和伊拉克进口原油的总量为1.51亿吨，占中国进口原油总量的39.7%。同年，中国从所有阿拉伯产油国进口的原油总量为1.60亿吨，占中国原油进口总量的41.93%。③2017年，中国从阿拉伯国家进口原油1.57亿吨，占进口总量的37.03%。

中阿经贸合作正在从传统的能源领域向立体、多维的领域拓展，农业、

---

① 高兰芳:《宁夏融入丝绸之路经济带建设的战略选择——兼谈中阿共建丝绸之路经济带》,《宁夏党校学报》2014年第6期，第104页；习近平:《弘扬丝路精神深化中阿合作——在中阿合作论坛第六届部长级会议开幕式上的讲话》,《人民日报》2014年6月6日，第2版。

② 上海外国语大学中东研究所、中阿合作论坛研究中心:《共建“一带一路”，推动中阿集体合作站上新起点——“中国—阿拉伯国家合作论坛”成就与展望》，2018，第14~15页，中阿合作论坛网，http://www.chinaarabcf.org/chn/zagx/ltdt/P020180614580301500634.pdf。

③ 杨言洪、田冉冉:《“一带一路”倡议背景下中国与阿拉伯国家经贸合作研究》,《国际商务——对外经济贸易大学学报》2018年第3期，第63页。

环境、高科技等日益成为中阿合作新的增长点。目前，中国已与阿曼、巴勒斯坦、叙利亚、埃及、阿尔及利亚、苏丹、毛里塔尼亚等国签署了农业合作备忘录或建立了农业工作组，与摩洛哥、埃及、约旦等国签署了双边环境合作文件。同时，中国还通过举办反应堆技术、中小反应堆方面的培训班，向阿拉伯国家传授和平利用核能的经验[①]，为今后中阿核能合作奠定坚实基础。2015 年，中阿举行环境合作论坛并签署环境合作谅解备忘录；2016 年，中阿荒漠化防治专业研讨会在苏丹举行；为加强相关交流合作和工作规范，中国于 2016 年发布了《支撑绿色“一带一路”建设：构建中阿绿色发展合作伙伴关系》、2017 年发布了《“一带一路”生态环境保护合作规划》。[②] 此外，中国电信企业在国际漫游、国际长途、国际数据业务等方面与阿联酋、沙特、埃及、卡塔尔等国开展合作，华为公司、中兴公司与近 20 个阿拉伯国家的电信企业开展固网、无线网、智能终端等领域合作。[③]

中阿在经贸合作过程中，都很重视双边与多边合作机制的建设，实现了“多边舞台谈合作、双边关系谈落实”的良性互动机制，建立了中国—沙特、中国—阿联酋、中国—阿尔及利亚企业家互访机制，中国与埃及、摩洛哥、突尼斯、阿联酋分别成立了双边商务理事会。2005 年至今，已举办 7 届中阿企业家大会；中国国际贸易促进委员会（中国贸促会）与阿拉伯农工商会总联盟、海合会工商联合会、非洲工商会联盟、阿拉伯银行联盟等 4 家机构建立了多边工商合作机制，与阿拉伯国家对口商协会机构、贸易投资促进机构和大型企业签署了 28 个合作协议。为促进中阿经贸合作、推动“一带一路”项目在中东落地生根，近年来中国四大国有银行相继在

① 《中阿合作论坛第十次高官会成果文件》，外交部网站，https://www.fmprc.gov.cn/zalt/chn/gylt/zywj/t1051545.htm，2013 年 5 月 29~30 日。

② 上海外国语大学中东研究所、中阿合作论坛研究中心：《共建“一带一路”，推动中阿集体合作站上新起点——“中国—阿拉伯国家合作论坛”成就与展望》，2018，第 19 页，中阿合作论坛网，http://www.chinaarabcf.org/chn/zagx/ltdt/P020180614580301500634.pdf。

③ 上海外国语大学中东研究所、中阿合作论坛研究中心：《共建“一带一路”，推动中阿集体合作站上新起点——“中国—阿拉伯国家合作论坛”成就与展望》，2018 年，第 15~16 页，中阿合作论坛网，http://www.chinaarabcf.org/chn/zagx/ltdt/P020180614580301500634.pdf。

中东开展业务，如中国农业银行在迪拜，中国银行在巴林，中国工商银行在卡塔尔、沙特、科威特和伊拉克等均设立分行。[①] 此外，中阿民航合作继续推进，中国与阿联酋、阿尔及利亚、沙特、伊拉克、阿曼、卡塔尔和埃及 7 个国家开通了直航航班，每周往来航班超过 180 架次。

1.3　中阿产能合作进展情况

产能合作是中阿经贸合作的重要组成部分，是中阿共建“一带一路”的重点领域之一。2014 年 6 月，习近平在中阿合作论坛第六届部长级会上提出中阿“1+2+3”合作格局，其中中阿产能合作是重要的组成部分。2017 年 1~4 月，中国企业与“一带一路”沿线国家新签对外承包项目达 1862 项，合同金额达 318.5 亿美元。在“一带一路”沿线国家中，海合会国家是最大的工程承包市场之一。除了数量上的增长，中国工程承包项目结构也在不断优化，逐步从以劳动密集型为主转变为劳动、技术、资金密集型相结合的模式，业务范围也从普通的房屋建设、路桥建设扩展到工业、能源、通信、石化等领域。[②]2016 年，中国企业在阿拉伯国家新签承包工程合同金额为 404 亿美元，同比增长 40.8%，完成营业额 336 亿美元，同比增长 10.6%。2017 年，中国在阿拉伯国家新签工程承包合同金额就已达 328.05 亿美元。

中阿双方在产能对接、石油炼化、港口基建等领域均推出重大项目；中阿在论坛框架下设立了技术转移中心，签署了“北斗”卫星导航系统落地协议，并就和平利用核能培训中心、清洁能源中心合作协议达成一致；中阿双方启动科技伙伴关系，将在新能源、卫生健康、现代农业、通信等领域建立 10 个国家联合实验室。中国已与埃及、阿尔及利亚、阿联酋、沙特、苏丹 5 国开展了双边航天合作，中国于 2017 年成功发射阿尔及利亚一号通信卫星，中国—阿拉伯国家北斗中心于 2018 在突尼斯成立。2017 年中

① 赵磊:《“四大行”加速中东布局》,《中国经济周刊》2013 年第 15 期，第 53~55 页。

② 刘欣路、许婷:《“一带一路”视角下中阿经贸合作》,《中国穆斯林》2018 年第 1 期，第 31 页。

国和沙特已确定第一批中沙产能与投资合作 30 个重点项目，其中 8 个项目已经开工建设。[①] 中国与海合会国家产能合作的主要领域为能源、钢铁、建材、建筑机械、五金、化工等，如山东电建沙特阿美 MGS 二期 EPC 项目、中石油 BGP 项目、中国通信服务沙特公司通信工程项目。[②]

截至 2018 年，中方企业在阿拉伯国家承建的多个“一带一路”倡议重点基建项目取得显著进展，其中包括阿尔及利亚中心港的项目筹备、埃及“斋月十日城”市郊铁路、埃及国家主电网输电线、埃及玻璃纤维生产线、埃及小卫星总装集成测试中心项目、阿联酋哈利法港二期集装箱码头、毛里塔尼亚友谊港扩建、摩洛哥“穆罕默德六世大桥”及包括摩洛哥北部新一代项目在内的中摩共建“一带一路”合作成就、卡塔尔路赛体育场、约旦阿塔拉特油页岩发电站、阿曼苏哈尔独立电站项目、苏丹上阿特巴拉水利枢纽、沙特延布炼油厂等。[③]

中国和阿尔及利亚产能合作也取得了重要阶段性成果。2017 年 10 月底，在中国工程师的努力下，阿尔及利亚北部甘塔斯隧道贯通，大城市奥兰到首都阿尔及尔的行程由原来的 4 小时缩短到 2 小时，其为阿尔及利亚北方铁路干线建设奠定了基础[④]，也体现出中国和阿尔及利亚产能合作潜力巨大。

中阿货币流通为“一带一路”和中阿产能合作提供融资支持。阿拉伯国家积极参与亚投行建设，沙特代表和埃及代表还分别担任亚投行中东选区和非洲选区的董事。目前，亚投行已批准 4 项涉及阿拉伯国家的项目——阿曼杜库姆港商业码头和作业区项目、阿曼铁路系统准备项目、阿曼宽带基础设施项目和埃及太阳能光伏发电项目，贷款承诺额共计 6.63 亿美元，

---

① 上海外国语大学中东研究所、中阿合作论坛研究中心:《共建“一带一路”，推动中阿集体合作站上新起点——“中国—阿拉伯国家合作论坛”成就与展望》，2018，第 12 页，中阿合作论坛网，http://www.chinaarabcf.org/chn/zagx/ltdt/P020180614580301500634.pdf。

② 刘欣路、许婷:《“一带一路”视角下中阿经贸合作》,《中国穆斯林》2018 年第 1 期，第 31 页。

③ 《中国和阿拉伯国家合作共建“一带一路”行动宣言》，中阿合作论坛网，http://www.cascf.org/chn/zagx/gjydyl/t1577010.htm，2018 年 7 月 10 日。

④ 《号称“工程师灾难”的北非第一长隧，中国用 7 年时间攻克》，http://dy.163.com/v2/article/detail/DTLGCL8D0511DTU9.html。

占亚投行已批准项目总额的 15.67%。2017 年 1 月，亚投行向阿曼提供贷款 2.65 亿美元，是亚投行首次向阿拉伯国家提供贷款。① 此外，为支持中东工业化，中国还设立 150 亿美元专项贷款和 100 亿美元优惠贷款，与阿联酋和卡塔尔等联合设立 200 亿美元共同投资基金。②

随着阿拉伯国家产业升级，尤其是随着沙特、埃及、阿联酋、卡塔尔、科威特、阿尔及利亚、摩洛哥等国在中长期发展规划中提出了经济多元化发展战略，减轻了对单一经济的依赖，为中国投资阿拉伯国家产能提供了有利条件。阿拉伯世界还是中国海外投资的重要目的地，中国投资带动了阿拉伯国家的产能升级。2012 年，中国对阿拉伯国家投资流量为 8.9 亿美元，当年末存量为 72 亿美元；2016 年底，中国对阿拉伯国家直接投资存量 151 亿美元；2017 年，中国对阿拉伯国家直接投资流量 12.6 亿美元，同比增长 9.3%。2014 年，中国企业在阿拉伯国家新签承包工程合同额达 359 亿美元，同比增长 23%，约占中国在全球新签承包工程合同总额的 1/5；2017 年，中国在阿拉伯国家新签承包工程合同额 328.05 亿美元。③

中国还成立研究中心和技术培训中心，为促进中阿产能合作提供智力支持。如中阿改革发展研究中心落户上海外国语大学，上海中医药大学海外中医中心落地摩洛哥，中阿北斗卫星导航系统卓越中心落地突尼斯，以及中阿技术转移中心、和平利用核能培训中心、清洁能源培训中心等，成为中阿双方产能合作与技术和经验交流的重要平台。

中阿双方重视在阿开展经贸合作区发展产能合作，积极推进沙特吉赞经济城中国产业园、阿曼杜库姆中国产业园、中国—阿联酋产能合作示范园、中埃（埃及）苏伊士经贸合作区、中国—苏丹农业合作开发区建设等。

---

① 上海外国语大学中东研究所、中阿合作论坛研究中心:《共建“一带一路”，推动中阿集体合作站上新起点——“中国—阿拉伯国家合作论坛”成就与展望》，2018，第 12~13 页，中阿合作论坛网，http://www.chinaarabcf.org/chn/zagx/ltdt/P020180614580301500634.pdf。

② 《中国和阿拉伯国家合作共建“一带一路”行动宣言》，中阿合作论坛网，http://www.cascf.org/chn/zagx/gjydyl/t1577010.htm，2018 年 7 月 10 日。

③ 上海外国语大学中东研究所、中阿合作论坛研究中心:《共建“一带一路”，推动中阿集体合作站上新起点——“中国—阿拉伯国家合作论坛”成就与展望》，2018，第 14~15 页，http://www.chinaarabcf.org/chn/zagx/ltdt/P020180614580301500634.pdf。

在设施联通方面，中国企业在阿拉伯国家广泛参与港口建设和投资，实施公路、铁路、输油管线、供水管网等项目。以港口建设为例，截至 2018 年，中资企业参与建设和运营了吉布提港、苏丹港、沙特吉达港、埃及塞得港和艾因苏赫纳港、阿尔及利亚哈姆达尼耶港、摩洛哥丹吉尔港和卡萨布兰卡港、毛里塔尼亚友谊港等近 10 个港口，成为中国在海上丝绸之路开展港口外交的重要对象。①

中阿产能合作着眼于未来，以高新技术合作和优势产能为合作新方向。自 2013 年中国科技部启动杰出青年科学家来华工作计划以来，已有 123 名阿拉伯国家科研人员在中国进行了短期科研工作；2014 年 12 月，国家主席习近平与访华的埃及总统塞西共同见证中国科技部与埃及科学研究部签署《关于共建中埃可再生能源联合实验室的谅解备忘录》；2015 年中阿技术转移中心正式揭牌成立；2015 年、2017 年举办了两届中阿技术转移暨创新合作大会；2016 年，习近平访问阿盟总部时宣布启动“中国—阿拉伯国家科技伙伴计划”；2016 年 3 月，中国和埃及共建的可再生能源实验室在埃及揭牌，目前该实验室建设正稳步推进，中国科技部也正与相关阿拉伯国家科技主管部门在共同感兴趣的领域就共建实验室事宜进行磋商。当前，埃及、摩洛哥、阿尔及利亚、沙特、约旦、突尼斯、利比亚 7 国与中国签订政府间科技合作协定，埃及、摩洛哥、沙特 3 国还与中国科技部建立了科技合作机制。② 科技合作使中阿产能合作更具可持续性。

近年来，阿拉伯国家也加大了对华投资。2015 年 12 月，中国和阿联酋就达成了 100 亿美元的“中国—阿联酋共同投资基金”，阿联酋对华投资主要包括先进制造业、可再生能源和能源、卫生医疗和医疗设备、农业、生物技术、创新科技、酒店、港口等。迪拜港口世界集团主席苏尔坦与青岛港集团主席签署协议，在青岛港投资 6.36 亿美元建设智能集装箱码头，实

---

① 孙德刚：《中国港口外交的理论与实践》，载《世界经济与政治》2018 年第 5 期，第 22~24 页。

② 上海外国语大学中东研究所、中阿合作论坛研究中心：《共建“一带一路”，推动中阿集体合作站上新起点——“中国—阿拉伯国家合作论坛”成就与展望》，2018，第 18~19 页，http://www.chinaarabcf.org/chn/zagx/ltdt/P020180614580301500634.pdf。

现远程装卸；迪拜港口世界集团还投资12亿美元，在天津建造新港口，已于2018年完工。[①]2018年国家主席习近平和国家副主席王岐山相继访问阿联酋，进一步带动阿拉伯国家对华投资。

2019年2月，沙特王储萨勒曼率团访华，就“一带一路”与沙特“2030愿景”实现对接、共建“中巴经济走廊”等，达成了广泛共识，签订280亿美元大单。沙特阿美公司与中国北方工业公司等在中国东北盘锦将开发投资规模达100亿美元的炼油和石化联合企业，组建华锦阿美石油化工项目合资公司，打造一家每天可生产30万桶石油的炼油厂。[②]

综上所述，中阿经贸合作已经拓展至立体多维领域，一是传统能源以及新能源合作，如石油、天然气、核能、太阳能、绿色低碳能源等，以“能源+”为重点；二是基础设施领域的产能合作，如道路、建筑、港口、智慧城市、产业园区和科技城等，中国参与投资30亿美元的埃及新行政首都中央商务区建设，包括修建一栋385米高的大楼，建成后将成为非洲第一高楼；[③]三是高科技领域合作，如航空航天、生物制药、新材料、“互联网+”、人工智能、大数据、电子商务、联合研发等。中国帮助阿尔及利亚和埃及发射卫星，中国与沙特联合探月与探测水星合作计划等，意味着中阿“空中丝绸之路”的延续和拓展。

宁夏在中阿经贸合作中扮演重要角色。自2010年起，商务部、中国贸促会和宁夏回族自治区人民政府共同举办了3届中阿经贸论坛和3届中阿博览会。[④]截至2017年底，2015年中阿博览会签署的108个投资类项目开工实施率已达70.4%，到位资金272.1亿元。[⑤]

---

① 中国港口机械网：《迪拜港口世界将在中国投资19亿美元》，http://www.21pi.cn/news/show.php? itemid=6944。

② 《沙特王储访华签280亿美元大单　表态支持“一带一路”倡议》，参考消息网，2019年2月24日，http://www.cankaoxiaoxi.com/china/20190224/2372626.shtml。

③ 杨福昌：《相向而行令中阿关系持续发展》，《环球时报》2018年7月9日，第14版。

④ 上海外国语大学中东研究所、中阿合作论坛研究中心：《共建“一带一路”，推动中阿集体合作站上新起点——“中国—阿拉伯国家合作论坛”成就与展望》，2018，第16页，http://www.chinaarabcf.org/chn/zagx/ltdt/P020180614580301500634.pdf。

⑤ 杨言洪、田冉冉：《“一带一路”倡议背景下中国与阿拉伯国家经贸合作研究》，《国际商务——对外经济贸易大学学报》2018年第3期，第65页。

1.4　结论

自 2014 年习近平在中阿合作论坛第六届部长级会议上提出中阿共建“一带一路”倡议以来，广大阿拉伯国家从追求政治变革转向探索符合各自国情的发展道路。五年来，阿拉伯国家普遍将工业化、信息化和产业多元化视为政府工作的重中之重，中阿合作领域从传统的能源领域向基础设施、产能合作、新能源、金融、航空航天、海洋、高科技等更加广阔的领域拓展，中阿在治国理政经验交流与政策沟通领域进一步密切合作。中阿从战略合作关系提升为战略伙伴关系，为“亚非合作”“南南合作”树立了成功典范，对于实现联合国 2030 可持续发展议程、宣传中国“新安全观”和“以发展促和平”理念，具有重要意义。

政治互信是中阿经贸合作的基础。中国是中东和平与发展事业的建设者，愿为促进地区和平稳定发挥积极作用。中国长期坚定支持巴勒斯坦人民正义事业，主张建立以 1967 年边界为基础、以东耶路撒冷为首都、享有完全主权、独立的巴勒斯坦国，支持以“两国方案”和“阿拉伯和平倡议”为基础，推动中东和平进程。2017 年 11 月 29 日，联合国举行“声援巴勒斯坦人民国际日”纪念大会，习近平向大会致贺电。同样，阿拉伯国家普遍坚持一个中国原则，在台湾、南海等涉及中国主权、安全和发展利益上，坚定支持中国立场。

总之，中国与阿拉伯国家共建“一带一路”、开展经贸合作，促进了亚非发展中国家在经贸领域的互联互通，促进了发展中国家内部的贸易便利化和产业升级。中国提出“以发展促和平”的理念，旨在化解冲突，为阿拉伯国家冲突解决提供了新方案，体现了“以综合治理促安全、以外交谈判谋安全、以经贸合作推动安全”的新理念和新实践。

第 2 章　阿拉伯世界主要经济体经济发展专题报告

2.1　研究对象的选取

2.1.1　阿拉伯世界简况

本章将研究对象锁定为阿拉伯世界。阿拉伯国家位于亚洲西部和非洲北部，处在亚、非两大洲的结合部，其非洲部分占 72%，亚洲部分占 28%，具有重要的战略地理位置。现有 22 个国家（包括阿盟 21 国和 2011 年被终止阿盟成员资格的叙利亚），它们是阿尔及利亚、阿联酋、阿曼、埃及、巴勒斯坦、巴林、吉布提、卡塔尔、科威特、黎巴嫩、利比亚、毛里塔尼亚、摩洛哥、科摩罗、沙特、苏丹、索马里、突尼斯、叙利亚、也门、伊拉克和约旦。阿拉伯国家的面积约为 1313 万平方千米，占世界陆地面积的 9.53%。阿拉伯国家的总人口数超过 3.59 亿人（2017 年，数据来自联合国报告），占世界总人口的 4.91%，其中劳动力约有 1.46 亿人。阿拉伯国家百分之九十以上的人口都信仰伊斯兰教。在阿拉伯国家中，海湾合作委员会（简称海合会，包括沙特、阿联酋、阿曼、科威特、卡塔尔、巴林 6 国）是伊斯兰文化圈中心地带，是世界主要能源生产和出口基地之一，已探明的石油、天然气储量分别占全球的 45% 和 23%。大部分阿拉伯国家属热带沙漠气候，夏季气候炎热，冬季气候温和，常年干旱少雨。

2.1.2　阿拉伯国家主要经济体

阿拉伯国家地域辽阔，各个国家经济发展水平不一，内部差距很大。目前，其经济延续复苏态势，但经济增速趋缓，不确定、不稳定因素增多，给中国企业开展对外投资合作带来了新的挑战。本章，我们将选定若干个与中国经贸关系紧密的阿拉伯国家主要经济体，从经济总量、经济增速、经济效益、经济结构、石油经济等方面，分别阐述其国民经济总体发展情况，希望能更好地帮助企业了解和熟悉阿拉伯国家的经济发展变化情况，掌握各国的主要经济发展政策和各国发展经济的主要侧重以及各国的营商环境，提升“走出去”的能力和海外经营水平；也希望为我国制订和实施更加科学、有利的阿拉伯国家政策，更好地促进我国与阿拉伯国家的关系，深入地推进我国“一带一路”建设，维护我国在阿拉伯地区的利益提供依据。基于此，本报告选取了沙特、阿联酋、阿曼、科威特、卡塔尔、巴林 6 个海湾国家和埃及 1 个传统地区大国以及阿尔及利亚、摩洛哥 2 个北非重要国家共 9 个中国在阿拉伯国家的主要贸易伙伴国家作为研究对象。

2.2　海湾国家经济发展情况

以沙特为首的海湾国家在阿拉伯地区区域经济合作中发挥着重要作用，是地区经济发展的重要带动力量，在中东乃至世界有着较强的影响力。这些国家人口较少，劳动力短缺。石油工业是其经济的支柱。凭借极其丰富的石油和天然气资源，赚得盆满钵满。其工业化水平较高，经济一体化程度较高，已经从自由贸易区发展为海湾共同市场。有关数据显示，目前其市场规模已超过 1.6 万亿美元，预计 2020 年将会达到 2 万亿美元。这些国家经济发展状况一般较好，收入都处于领先水平。

表 2.1　2017 年海湾 6 国经济发展指标在中东国家排名（2010 年不变价美元）

国家	GDP		GDP 增幅		人均 GDP	
	金额（亿美元）	位次	增幅（%）	位次	金额（美元／人）	位次
沙特	6849.94	2	–0.74	19	20796.32	7
阿联酋	3872.59	4	0.79	17	41197.17	2
卡塔尔	1733.87	9	1.60	16	65696.39	1
科威特	1387.62	10	–2.87	21	33545.62	4
阿曼	748.50	13	–0.27	18	16144.41	8
巴林	330.03	17	3.88	8	22111.48	6

数据来源：世界银行。

2.2.1　沙特

沙特的经济发展属于典型的石油经济模式。石油出口额占沙特国内生产总值的 40%、政府收入的 80%、外汇收入的 90% 以上。从经济总量上看，2017 年，沙特国内生产总值 6838.27 亿美元，经济规模有所扩大，在中东位居第 2。其中，第一产业增加值 173.93 亿美元，第二产业增加值 3076.97 亿美元，第三产业增加值 3587.37 亿美元。从经济增速上看，2017 年比上年下降 0.74%，在中东位居第 19，面临低增长、高失业和高通胀等经济困难。从经济结构上看，2017 年，第一产业增加值占比为 2.54%，第二产业增加值比重为 45%，第三产业增加值比重为 52.46%（比上年下降 1.7%），表明经济结构在不断调整，但石油利润对 GDP 的贡献占比超过 26%，仍然较大，产业结构需要继续完善。从经济效益上看，全年国民总收入 6956 亿美元，人均国内生产总值 20796.32 美元，比上年下降 2.73%，在中东位居第 7。从开放经济的角度看，2016 年，沙特对外贸易总额 3374 亿美元；2017 年底外汇储备余额 4889 亿美元；经常项目差额为 –238 亿美元（表明其国外财产净额有所减少，会影响对外收支情况和外汇储备的增长）。从改革发展的角度看，为应对石油经济危机，2016 年 4 月沙特政府提出了“2030 愿景”规划。其发展目标包括：利用沙特廉价能源，建立工业部门；提高水资源和电力管理水平，摆脱高度依赖补贴的现状；发展小型公共投资基金和战略投资；发展农业和娱乐业；建造 16 个核反应堆替代石油发电；将非石油出口占 GDP 比重从 16% 提高到 50%，将非石油收入占总收入的比重从 10%

提升到 70%；将武器国产化率从 2% 提高到 50%；将失业率从 11% 降至 7.6%；将沙特在世界经济体中排名从第 19 位升至第 15 位。为此，沙特政府在政策执行层面出台了一系列配套举措，具体包括 3 个方面。一是减少政府财政支出、增加收入来源。主要办法有停发住房补贴，压缩国内油价补贴，紧缩购买新汽车、家具和其他设备的费用，提高电价和汽油价格等。二是加大经济开放力度。主要办法有设立自由经济区，鼓励发展商业、金融业和高科技产业，重点包括能源和水、交通、生物技术、食品工业、电子技术、先进制造业、媒体和娱乐业以及机器人、可再生能源和未来运输解决方案等高科技行业。开放旅游市场，允许外国游客入境，以促进旅游产业的发展。鼓励与沙特大学合作，对学生进行全面的金融培训，以加快人才培养。三是大力发展私营经济。主要办法有重整大部分国有部门，出售国有石油公司股票，将国际机场全部私有化等。[①] 目前沙特大力推行经济多样化发展战略，轻工业等非石油产业已取得一定发展，但经济效果远低于预期。经济体制还不完善，生产力发展仍面临诸多体制性障碍，还需要建立一个完整的产业结构，在工业、农业和服务业之间达到平衡。

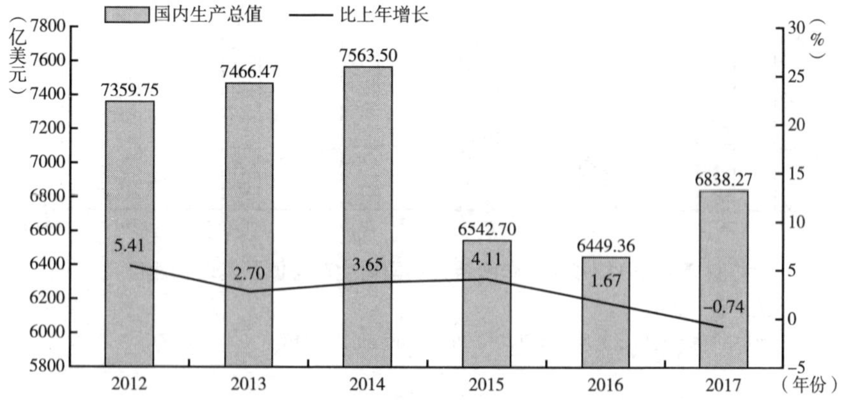

图 2.1　2012~2017 年沙特国内生产总值及其增长速度

数据来源：世界银行。

注：国内生产总值按现价美元计算；增长速度按 2010 年不变价美元计算。

---

① 林海虹：《沙特经济转型：愿景与挑战》，《国际问题研究》2018 年第 3 期。

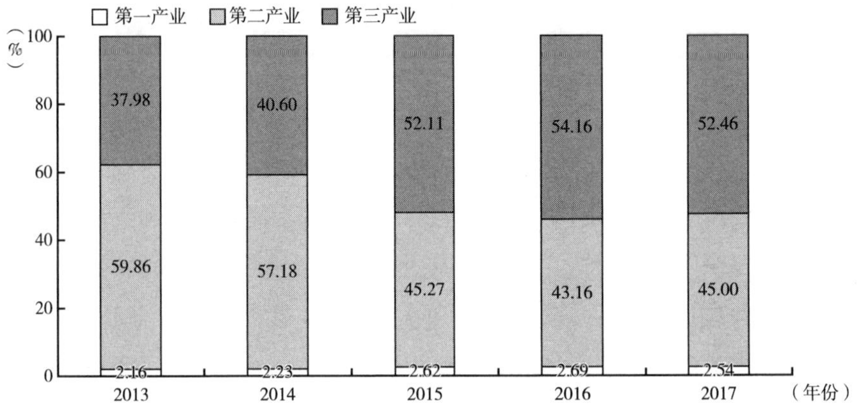

图 2.2　2013~2017 年沙特三次产业增加值占国内生产总值比重

数据来源：世界银行，按现价美元计算整理得出。

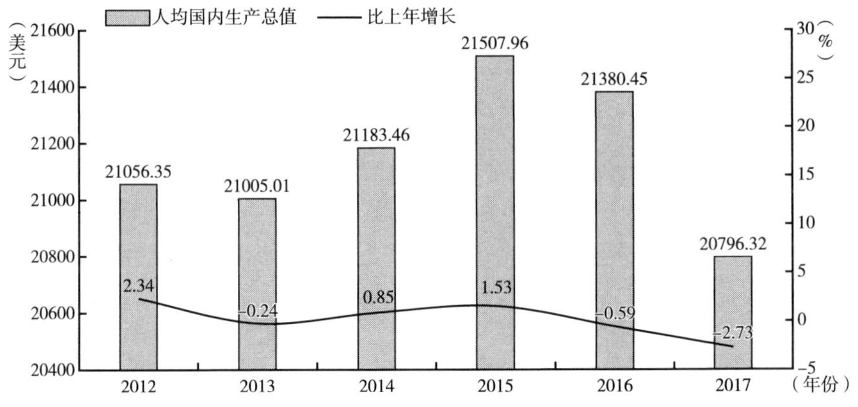

图 2.3　2012~2017 年沙特人均国内生产总值及其增长速度

数据来源：世界银行。

注：人均国内生产总值及其增长速度均按 2010 年不变价美元计算。

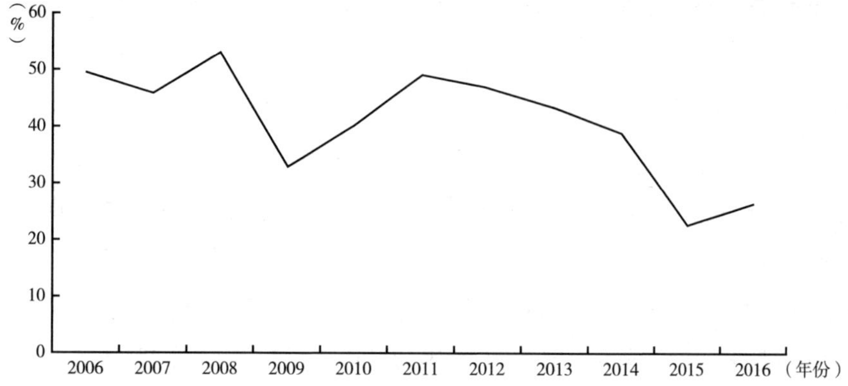

图 2.4　2006~2016 年沙特石油租金

数据来源：世界银行。

注：石油租金指石油利润占 GDP 的百分比。石油租金在石油国家的财政中占有很大比率。

2.2.2　阿联酋

阿联酋是阿拉伯地区发展经济现代化最成功的国家之一，其在旅游、商业、贸易、运输和航空业方面表现卓越。根据《2015 年全球旅游业竞争力报告》数据显示，阿联酋在 141 个参评国家中位列第 24 位，比 2014 年上升 4 位。根据世界银行发布的 2016 年世界物流绩效指数排行，在全球 160 个国家排名中，阿联酋位列全球物流表现指数第 13 位，是阿拉伯地区物流绩效最高的国家。目前，非石油经济成为阿联酋经济发展的核心，[①] 其对国内生产总值的贡献率超过 75%。

从经济总量上看，2017 年，阿联酋国内生产总值 3825.75 亿美元，在中东位居第 4。其中，第一产业增加值 29.19 亿美元，第二产业增加值 1667.9 亿美元，第三产业增加值 2128.65 亿美元。从经济增速上看，2017 年比上年增长 0.79%，增长缓慢，在中东位居第 17。从经济结构上看，2017 年，第一产业增加值比重为 0.76%，份额极小，粮食作物都要依赖进口；第二产业增加值比重为 43.6%，占比提升 2.15%；第三产业增加值比重为 55.64%，占比下降 2.14%，产业结构需要继续完善。从经济效益上看，全年国民总收

① 韩露、林梦等:《阿联酋非石油经济的发展及中阿合作建议》,《国际经济合作》2017 年第 4 期。

入 3854 亿美元，全年人均国内生产总值 41197.17 美元，虽稍有下降，但在中东位居第 2，属于高水平富裕国家，其实力很强。从开放经济的角度看，2016 年阿联酋对外贸易总额 5109 亿美元。在对外政策上，阿联酋与沙特密切配合；对内政策上，阿联酋与海合会各成员国之间配合默契、政局基本稳定。从改革的角度看，阿联酋提出了“2021 战略规划”，大力发展现代服务业，经济竞争力逐年提高。目前阿联酋投资环境不断改善，经济处于快速发展时期，工程建设项目量非常大，生产设备、机械设备以及建筑材料等都需要进口。根据世界银行 2017 年营商环境指数显示，阿联酋商业环境排名为 26 位，比 2016 年上升 8 位。这主要是因为阿联酋对投资管理较为细致，外商投资行业限制较多，且法律较为完备，在打击诈骗、贿赂、假冒伪劣、洗钱等经济金融领域不法行为方面，在对投资者保护方面，工作做得较好。再者，阿联酋是个低税国家，境内无企业所得税和个人所得税、增值税、印花税等税种。其对一般商品只征收 5% 的进口关税，部分农产品和药品免税，但对奢侈品征收重税，如烟草税为 50%~70%。① 相信阿联酋优越的市场和金融环境以及稳定的政治现状，对各国投资者会有极大的吸引力。

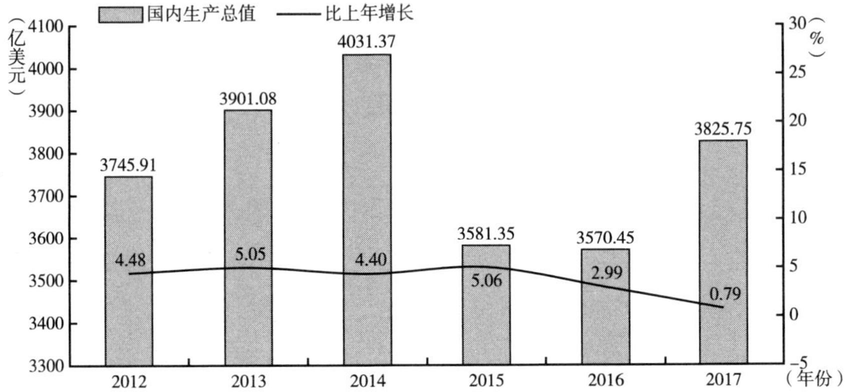

图 2.5　2012~2017 年阿联酋国内生产总值及其增长速度

数据来源：世界银行。

注：国内生产总值按现价美元计算；增长速度按 2010 年不变价美元计算。

① 《阿联酋经济与商业环境风险分析报告（2017 版）》,《国际融资》2018 年第 9 期。

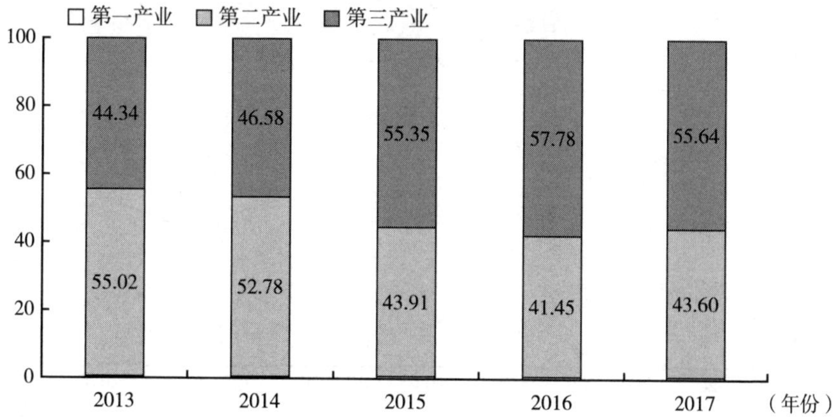

图 2.6　2013~2017 年阿联酋三次产业增加值占国内生产总值比重

数据来源：世界银行，按现价美元计算整理得出。

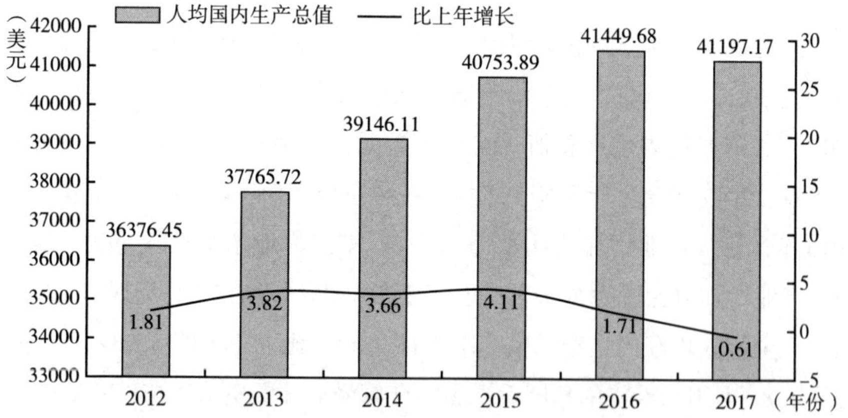

图 2.7　2012~2017 年阿联酋人均国内生产总值及其增长速度

数据来源：世界银行。

注：人均国内生产总值及其增长速度均按 2010 年不变价美元计算。

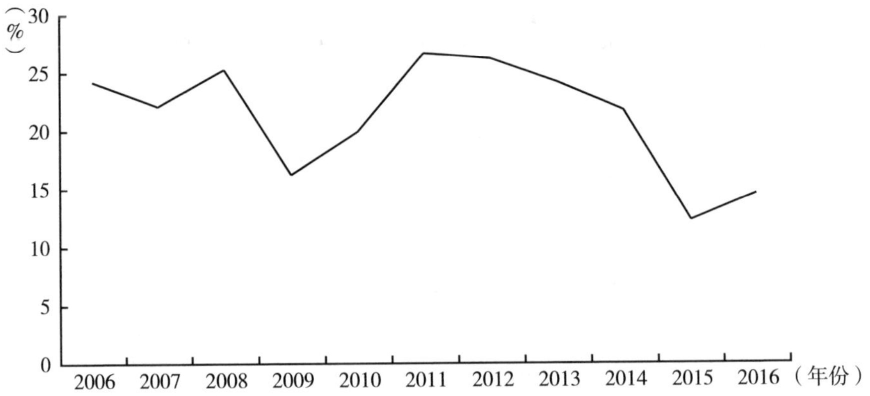

图 2.8　2006~2016 年阿联酋石油租金

数据来源和注同图 2.4。

2.2.3　阿曼

阿曼是典型的资源输出型国家，油气产业是国民经济的支柱，产值占GDP 近 30%，出口收入在政府财政收入中占比近 70%。从经济总量上看，2017 年，阿曼国内生产总值 726.43 亿美元，在中东位居第 13。从经济增速上看，2017 年比上年下降 0.27%，在中东位居第 18。从经济结构上看，2016 年，第一产业增加值比重为 1.97%；第二产业增加值比重为 47.17%；第三产业增加值比重为 50.86%。从经济效益上看，全年国民总收入 701 亿美元，全年人均国内生产总值 16144.41 美元，比上年下降 4.82%，在中东位居第 8。从开放经济的角度看，2017 年阿曼对外贸易总额 539 亿美元，连续保持贸易顺差。主要贸易伙伴为中国、阿联酋、日本、印度、沙特、韩国、美国、欧盟等。其最主要的出口商品是石油、天然气；主要进口货物有运输工具、机电产品、五金矿产、化工产品、轻工纺织、食品和农产品等。2017 年，阿曼通货膨胀率为 0.58%。从改革的角度看，近年来，其全力推进经济多元化战略，大力优化引资环境，以杜库姆等经济特区、工业园区为载体吸引外资，以新机场、高速公路等重大项目为重点完善基础设施，积极扶持制造业、物流业、旅游业、渔业和矿业五大非油气产业发展。

世界经济论坛《2017–2018 年全球竞争力报告》显示，在全球最具竞争力的 137 个国家和地区中阿曼排第 62 位。在世界银行《2018 年全球营商环境报告》排名中，阿曼位列创业手续简便度排名的第 31 位，列营商便利度排名的第 71 位。[①] 这会提振市场人气，促进其成为强劲的经济活动区域。

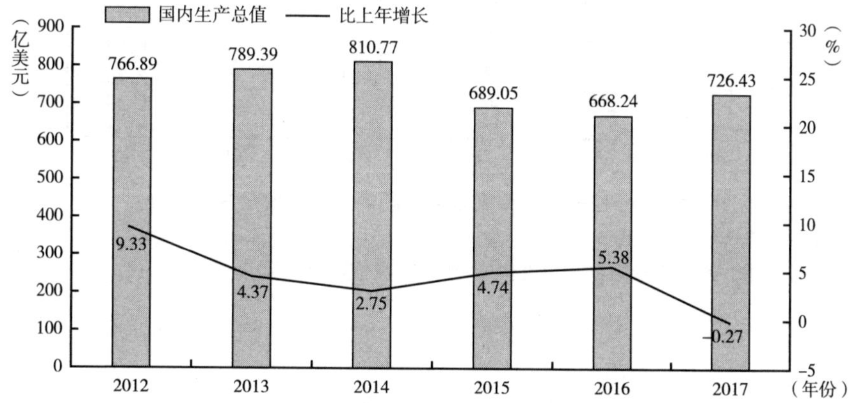

图 2.9　2012~2017 年阿曼国内生产总值及其增长速度

数据来源：世界银行。

注：国内生产总值按现价美元计算；增长速度按 2010 年不变价美元计算。

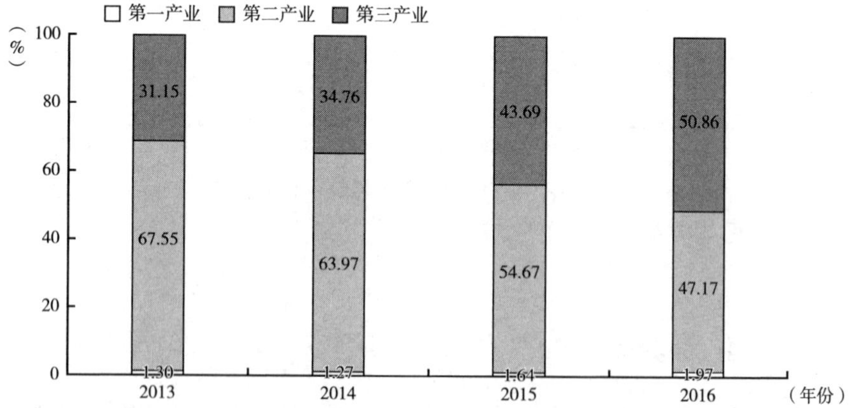

图 2.10　2013~2016 年阿曼三次产业增加值占国内生产总值比重

数据来源：世界银行，按现价美元计算整理得出。

注：2017 年数据缺失。

① 国际贸易经济合作研究院等:《对外投资合作国别（地区）指南：阿曼（2018 年版）》。

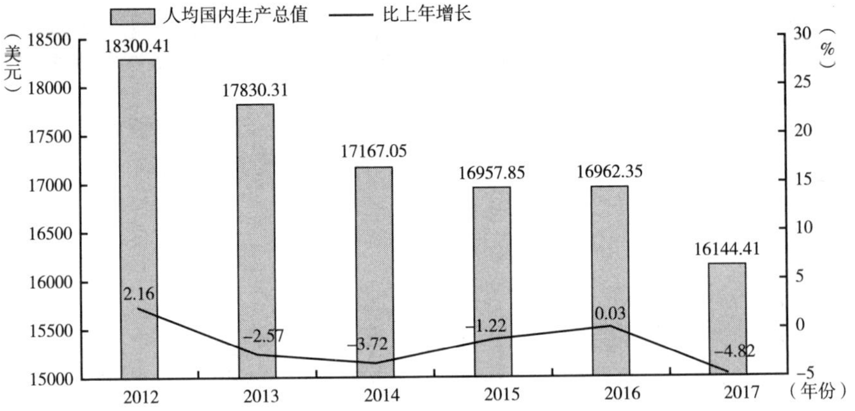

图 2.11　2012~2017 年阿曼人均国内生产总值及其增长速度

数据来源：世界银行。

注：人均国内生产总值及其增长速度均按 2010 年不变价美元计算。

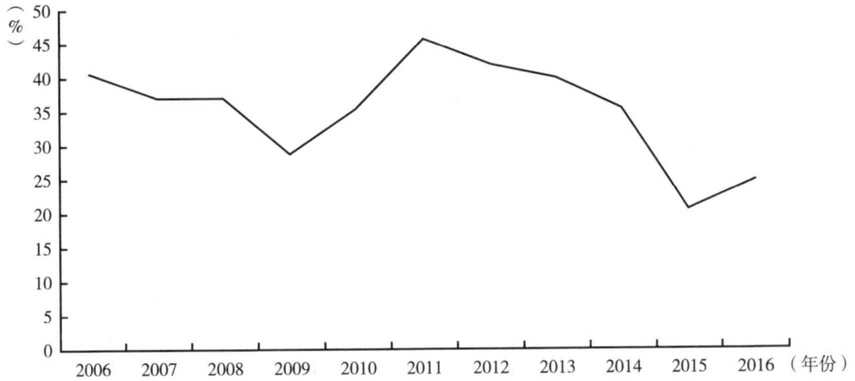

图 2.12　2006~2016 年阿曼石油租金

数据来源和注同图 2.4。

2.2.4　科威特

科威特经济总体上以石油、天然气和石化工业为主，结构相对单一。其 GDP 的 50% 和政府收入的 85% 来自石油。为减轻对石油经济的依赖程度，政府强调发展多种经济。其对外开放程度较高。在世界经济论坛发布的《2017–2018 年全球竞争力报告》中，科威特在全球 137 个国家（地区）

中排名第 52 位。在世界银行发布的《2018 年营商便利指数排名》中，科威特在 190 个经济体中位列第 96 位，较上年提升 6 个位次。各项指标排名：开业便利度排名第 149 位，办理施工许可便利度排名第 129 位，电力供应便利度排名第 97 位，登记财产便利度排名第 70 位，纳税便利度排名第 6 位。①

从经济总量上看，2017 年，科威特国内生产总值 1201.26 亿美元，在中东位居第 10。从经济增速上看，2017 年比上年下降 2.87%，在中东位居第 21。从经济结构上看，2016 年，第一产业增加值比重偏小（0.56%），但政府重视发展农业，以生产蔬菜为主，农牧产品主要依靠进口。渔业资源丰富，盛产大虾、石斑鱼和黄花鱼。第二产业增加值比重为 51.64%，占比下降 4.3%。第三产业增加值比重为 47.8%，占比大幅增长 4.27%。从经济效益上看，全年国民总收入 1391 亿美元，全年人均国内生产总值 33545.62 美元，虽比上年下降 4.84%，但在中东仍位居第 4。从开放经济的角度看，2017 年科威特对外贸易总额 884 亿美元，外贸总体顺差。其主要出口商品为石油等燃料及矿产品、化学制品、塑料及橡胶制品、交通运输设备、珠宝首饰等；主要进口商品为机械及电器产品、金属制品、车辆及其部件、化学制品、服装纺织品等。截至 2017 年底其外汇储备总额 368.9 亿美元。经常项目差额为 76 亿美元，盈余增长较快。2017 年其财政余额出现赤字，且债务有所增加。2017 年科威特通胀率为 1.5%。从改革的角度看，为吸引外国投资，其制定颁布了一系列相关法律法规，形成了比较完整的鼓励外国投资法制框架。其整体关税水平较低。一般商品的进口关税统一为 5%；对于食品、生活必需品、药品以及新设企业所需进口的机械设备，则免征关税；来自 GCC 其他国家的工业产品及部分农产品享受免关税待遇。2015~2020 年科威特发展计划的重点是推进经济改革进程和实施大型战略项目。其引资重点领域是高新科技产业，包括电子网络建设、电信、环保、先进的石油技术等。其不鼓励投资产能过剩的行业，如旅馆业等。近年来，

① 国际贸易经济合作研究院等：《对外投资合作国别（地区）指南：科威特（2018 年版）》。

科威特大搞基础建设和土木工程，陆续推出了一批大型基础设施工程项目和多个市区公路建设和改造项目，这为外企在当地拓展工程承包和劳务市场带来了机遇。

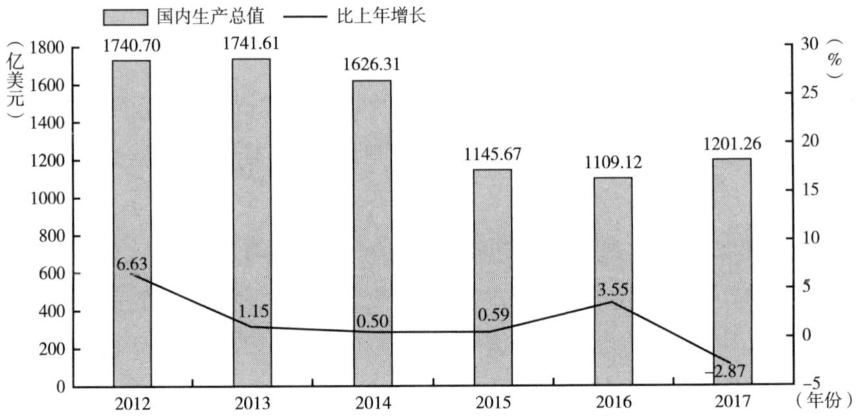

图 2.13　2012~2017 年科威特国内生产总值及其增长速度

数据来源：世界银行。

注：国内生产总值按现价美元计算；增长速度按 2010 年不变价美元计算。

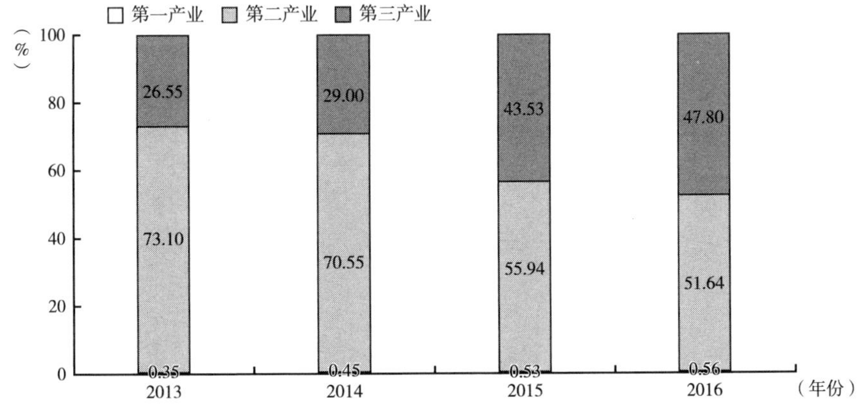

图 2.14　2013~2016 年科威特三次产业增加值占国内生产总值比重

数据来源：世界银行，按现价美元计算整理得出。

注：2017 年数据缺失。

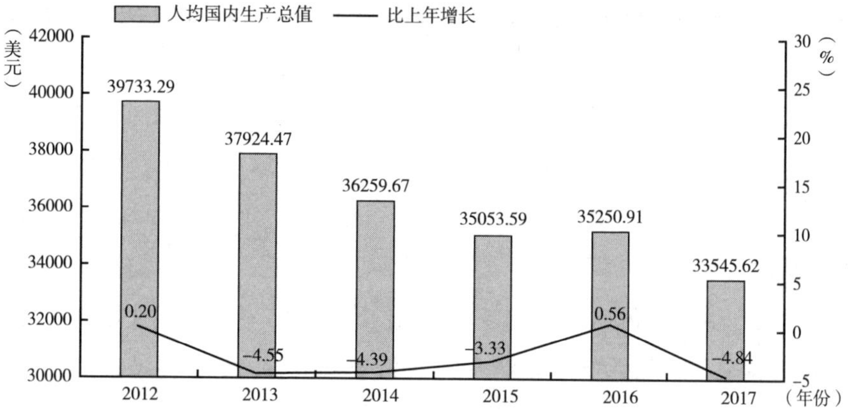

图 2.15　2012~2017 年科威特人均国内生产总值及其增长速度

数据来源：世界银行。

注：人均国内生产总值及其增长速度均按 2010 年不变价美元计算。

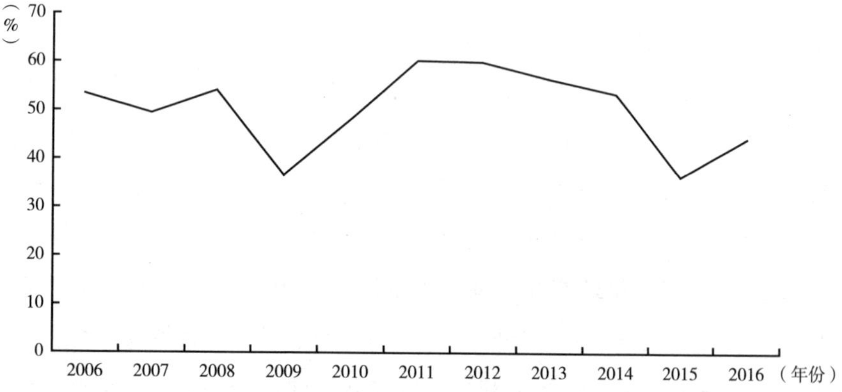

图 2.16　2006~2016 年科威特石油租金

数据来源和注同图 2.4。

2.2.5　卡塔尔

卡塔尔油气资源丰富，油气产业的快速发展带动了卡塔尔经济高速增长，并为其带来了巨额财富，其人均国内生产总值名列世界前茅。卡塔尔选择的是外向型经济发展模式，其法律法规体系日益健全，营商环境不断改善。世界经济论坛《2017–2018 年全球竞争力报告》显示，在全球最具竞

争力的137个国家和地区中，卡塔尔排第25位。世界银行《2018年营商环境报告》中，卡塔尔经商环境在190个国家（地区）中排名第83位。

从经济总量上看，2017年，卡塔尔国内生产总值1676.05亿美元，在中东位居第9。从经济增速上看，2017年比上年增长1.6%，在中东位居第16。从经济结构上看，2016年，其第一产业增加值比重为0.18%，主要农产品包括水果、蔬菜、禽类、奶制品、牛肉和鱼，粮食作物都要依赖进口；第二产业增加值比重为51.9%，占比下降6.6%；第三产业增加值比重为47.92%，占比大幅增长6.58%。从经济效益上看，全年国民总收入1672亿美元，全年人均国内生产总值65696.39美元，虽然比上年有所下降，但在中东仍位居第1。这远远超过了一般发达国家的收入水平，属于高水平富裕国家，其实力很强。从开放经济的角度看，2016年卡塔尔对外贸易总额894亿美元，外贸总体顺差。2017年其前四大贸易伙伴分别是：日本（占比13.49%）、韩国（占比11.5%）、中国（占比10.89%）、印度（占比10.09%）。主要出口产品是原油、汽油、液化气、凝析油、尿素、乙烯等；主要进口产品是飞机及直升机配件、轿车、电缆等建筑材料、工程机械及配件、通信网络设备及配件、食品等。2017年卡塔尔经常项目差额为64亿美元，盈余增长较快。2017年卡塔尔通货膨胀率为0.4%。从改革的角度看，为筹备2022世界杯足球赛和实现“2030国家愿景规划”，近年来，卡塔尔推行经济多元化战略，鼓励外资参与非油气产业发展，强调支持粮食安全项目、中小企业发展、经济区和自由区的开发建设等领域，经济逐渐由单一油气经济向多元化发展。2017年非油气领域经济比重进一步提高，达到67.3%。未来卡塔尔政府将会优先确保世界杯场馆和相关基础设施项目的建设，大力鼓励金融、建筑、加工制造、航空海运、物流、旅游和商贸服务等行业的发展，上述行业的投资机会将会为外资的参与和投入开辟更加广阔的空间。①在改善投资环境，吸引外国资金和技术方面，规定外资在卡塔尔可享有优惠政策。例如，外国投资者可在当地长期租赁土地，可享受投

① 国际贸易经济合作研究院等：《对外投资合作国别（地区）指南：卡塔尔（2018年版）》。

资资本所得税、进口设备关税等免税优惠，外企资金可自由汇入和汇出等。此外，对于农业、工业、卫生、教育、旅游等政府鼓励投资的行业，外国投资者经批准可持有项目投资总额 49% 以上直至 100% 的股份。这些优惠政策的实施为外资提供了保障和优惠，将促进卡塔尔经济可持续发展。①

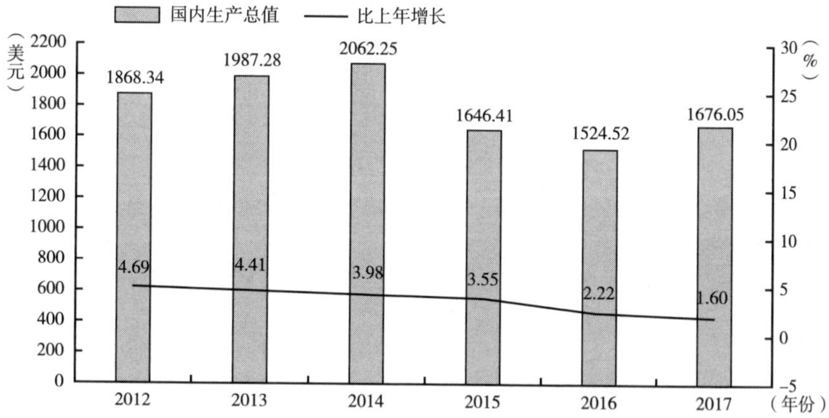

图 2.17　2012~2017 年卡塔尔国内生产总值及其增长速度

数据来源：世界银行。

注：国内生产总值按现价美元计算；增长速度按 2010 年不变价美元计算。

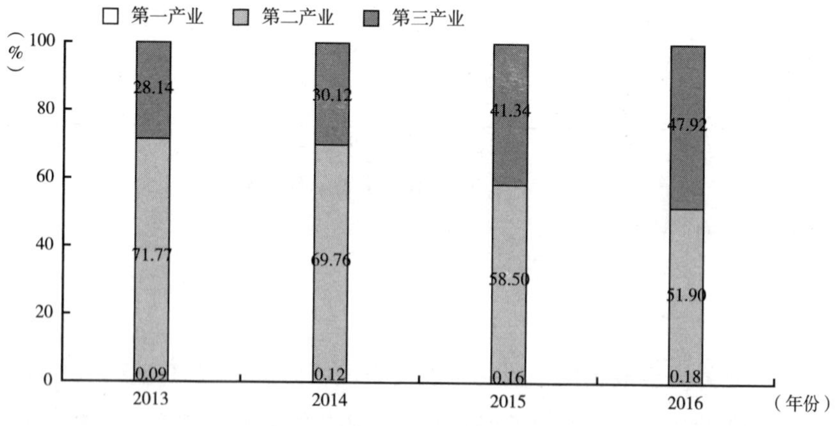

图 2.18　2013~2016 年卡塔尔三次产业增加值占国内生产总值比重

数据来源：世界银行，按现价美元计算整理得出。

注：2017 年数据缺失。

① 姜英梅：《卡塔尔经济发展战略与“一带一路”建设》，《阿拉伯世界研究》2016 年第 6 期。

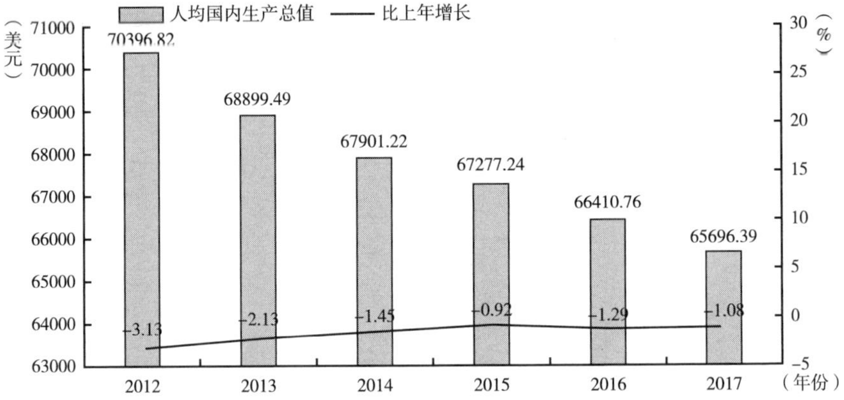

图 2.19　2012~2017 年卡塔尔人均国内生产总值及其增长速度

数据来源：世界银行。

注：人均国内生产总值及其增长速度均按 2010 年不变价美元计算。

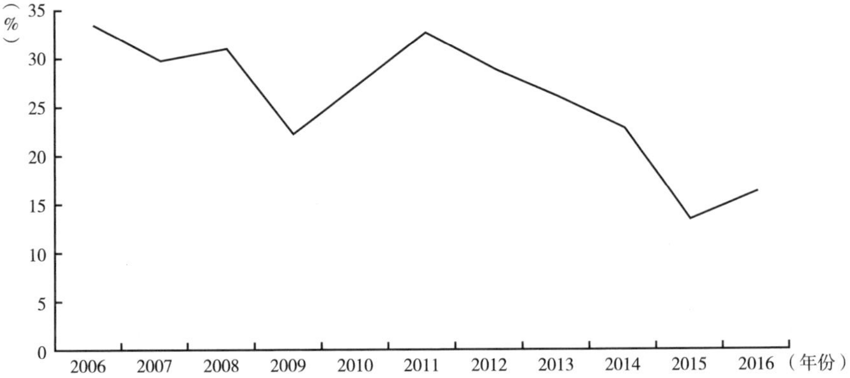

图 2.20　2006~2016 年卡塔尔石油租金

数据来源和注同图 2.4。

2.2.6　巴林

巴林是海合会成员国中第一个发现石油的国家。从 20 世纪 70 年代末起，巴林开始实行自由开放的经济政策，积极推进经济多元化战略，重点发展了金融、贸易、旅游和会展等产业，减少对油气产业的过度依赖。目前，其已成为海湾地区金融中心之一。世界经济论坛《2017–2018 年全球竞争力报告》显示，在全球最具竞争力的 137 个国家和地区中，巴林排第 44

位。世界银行发布的《2018 营商环境报告》显示，巴林在全球 190 个经济体中营商便利度排名第 66 位。①

从经济总量上看，巴林规模较小。2017 年，巴林国内生产总值 353.07 亿美元，在中东位居第 17。其中，第一产业增加值 1.03 亿美元，第二产业增加值 146.37 亿美元，第三产业增加值 205.68 亿美元。从经济增速上看，2017 年比上年增长 3.88%，经济增长主要依靠非石油产业的推动，在中东位居第 8。从经济结构上看，2017 年，巴林第一产业增加值占比仅为 0.29%。表明其农业规模很小，农产品绝大部分依靠进口。第二产业增加值比重为 41.46%。冶炼和石化是巴林重要的工业部门，石化产品、球团铁矿、铝线、铝板等资源类产品是其优势产品；大型机电产品、纺织品、建筑材料、家电和轻工产品等主要依靠进口。第三产业增加值比重为 58.25%，比上年下降 1.99 个百分点。由于巴林社会环境较为开放和宽松，交通相对便利，宾馆餐饮、旅游、金融等服务业比较发达；每年有较大规模的展会 10 余次，目前巴林已经成为中东地区的重要会展中心。从经济效益上看，全年人均国内生产总值 22111.48 美元，比上年减少近 180 美元，在中东位居第 6。从开放经济的角度看，巴林主要贸易伙伴包括沙特、中国、美国和阿联酋等国家和地区。受国际油价低迷影响，巴林财政赤字大幅攀升。2017 年财政赤字占 GDP 比重超过 10%。截止到 2017 年底，巴林外汇储备约为 21.7 亿美元，公共债务余额 297 亿美元，占 GDP 比重为 84%。2017 年巴林的通货膨胀率为 1.4%。从改革发展的角度看，巴林专门设立了经发会，负责全面制定并监督落实巴林的经济发展战略，创造良好的营商环境以吸引更多外商直接投资，为境外投资者提供信息咨询服务。近年来，政府一方面采取了一系列措施增收节支；另一方面进一步推动经济转型，尤其是抓住数字化进程带来的机遇，不断促进非石油部门、石油部门发展。具体来看，巴林不鼓励重工业型的企业进入巴林；其技术转型将集中在金融、旅游、轻工业、物流及科技等五个领域；未来几年巴林政府拟对一些领域基础设施进行升级改造和将投资更广泛的数据生态系统，以帮助新的数据产

① 国际贸易经济合作研究院等:《对外投资合作国别（地区）指南：巴林（2018 年版）》。

业集群蓬勃发展。[①] 巴林政府欢迎外国投资者参与当地基础设施投资。在融资条件方面，规定外资企业与巴林本地企业享受同等待遇。在税收方面，巴林是低税国家，税收体系较为简单，无所得税，商务成本低于迪拜、卡塔尔等周边市场。对进口商品只征收关税。在专属工业区内投资可享受更加优惠的待遇，包括廉价工业用地、优惠劳工措施、免除原材料及设备进口关税等。巴林希望提供一个可持续增长和公平竞争的环境，让经济走上正确道路。

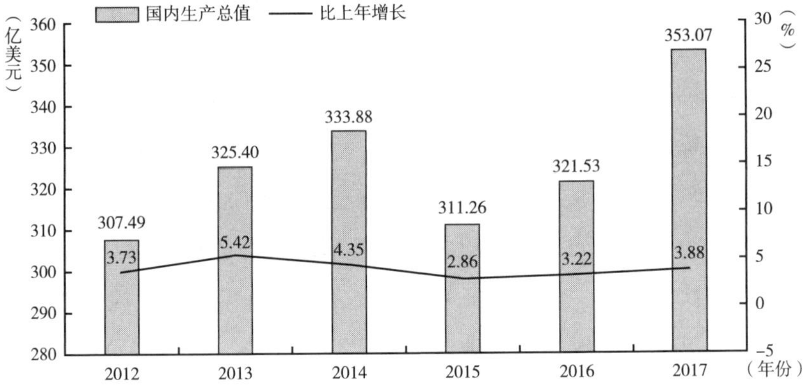

图 2.21　2012~2017 年巴林国内生产总值及其增长速度

数据来源：世界银行。

注：国内生产总值按现价美元计算；增长速度按 2010 年不变价美元计算。

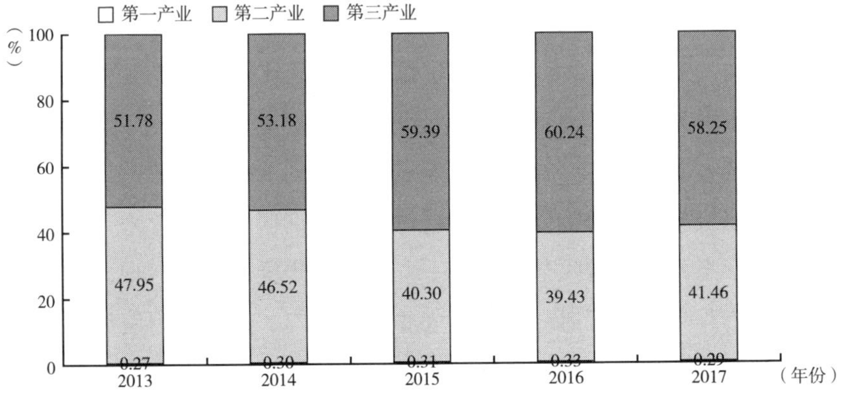

图 2.22　2013~2017 年巴林三次产业增加值占国内生产总值比重

数据来源：世界银行，按现价美元计算整理得出。

① 周智宇：《油价波动困扰经济巴林加速数字化转型》，《商讯》2018 年第 12 期。

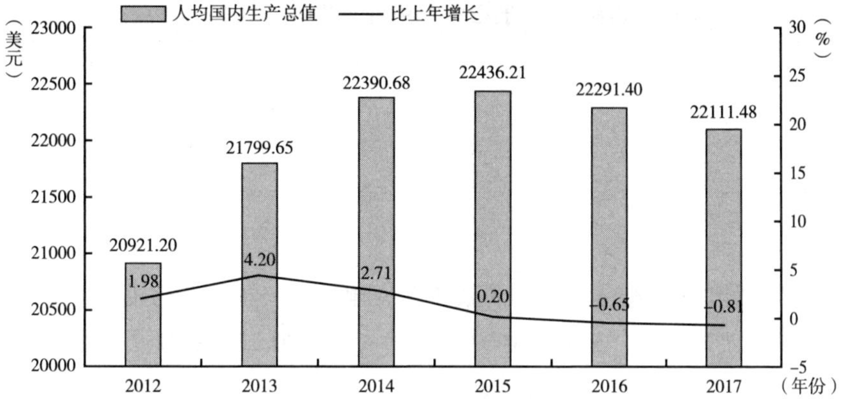

图 2.23　2012~2017 年巴林人均国内生产总值及其增长速度

数据来源：世界银行。

注：人均国内生产总值及其增长速度均按 2010 年不变价美元计算。

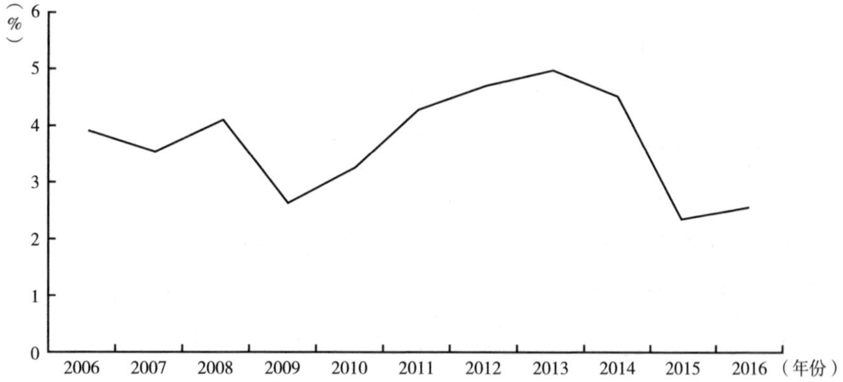

图 2.24　2006~2016 年巴林石油租金

数据来源和注同图 2.4。

2.3　传统地区大国经济发展情况

2.3.1　埃及经济发展概况

埃及是中东前 6 大经济体之一，是中东非常重要的传统地区大国，属于重要支点国家，地位不容小觑。

表 2.2　2017 年埃及经济发展指标在中东国家排名（2010 年不变价美元）

国家	GDP		GDP 增幅		人均 GDP	
	金额（亿美元）	位次	增幅（%）	位次	金额（美元 / 人）	位次
埃及	2717.22	6	4.18	5	2785.37	18

数据来源：世界银行。

埃及农业人口较多，旅游资源丰富，旅游收入是外汇的主要来源。与中东其他国家相比，虽然近年经济增长较快，但内部动荡，失业率居高不下，经济复苏缓慢，经济发展仍然比较困难。从经济总量上看，2017 年，埃及国内生产总值 2353.69 亿美元，经济规模出现大幅减少，在中东位居第 6。其中，第一产业增加值 270.33 亿美元，第二产业增加值 794.39 亿美元，第三产业增加值 1288.97 亿美元。从经济增速上看，2017 年比上年增长 4.18%，在中东位居第 5。从经济结构上看，仍然属于发展中国家。2017 年，第一产业增加值比重为 11.49%，第二产业增加值比重为 33.75%，第三产业增加值比重为 54.76%。从经济效益上看，综合国力在不断增强。全年国民总收入 2309 亿美元，全年人均国内生产总值 2785.37 美元，比上年增长 2.19%，在中东位居第 18。从开放经济的角度看，2017 年，埃及对外贸易总额 922 亿美元；经常项目差额为 –93 亿美元（表明其国外财产净额有所减少）。从改革发展的角度看，埃及政府出台了《埃及 2030 年愿景》，目前正在重点推进与民生关系密切的经贸与投资合作项目的建设，许多重大项目纷纷上马，各类投资机会涌现，发展潜力巨大。但是，根据《2018 年世界银行营商环境报告》，埃及在全球 190 个国家和地区中排第 128 名。跨境贸易、税负、履约能力均排在 160 名以后。这表明，埃及在政策持续性、通货膨胀、腐败、低效政府和官僚主义、劳动力受教育程度低、金融市场准入等影响营商环境的 6 个主要问题上有待改善。

2.3.2　埃及经济发展具体指标情况

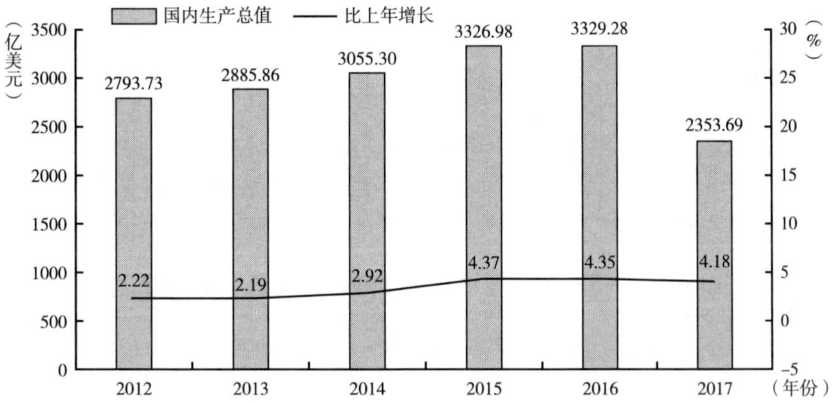

图 2.25　2012~2017 年埃及国内生产总值及其增长速度

数据来源：世界银行。

注：国内生产总值按现价美元计算；增长速度按 2010 年不变价美元计算。

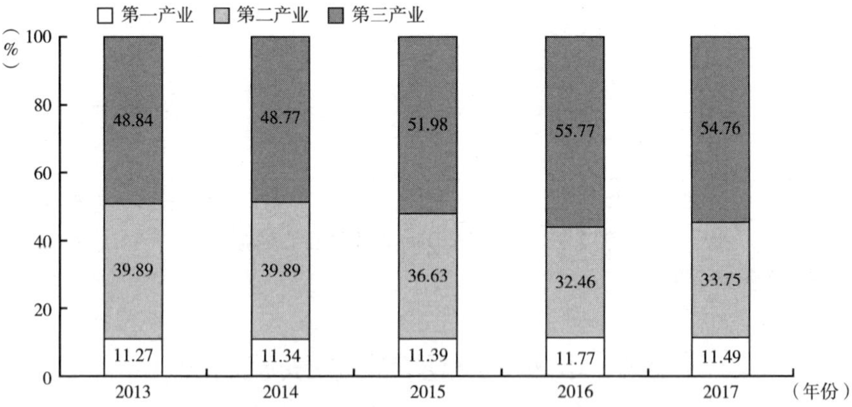

图 2.26　2013~2017 年埃及三次产业增加值占国内生产总值比重

数据来源：世界银行，按现价美元计算整理得出。

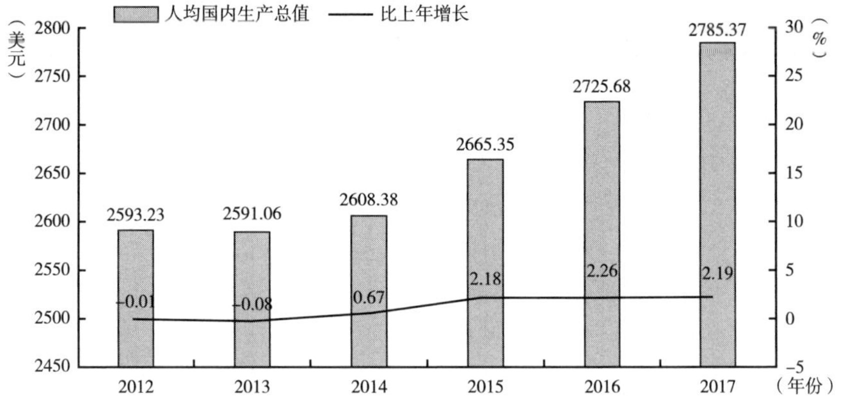

图 2.27　2012~2017 年埃及人均国内生产总值及其增长速度

数据来源：世界银行。

注：人均国内生产总值及其增长速度均按 2010 年不变价美元计算。

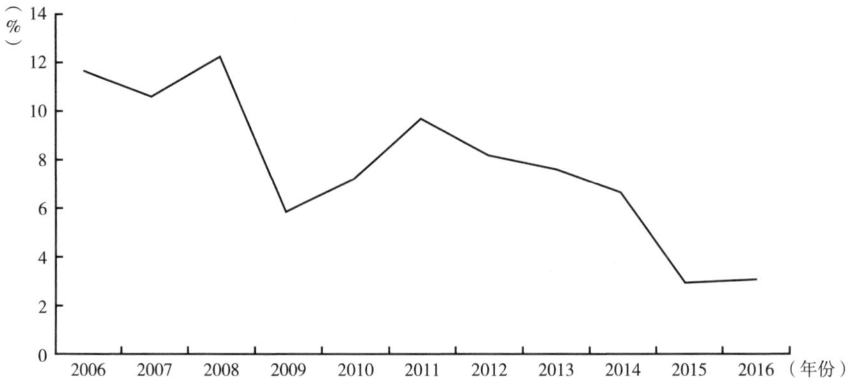

图 2.28　2006~2016 年埃及石油租金

数据来源和注同图 2.4。

2.4　北非重要国家经济发展情况

阿尔及利亚和摩洛哥是非洲北部两个重要的发展中国家，其旅游资源丰富，地理位置优越，可以辐射欧洲、美洲、非洲内陆市场和阿拉伯世界，是发展全球贸易的良好切入点。具有成为“一带一路”支撑点的潜质，理应受到更多的关注。

表 2.3　2017 年北非 2 个重要国家经济发展指标在中东国家排名（2010 年不变价美元）

国家	GDP	GDP 增幅	人均 GDP			
	金额（亿美元）	位次	增幅（%）	位次	金额（美元 / 人）	位次
阿尔及利亚	1714.67	8	1.70	15	4825.18	14
摩洛哥	1010.60	11	4.10	6	3292.45	16

数据来源：世界银行。

2.4.1　阿尔及利亚

阿尔及利亚经济发展水平较落后。从经济总量上看，2017 年，国内生产总值 1703.71 亿美元，在中东位居第 8。其中，第一产业增加值 208.96 亿美元，第二产业增加值 618.11 亿美元，第三产业增加值 876.64 亿美元。从经济增速上看，2017 年比上年增长 1.7%，增长缓慢，在中东位居第 15。从经济结构上看，2017 年，第一产业增加值比重为 12.26%，第二产业增加值比重为 36.28%，第三产业增加值比重为 51.46%（比上年下降 1.37%）。劳动密集型产业仍占较大比例，产业结构还不尽合理，亟待进一步调整。从经济效益上看，全年人均国内生产总值 4825.18 美元，比上年下降 0.05%，在中东位居第 14。全年国民总收入 1679 亿美元。从开放经济的角度看，2017 年，对外贸易总额 812 亿美元；2016 年，经常项目差额为 –262 亿美元，国外财产净额有所减少。从改革发展的角度看，目前其正在实行经济改革，积极发展石油化工、轻工业、旅游业等产业。希望通过产业多元化、私有化等措施促进经济发展。其在石油、天然气、电力、通信、住建等方面加强了和外资的合作，以求和各国实现在平等互利基础上的合作共赢。另外，其投资环境整体欠佳。在银行、海关、税收、签证等方面存在着手续繁杂、等待时间较长等诸多不便之处，使外商在阿的经贸活动受到了很大限制。目前其已经放宽了进口付款方式，加强了国内基础设施建设，还开始实施了一项旨在促进投资的新法规。这项法规的实施是阿尔及利亚发展战略的一部分，其目的是借助改善国家整体的营商环境来提振经济，同时通过吸引外国直接投资来减少进口的数量和实现出口的多样化。根据阿尔及利亚

新投资法规定，投资项目根据其所处的地理位置以及对国家经济和社会发展产生的影响，可以享受不同税收减免的待遇；对优先考虑发展领域和能够创造就业的投资项目将提供额外的优惠；对于那些对国民经济发展具有重大意义的投资项目将给予特殊补贴。正在改善且不断优化的国内环境，将为阿尔及利亚的外资创造良好的投资环境。①

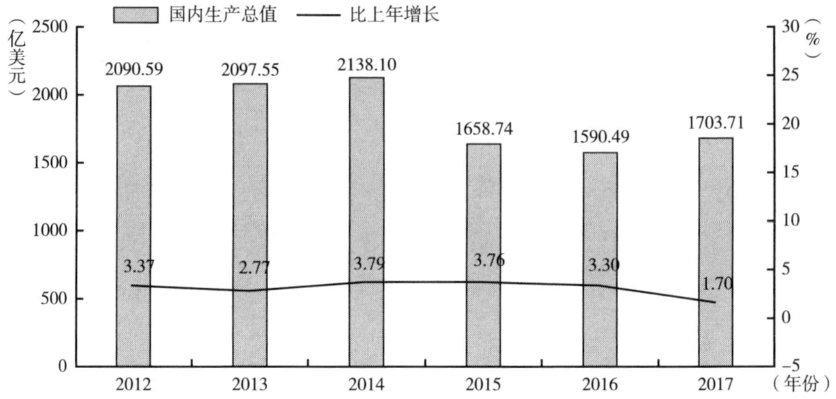

图 2.29　2012~2017 年阿尔及利亚国内生产总值及其增长速度

数据来源：世界银行。

注：国内生产总值按现价美元计算；增长速度按 2010 年不变价美元计算。

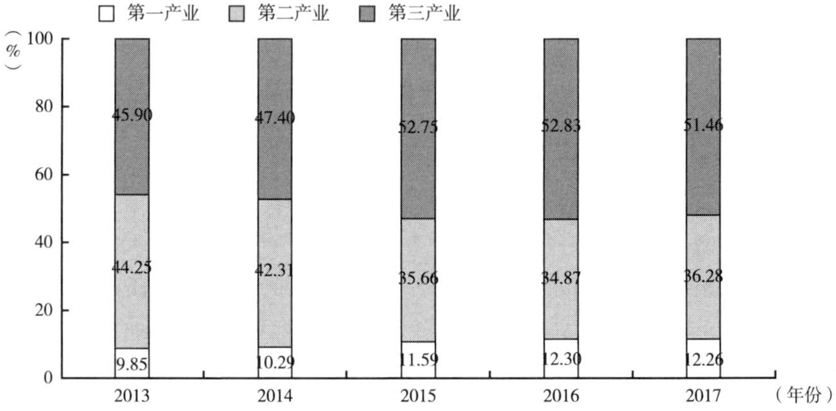

图 2.30　2013~2017 年阿尔及利亚三次产业增加值占国内生产总值比重

数据来源：世界银行，按现价美元计算整理得出。

① 阿布德努·贺利菲、王晓波：《阿尔及利亚投资指南》，《中国投资》2017 年第 20 期。

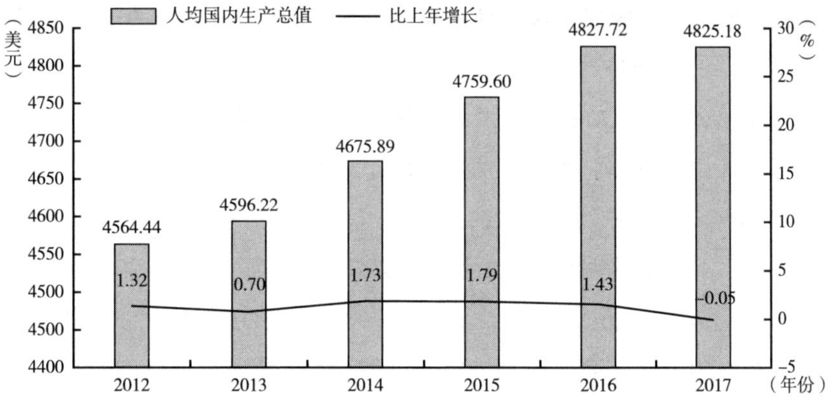

图 2.31　2012~2017 年阿尔及利亚人均国内生产总值及其增长速度

数据来源：世界银行。

注：人均国内生产总值及其增长速度均按 2010 年不变价美元计算。

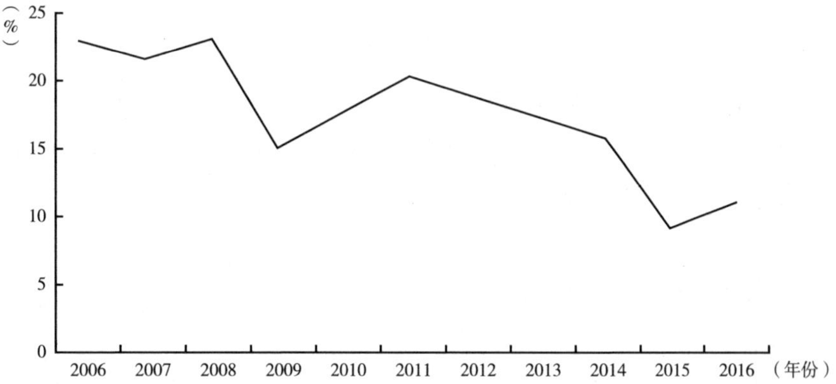

图 2.32　2006~2016 年阿尔及利亚石油租金

数据来源和注同图 2.4。

2.4.2　摩洛哥

摩洛哥经济发展条件较差，没有海湾国家那样的石油资源优势，经济受农业影响较大，主要依赖出口原料和初级农产品来维持国家经济。在过去的 6 年间，经济总体呈现平稳向好态势，年平均增长速度为 2.13%。从经济总量上看，总体规模较小。2017 年，国内生产总值 1091.39 亿美元，在中东位居第 11。其中，第一产业增加值 142.5 亿美元，第二产业增加值 279.13

亿美元，第三产业增加值 669.77 亿美元。从经济增速上看，2017 年比上年增长 4.1%，在中东位居第 6，居非洲国家前列，高于全球 GDP 增长率，是非洲大陆经济发展较好的国家之一。从经济结构上看，2017 年，第一产业增加值比重为 13.06%，第二产业增加值比重为 25.58%，第三产业增加值比重为 61.36%，是以服务业为主的产业结构，但仍然属于农业国家。从经济效益上看，实力在不断提升。全年人均国内生产总值 3292.45 美元，比上年增长 2.73%，在中东位居第 16。全年国民总收入 1071 亿美元。从开放经济的角度看，2016 年，摩洛哥对外贸易总额 646 亿美元，出口的商品还主要集中在矿产品、航空器、航天器及其零件和优质农、牧、渔业商品等方面；2017 年经常项目差额为 39.5 亿美元，出现盈余。从改革发展的角度看，近年来，摩洛哥积极推行企业私营化和贸易自由化，不断加大对基础设施的投资力度，每年都有电信、公路、供水和水坝等重大工程上马，卫星城镇建设如火如荼，工程承包市场潜力巨大。有效缓解了当地的失业问题，并带动了摩洛哥仓储、运输和进出口等相关产业的发展。根据 2017 年《非洲经济展望》报告显示，摩洛哥已成为非洲最具投资吸引力的国家，也是非洲内部第五大对外投资国。

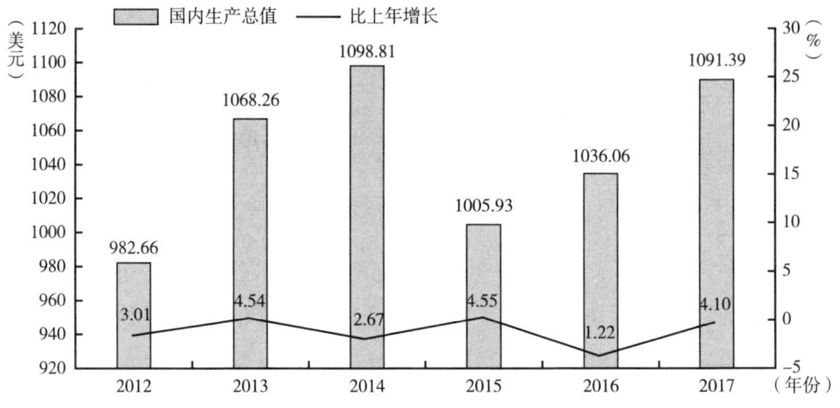

图 2.33　2012~2017 年摩洛哥国内生产总值及其增长速度

数据来源：世界银行。

注：国内生产总值按现价美元计算；增长速度按 2010 年不变价美元计算。

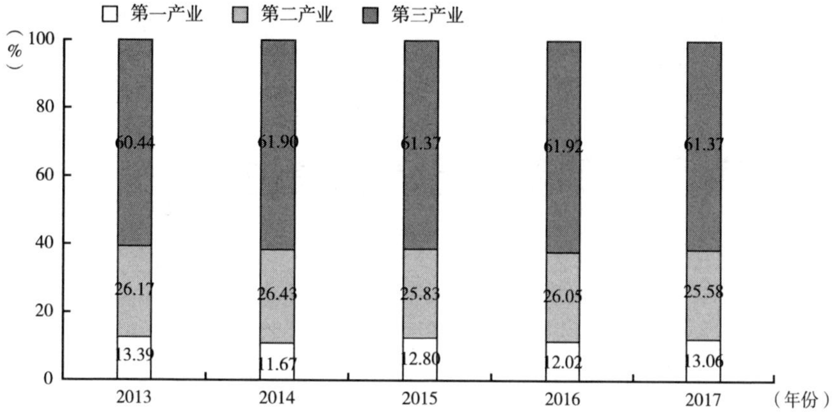

图 2.34　2013~2017 年摩洛哥三次产业增加值占国内生产总值比重

数据来源：世界银行，按现价美元计算整理得出。

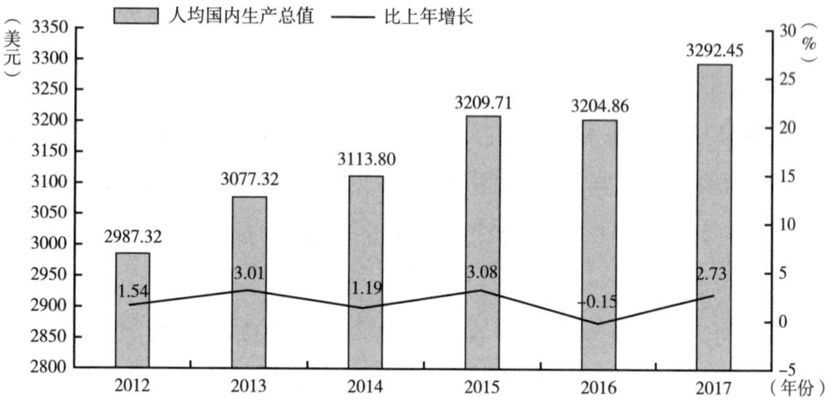

图 2.35　2012~2017 年摩洛哥人均国内生产总值及其增长速度

数据来源：世界银行。

注：人均国内生产总值及其增长速度均按 2010 年不变价美元计算。

第 3 章　中阿贸易合作专题报告

2017 年，全球经济逐步复苏，经济增速回升，逐渐走出了危机后的深度调整阶段。根据世界银行数据，2017 年全球经济增长率超过 3%，世界经济迎来逐步向好局面。虽然在世界经济增速回升的同时，全球经济面临诸多风险和威胁，如保护主义和逆全球化风潮盛行、全球债务水平过高等，但是各国努力推进全球宏观经济政策协调，积极应对，尤其是中国有关建立新型国际关系和建设人类命运共同体的倡议深入人心，为继续推进经济全球化指明了方向，中国所倡议的“一带一路”建设为开拓国际合作新空间和新领域提供了可能性，也为沿线国家经济发展带来了新的增长动力。

虽然美国宣布退出跨太平洋伙伴关系协定（TPP），美国与欧盟的跨大西洋贸易与投资伙伴关系（TTIP）谈判以及美国与中国的双边投资条约（BIT）谈判基本陷入停滞，全球范围内的贸易保护加剧，但是根据世界贸易组织（WTO）的数据，2017 年世界货物出口总额增长率转负为正，国际贸易增长表现出了量价齐升的特点。

在上述背景下，中阿贸易合作克服了诸多困难，合作水平得到了一定的提升，为“一带一路”建设起到了积极的作用，为促进双方互利共赢打造命运共同体奠定了良好的基础。

3.1　中国与阿拉伯国家对外贸易基本状况

3.1.1　中国对外贸易基本状况

2017 年，中国经济增速达到 6.9%，为世界经济贡献达到 15%。在 2015 年、2016 年中国连续两年进出口总额下降（2015 年进出口总额跌至 40000 亿美元以下，降速达 8.35%，2016 年则继续下降，进出口总额仅为 36855.58 亿美元）之时，2017 年进出口贸易扭转了下降趋势，进出口总额达到 39747.95 美元，相比 2016 年增速达到 7.85%，出现增长。其中，出口额达 22633.71 亿美元，比上年增长 7.9%；进口额达 17114.24 亿美元，比上年增长 7.78%。同时，贸易差额继续保持顺差，顺差额为 5519.47 亿美元。

表 3.1　2010~2017 年中国对外贸易额及增长速度

指标 年份	进出口贸易		出口贸易		进口贸易		贸易差额	
	总额（亿美元）	同比变化（%）	金额（亿美元）	同比变化（%）	金额（亿美元）	同比变化（%）	金额（亿美元）	同比变化（%）
2010	28668.98	35.18	15777.64	31.30	12891.34	40.25	2886.30	2.17
2011	35191.68	22.75	18983.88	20.32	16207.8	25.73	2776.08	−3.82
2012	37240.51	5.82	20487.82	7.92	16752.69	3.36	3735.13	34.55
2013	40014.58	7.45	22090.07	7.82	17924.51	6.99	4165.56	11.52
2014	41566.47	3.88	23422.93	6.03	18143.54	1.22	5279.39	26.74
2015	38096.63	−8.35	22734.68	−2.94	15361.95	−15.33	7372.73	39.65
2016	36855.58	−3.26	20976.37	−7.73	15879.21	3.37	5097.16	−30.86
2017	39747.95	7.85	22633.71	7.90	17114.24	7.78	5519.47	8.29

数据来源：根据联合国国际贸易数据库数据整理计算。

注：以中国为报告国。

从中国在国际贸易中的地位来看，2007 年进出口总额占世界贸易额的比重为 17.6%，2010 年进出口总额占世界贸易额比重上升到 21.7%，2017 年则达到 25.2%。从出口来看，2010 年中国出口额已经世界第一，超过美国、德国和日本；出口额占世界总出口额的 12.3%，2017 年出口额占世界

贸易额比重进一步上升，达到 13.96%。从进口来看，2010 年中国进口额位居世界第三，居于美国和德国之后，占世界总进口额的 6.7%；2017 年，位居世界第二，仅次于美国，进口额占世界总进口额的 7.07%。这表明，中国在国际贸易中的地位不断上升且越来越重要。

3.1.2 阿拉伯国家对外贸易基本状况

2017 年，中东地区局势仍比较复杂，地区安全状况频出。但是随着石油价格的逐步上涨，阿拉伯国家出口贸易额出现小幅回升，从而改变了自 2014 年以来由于石油价格下降等因素造成的出口额不断下降的趋势。2017 年，阿拉伯国家出口额达到 6744.687 亿美元，比上年增长 7.67%。但即使如此，阿拉伯国家出口额也没有达到 2012 年超过万亿美元的水平。同时，阿拉伯国家进口额进一步下降，降为 6093.740 亿美元，降幅达 9.63%，这主要是由于许多阿拉伯国家财政收入、经济增长趋缓导致的财政收缩所致。总体来看，阿拉伯国家进出口总额为 12838.43 亿美元，比上年小幅下降。2010 年阿拉伯国家的出口占世界总出口的 5.71%，到 2017 年降为 4.59%；2010 年阿拉伯国家的进口占世界进口的 3.73%，到 2017 年增长为 3.86%。总的来说，从阿拉伯国家在国际贸易中的地位变动不大。

表 3.2　2010~2017 年阿拉伯国家对外贸易额及增长速度

指标 / 年份	进出口贸易		出口贸易		进口贸易		贸易差额	
	总额（亿美元）	同比变化（%）	金额（亿美元）	同比变化（%）	金额（亿美元）	同比变化（%）	金额（亿美元）	同比变化（%）
2010	13439.29	24.02	7960.126	34.32	5479.169	11.59	2480.957	144.16
2011	17392.17	29.41	10906.28	37.01	6485.896	18.37	4420.379	78.17
2012	19446.23	11.81	12289.56	12.68	7156.672	10.34	5132.887	16.12
2013	19903.86	2.35	12088.3	−1.64	7815.563	9.21	4272.736	−16.76
2014	19208.59	−3.49	11205.41	−7.30	8003.181	2.40	3202.229	−25.05
2015	14392.32	−25.07	7090.995	−36.72	7301.324	−8.77	−210.329	−106.57
2016	13007.05	−9.63	6264.124	−11.66	6742.926	−7.65	−478.802	−127.64
2017	12838.43	−1.30	6744.687	7.67	6093.74	−9.63	650.947	235.95

数据来源：根据联合国国际贸易数据库数据整理计算。

注：由于以阿拉伯国家为报告国的部分数据缺失，表中数据以世界所有国家为报告国。

3.2　中国与阿拉伯国家对外贸易情况

3.2.1　中阿双边贸易规模及增长速度

2017 年，中国双边贸易额有所回升，达到 1917.57 亿美元，增幅达 12.12%。其中，中国向阿拉伯国家出口 986.73 亿美元，下降 1.99%；自阿拉伯国家进口 930.84 亿美元，增长 32.30%。贸易差额（出口减进口）为 55.89 亿美元，比上年下降 247.29 亿美元，这表明，中国对阿拉伯国家的贸易顺差在减小，且幅度较大（见表 3.3 和图 3.1）。2016 年阿拉伯国家是中国第七大进口来源国，中国自阿拉伯国家进口占全部进口额的 4.43%。阿拉伯国家是中国第五大出口目的地，占比 4.80%，居于美国、欧盟、中国香港、日本之后。2017 年阿拉伯国家是中国第七大进口来源地，占比 5.44%，居于欧盟、韩国、日本、美国、德国、澳大利亚等国之后。阿拉伯国家是中国第六大出口目的地，占比 4.4%，居于欧盟、韩国、日本、美国、德国、澳大利亚之后（见表 3.4）。

表 3.3　2010~2017 年中国对阿拉伯国家贸易总体情况

指标	进出口贸易		出口贸易		进口贸易		贸易差额	
年份	总额（亿美元）	同比变化（%）	金额（亿美元）	同比变化（%）	金额（亿美元）	同比变化（%）	金额（亿美元）	同比变化（%）
2010	1368.58	34.37	629.37	16.00	739.21	55.32	-109.83	-264.77
2011	1843.58	34.71	758.61	20.53	1084.96	46.77	-326.35	197.13
2012	2224.20	20.65	912.79	20.32	1311.41	20.87	-398.62	22.14
2013	2388.97	7.41	1013.52	11.03	1375.45	4.88	-361.93	-9.20
2014	2510.51	5.09	1138.21	12.30	1372.30	-0.23	-234.09	-35.32
2015	2025.41	-19.32	1150.40	1.07	875.01	-36.24	275.38	-217.64
2016	1710.29	-15.56	1006.74	-12.49	703.56	-19.59	303.18	10.09
2017	1917.57	12.12	986.73	-1.99	930.84	32.30	55.89	-81.57

分类依据：HS3。

数据来源：根据联合国国际贸易数据库数据整理计算。

注：以中国为报告国。

表 3.4　2016、2017 年中国进出口主要贸易伙伴排名情况

排名	国家和地区	2016 年中国对各国的出口额（亿美元）	比重（%）	国家和地区	2016 年中国自各国的进口额（亿美元）	比重（%）
1	美国	3856.78	18.39	欧盟（27 国）	2079.82	13.10
2	欧盟（27 国）	3383.06	16.13	韩国	1589.75	10.01
3	中国香港	2872.52	13.69	日本	1456.71	9.17
4	日本	1292.68	6.16	美国	1351.20	8.51
5	阿盟	1006.74	4.80	德国	861.09	5.42
6	韩国	937.07	4.47	澳大利亚	708.95	4.46
7	德国	652.14	3.11	阿盟	703.56	4.43
排名	国家和地区	2017 年中国对各国的出口额（亿美元）	比重（%）	国家和地区	2017 年中国自各国的进口额（亿美元）	比重（%）
1	美国	4303.28	19.01	欧盟（27 国）	2447.95	14.30
2	欧盟（27 国）	3711.73	16.40	韩国	1775.53	10.37
3	中国香港	2792.11	12.34	日本	1657.94	9.69
4	日本	1372.59	6.06	美国	1544.42	9.02
5	韩国	1027.04	4.54	德国	969.40	5.66
6	阿盟	986.73	4.36	澳大利亚	950.09	5.55
7	越南	716.17	3.16	阿盟	930.84	5.44

分类依据：HS3。

数据来源：根据联合国国际贸易数据库数据整理计算。

注：以中国为报告国。

由图 3.1 所示，2010~2014 年中阿双边贸易整体保持快速增长的态势，2014 年双边贸易额达到 2510.51 亿美元，达到这期间最高水平。2015 年，双边贸易额急剧下降，下降近 500 亿美元，这一下降趋势到 2017 年出现了转折，2017 年进口额大幅上升，使得双边贸易总额提升。

3.2.2　中国与阿拉伯国家主要贸易伙伴的进出口基本状况

由表 3.5 可知，2017 年，中国在阿拉伯国家的第一大贸易伙伴是沙特，贸易额为 501.37 亿美元。排名第二的是阿联酋，贸易额为 410.35 亿美元，伊拉克、阿曼、科威特、埃及、卡塔尔和阿尔及利亚分别位居第 2~8 位，其中，伊拉克、阿曼、科威特、埃及与中国的贸易额超过了 100 亿美元，

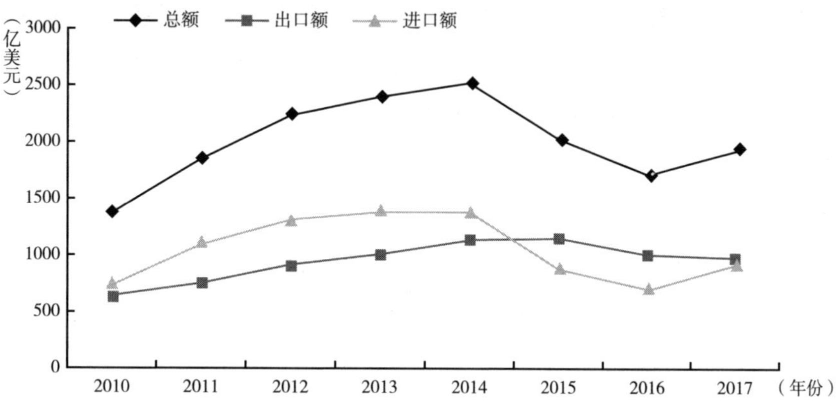

图 3.1　2010~2017 年中国与阿拉伯国家贸易趋势

贸易额分别为 221.44 亿美元、156.99 亿美元、120.48 亿美元和 108.28 亿美元。在前十位的贸易伙伴中，与中国贸易额增幅最大的是卡塔尔，增幅达 46.2%，科威特和伊拉克增幅也较大，分别达到了 28.56% 和 21.60%。从出口来看，中国对阿联酋出口额最多，达到 287.24 亿美元，其次是沙特，达到 183.75 亿美元。对埃及和伊拉克的出口紧随其后，分别为 94.86 亿美元和 83.30 亿美元。出口增速最大的是卡塔尔，达到了 11%，其次是伊拉克，达到了 10.37%。从进口来看，中国在该地区最大的进口来源国是沙特，2017 年，进口额为 317.62 亿美元。其次是伊拉克、阿曼、阿联酋和科威特，进口额分别达到了 138.14 亿美元、133.83 亿美元、123.11 亿美元和 89.35 亿美元。中国从这 5 个国家的进口占从阿拉伯国家进口总额的绝大部分，比重达到了 86.16%。造成这一现象的最主要原因是中国从阿拉伯国家进口的主要是原油，这 5 国是中国重要的原油进口来源国。其中需要注意的是在这 5 个国家中，除阿联酋，其他 4 国对中国都存在贸易顺差。

总体来看，与 2016 年相比，中国与阿拉伯国家主要贸易伙伴的变化不大，但是，进出口增速发生了变化。2016 年中国与前七大贸易伙伴国的进出口都是负增长，但到了 2017 年，仅对埃及的贸易为负增长，其他均为正增长（如表 3.5 所示）。

海合会六国依然是中国在阿拉伯国家最大的区域性贸易合作伙伴，2017 年，中国与海合会国家的双边贸易额为 1280.18 亿美元，占中国与阿拉伯国家贸易总额的 66.76%，与 2016 年的 1124 亿美元相比，略有上升，占比也上升了 1 个百分点。

表 3.5　2017 年中国在阿拉伯国家的主要贸易伙伴情况

序号	国家	金额（亿美元）			同比增长（%）		
		进出口	出口	进口	进出口	出口	进口
1	沙特	501.37	183.75	317.62	18.59	–1.48	34.44
2	阿联酋	410.35	287.24	123.11	2.43	–4.47	23.18
3	伊拉克	221.44	83.30	138.14	21.60	10.37	29.55
4	阿曼	156.99	23.16	133.83	10.64	7.86	11.15
5	科威特	120.48	31.13	89.35	28.56	3.73	40.26
6	埃及	108.28	94.86	13.42	–1.47	–9.11	142.57
7	卡塔尔	80.82	16.82	64.00	46.20	11.00	59.51
8	阿尔及利亚	72.33	67.85	4.48	–9.36	–11.29	35.08
9	摩洛哥	38.27	31.76	6.51	5.36	3.17	17.55
10	约旦	30.83	28.04	2.79	–2.61	–5.10	32.21
11	苏丹	28.13	22.22	5.91	6.78	4.32	17.06
12	也门	23.03	16.43	6.60	23.93	–2.91	297.50
13	吉布提	21.75	21.75	0.00	1.23	1.26	–88.44
14	黎巴嫩	20.34	20.11	0.23	–3.97	–4.27	30.37
15	突尼斯	15.26	13.28	1.98	6.36	2.48	42.72

分类依据：HS3。

数据来源：根据联合国国际贸易数据库数据整理计算。

注：以中国为报告国。

3.2.3　中阿双边贸易结构

一直以来，中国与阿拉伯国家因为各自的资源禀赋、产业结构和工业体系等存在极大的贸易互补性。

联合国贸易和发展会议将贸易商品分为原材料、中间品、消费品和资本品四大类，这种分类，能够比较具体地表现国家之间相互的贸易关系、各自在国际分工中的地位和产业结构状况。

根据以上分类方法，我们对中阿双边贸易结构进行统计分析。2017 年，中国对阿拉伯国家的出口主要是消费品和资本品，出口额分别为 464.20 亿美元和 310.08 亿美元，这两大类出口商品占全部出口商品的比重达 78.46%，从出口额和占比来看都比 2009 年有所增长。但中国对阿拉伯国家出口的原材料仅为 11.69 亿美元，占比 1.19%，这表明，中国对阿拉伯国家出口以制成品为主。从进口来看，中国从阿拉伯国家进口最多的商品是原材料，2017 年进口额为 644.81 亿美元，比 2009 年增加近一倍，占中国从阿拉伯国家全部进口额的 69.27%；同时，中国从阿拉伯国家的中间品进口额位居第二，进口额为 170.30 亿美元，占比达 18.30%。中国从阿拉伯国家进口的消费品和资本品分别占全部进口额的 12.02 和 0.40%。回看 2016 年，中阿双边贸易基本也是这样的贸易格局，2017 年与之相比变化不大。这表明，近年来中阿双边贸易结构相对稳定。

表 3.6　中国与阿拉伯国家大类商品贸易结构

UNCTAD 分类产品	贸易额和比重	2009 年	2016 年	2017 年
原材料	出口额（亿美元）	7.08	11.52	11.69
	比重（%）	1.31	1.14	1.19
	进口额（亿美元）	387.97	494.82	644.81
	比重（%）	81.52	70.33	69.27
中间品	出口额（亿美元）	107.86	194.60	191.86
	比重（%）	19.88	19.33	19.44
	进口额（亿美元）	62.05	127.95	170.30
	比重（%）	13.04	18.19	18.30
消费品	出口额（亿美元）	232.62	492.37	464.20
	比重（%）	42.87	48.91	47.04
	进口额（亿美元）	23.44	77.38	111.87
	比重（%）	4.93	11.00	12.02
资本品	出口额（亿美元）	191.30	299.58	310.08
	比重（%）	35.26	29.76	31.42
	进口额（亿美元）	2.18	3.24	3.69
	比重（%）	0.46	0.46	0.40

分类依据：HS3。

数据来源：根据联合国国际贸易数据库数据整理计算。

商品分类：根据联合国贸易和发展会议分类的分类整理计算。

注：以中国为报告国。

从更为具体的产品分类来看，2017 年，中国对阿拉伯国家的主要出口产品是机械设备和电气产品、纺织和服装以及金属产品，其出口额占出口总额的比重较高，分别达 32.35%、18.22% 和 11.94%，三大类产品占比超过了 60%。同时，中国还向阿拉伯国家出口杂项制品、运输设备、塑料和橡胶产品、矿石和玻璃以及化学制品等。与 2009 年出口结构相比，2017 年出口结构变化不大，仅运输设备位次变化较大，从 2009 年的第 5 位下降到 2017 年的第 7 位。与 2016 年相比，2017 年出口结构基本无变化，只是各类商品出口额有增有减，但起伏较小。总体来看，中国对阿拉伯国家的出口结构相对稳定。

表 3.7　2017 年中国对阿拉伯国家出口商品结构

产品编码	大类产品名称	2009 年出口额（亿美元）	2016 年出口额（亿美元）	2017 年出口额（亿美元）	2017 年占全部出口额比重（%）
84–85	机械设备和电气产品	183.06	312.02	319.16	32.35
50–63	纺织和服装	102.98	192.18	179.74	18.22
72–83	金属产品	63.37	122.61	117.85	11.94
90–99	杂项制品	41.40	92.22	95.74	9.70
86–89	运输设备	32.32	42.79	36.52	3.70
39–40	塑料和橡胶产品	25.32	57.59	59.15	5.99
68–71	矿石和玻璃	24.18	48.22	42.06	4.26
28–38	化学制品	16.23	31.64	33.16	3.36
64–67	鞋靴类产品	15.85	34.05	32.71	3.31
44–49	木及木制品	10.39	27.74	25.00	2.53
06–15	蔬菜	8.19	11.60	11.56	1.17
41–43	皮革和毛皮制品	7.75	15.63	15.17	1.54
16–24	食品	5.02	7.88	8.50	0.86
27–27	矿物燃料和矿物油	4.00	7.28	6.90	0.70
25–26	矿产品	1.37	1.40	1.36	0.14
01–05	动物产品	1.14	1.89	2.14	0.22

分类依据：HS3。

数据来源：根据联合国国际贸易数据库数据整理计算。

注：以中国为报告国。

2017 年，中国从阿拉伯国家进口商品结构也基本延续了 2016 年的状况，较为稳定。进口额居第一位的依然是矿物燃料和矿物油，进口额为 732.10 亿美元，占到进口总额的 78.65%。其次是化学产品，进口额为 81.27 亿美元，占比为 8.73%，第三位的是塑料和橡胶产品，进口额为 75.40 亿美元，占比为 8.10%。其他产品进口额比较低，所占比重也比较低。这种贸易结构反映了阿拉伯国家产业结构相对单一，石油产业为支柱产业，制造业和农业相对薄弱，工业体系有待完善。

表 3.8　2017 年中国自阿拉伯国家进口商品构成

产品编码	大类产品名称	2009 年进口额（亿美元）	2016 年进口额（亿美元）	2017 年进口额（亿美元）	2017 年占全部进口额比重（%）
27–27	矿物燃料和矿物油	396.14	553.04	732.10	78.65
28–38	化学产品	35.28	58.94	81.27	8.73
39–40	塑料和橡胶产品	21.75	57.09	75.40	8.10
25–26	矿产品	12.67	18.18	22.11	2.38
72–83	金属产品	5.65	4.19	4.82	0.52
84–85	机械设备和电器产品	2.16	3.33	3.92	0.42
06–15	蔬菜	0.27	1.99	3.53	0.38
50–63	纺织和服装	1.15	2.92	3.48	0.37
16–24	食品	0.01	0.49	1.47	0.16
68–71	矿石和玻璃	0.40	2.24	1.24	0.13
41–43	皮革和毛皮制品	0.20	0.30	0.44	0.05
44–49	木及木制品	0.04	0.06	0.32	0.03
90–99	杂项制品	0.06	0.30	0.31	0.03
01–05	动物产品	0.10	0.28	0.23	0.02
86–89	运输设备	0.01	0.10	0.16	0.02
64–67	鞋靴类产品	0.04	0.11	0.04	0.00

分类依据：HS3。
数据来源：根据联合国国际贸易数据库数据整理计算。
注：以中国为报告国。

进入21世纪以来，中国与阿拉伯国家的能源合作一直是双边贸易合作的重要组成部分，阿拉伯国家一直是中国最大的原油进口来源地。2007年中国原油进口额为798.58亿美元，其中，从阿拉伯国家进口286.66亿美元，占进口总额的35.90%。2016年中国原油进口总额为1166.61亿美元，从阿拉伯国家进口473.04亿美元，占进口总额的40.55%，占比有较大幅度的增加。2017年中国原油进口额为1638.21亿美元，从阿拉伯国家进口616.11亿美元，占比为37.61%，出现小幅下降。

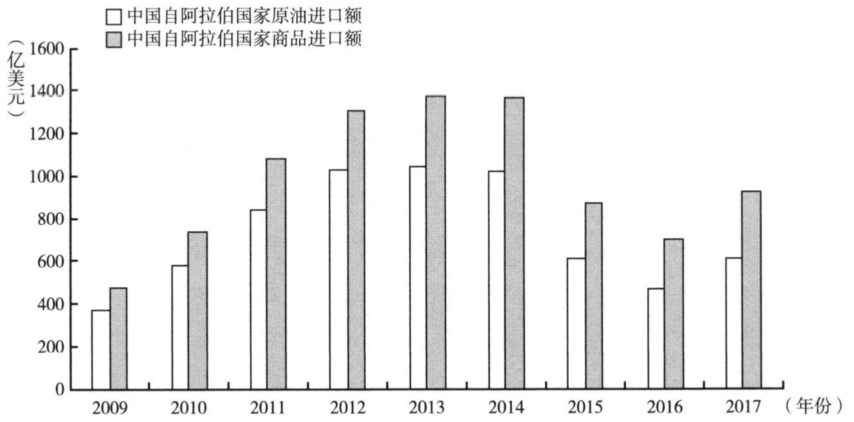

图 3.2　2009~2017 年中国自阿拉伯国家进口原油贸易额和总进口额

分类依据：HS2003。

数据来源：WITS 数据库。

2009年，在中国原油进口来源国排名前十位国家中，阿拉伯国家有6个，包括沙特、阿曼、苏丹、伊拉克、利比亚和科威特，其中沙特位居第一。2016年，这一进口格局发生了变化，俄罗斯取代沙特阿拉伯位居第一，伊拉克也从原来的第7位而升至第5位。居前十位的阿拉伯国家有沙特、阿曼、伊拉克、科威特、阿联酋，其所占中国进口原油总额的比重分别为13.35%、9.56%、9.14%、4.14%和3.31%。2017年，这一格局基本延续，沙特依然居于第2位，伊拉克则从第5位上升到第4位。

表 3.9　中国进口石油原油（HS2709 类商品）主要进口来源国状况

排名	进口来源国	2016 年进口金额（亿美元）	2016 年进口比重（%）	2017 年进口额（亿美元）	2017 年进口比重（%）
1	俄罗斯	168.90	14.48	238.84	14.58
2	沙特	155.69	13.35	205.15	12.52
3	安哥拉	138.66	11.89	201.23	12.28
4	阿曼	111.48	9.56	138.13	8.43
5	伊拉克	106.60	9.14	123.75	7.55
6	伊朗	93.57	8.02	119.29	7.28
7	巴西	60.37	5.17	91.77	5.60
8	科威特	48.29	4.14	70.83	4.32
9	委内瑞拉	45.87	3.93	65.66	4.01
10	阿联酋	38.62	3.31	41.57	2.54
—	世界	1166.61	100	1638.21	100

分类依据：HS3。

数据来源：根据联合国国际贸易数据库数据整理计算。排名依据 2016 年数据。

注：以中国为报告国。

总体来看，中国原油进口对阿拉伯国家依赖程度较高，其中，沙特、阿曼、科威特和阿联酋等海合会国家是非常重要的合作伙伴，同时，伊拉克的进口地位也越来越重要。

表 3.10　中国自阿拉伯国家进口石油原油（HS2709 类商品）状况

排名	进口来源国	2016 年进口金额（亿美元）	2016 年进口比重（%）	2017 年进口额（亿美元）	2017 年进口比重（%）
1	沙特	155.69	13.35	205.15	12.52
2	阿曼	111.48	9.56	123.75	7.55
3	伊拉克	106.60	9.14	138.13	8.43
4	科威特	48.29	4.14	70.83	4.32
5	阿联酋	38.62	3.31	41.57	2.54
6	利比亚	3.45	0.30	13.62	0.83
7	苏丹	3.38	0.29	2.93	0.18

续表

排名	进口来源国	2016 年进口金额（亿美元）	2016 年进口比重（%）	2017 年进口额（亿美元）	2017 年进口比重（%）
8	埃及	2.53	0.22	8.80	0.54
9	卡塔尔	1.57	0.13	3.81	0.23
10	也门	1.43	0.12	6.33	0.39
—	阿盟	473.04	40.55	616.11	37.61

分类依据：HS3。

数据来源：根据联合国国际贸易数据库数据整理计算。排名依据 2016 年数据。

注：以中国为报告国。

3.3 中国与阿拉伯国家服务贸易状况

3.3.1 中国服务贸易规模及结构

中国商务部数据显示，2009 年中国服务贸易进出口总额为 3025 亿美元，2009 年受金融危机影响有小幅下降，之后进出口总额一直持续增长，2017 年中国服务贸易总额达 6957 亿美元，同比增长 5.0%。出口方面，2009 年中国服务贸易出口额为 1436 亿美元，2017 年达到 2281 亿美元，为历史最高水平，同比增长 8.9%。进口方面，2009 年进口额为 1589 亿美元，2017 年达 4676 亿美元，同比增长 3.4%。

表 3.11　2009~2017 年中国服务贸易进出口额

年份	中国进出口		中国出口		中国进口		差额（亿美元）
	金额（亿美元）	同比（%）	金额（亿美元）	同比（%）	金额（亿美元）	同比（%）	
2009	3025	–6.1	1436	–12.1	1589	0	–153
2010	3717	22.9	1783	24.2	1934	21.7	–151
2011	4489	20.8	2010	12.7	2478	28.2	–468
2012	4829	7.6	2016	0.3	2813	13.5	–797
2013	5376	11.3	2070	2.7	3306	17.5	–1236

续表

年份	中国进出口		中国出口		中国进口		差额（亿美元）
	金额（亿美元）	同比（%）	金额（亿美元）	同比（%）	金额（亿美元）	同比（%）	
2014	6520	21.3	2191	5.9	4329	30.9	–2137
2015	6542	0.3	2186	–0.2	4355	0.6	–2169
2016	6616	1.1	2095	–4.2	4521	3.8	–2426
2017	6957	5.0	2281	8.9	4676	3.4	–2395

数据来源：中国商务部网站。

中国服务贸易出口占世界比重一直徘徊在4%左右，2009年为3.58%，2012年增长到4.44%，而2017年又下降到4.30%。2017年出口额低于美国、英国、德国和法国这几个发达国家。2017年与2009年相比较出口位居世界位次没有变化，都居第5位。中国服务贸易进口占世界进口比重在不断增加，2009年仅为4.36%，2017年就达到了9.2%。2009年进口位居世界第6位，到2017年就上升到世界第2位，仅次于美国。总体来看，中国服务贸易呈现逆差状态，且逆差额不断扩大。2009年逆差额为153亿美元，2017年逆差额已达到了2395亿美元。据表3.13可以看出，中国逆差差额相对较大。

表3.12　主要经济体服务贸易进出口额占世界比重（%）

国家和地区＼年份	2009		2012		2016		2017	
	出口比重	进口比重	出口比重	进口比重	出口比重	进口比重	出口比重	进口比重
澳大利亚	1.29	1.40	1.29	1.67	1.17	1.28	1.22	1.33
加拿大	2.00	2.48	1.97	2.53	1.66	2.06	1.64	2.09
中国	3.58	4.36	4.44	6.35	4.23	9.34	4.30	9.20
法国	5.66	5.26	5.17	4.57	4.75	4.86	4.70	4.73
德国	6.50	7.47	5.56	6.65	5.68	6.30	5.73	6.37
印度	2.71	2.40	3.21	2.93	3.27	2.76	3.47	3.03
意大利	2.84	3.27	2.39	2.45	2.03	2.14	2.09	2.26
日本	3.53	4.65	3.02	4.17	3.51	3.81	3.48	3.76
韩国	2.12	2.46	2.28	2.45	1.92	2.33	1.65	2.40

续表

年份 国家和地区	2009		2012		2016		2017	
	出口比重	进口比重	出口比重	进口比重	出口比重	进口比重	出口比重	进口比重
俄罗斯	1.34	1.89	1.37	2.46	1.02	1.54	1.09	1.74
英国	7.75	5.47	6.94	4.42	6.69	4.27	6.61	4.23
美国	14.96	11.55	14.47	10.20	15.19	10.43	14.72	10.59
阿拉伯国家	0.03	6.32	0.03	6.26	0.04	6.27	0.04	5.78

数据来源：根据 WTO 网站数据整理计算。

表 3.13　2009~2017 年主要经济体服务贸易进出口差额

单位：亿美元

年份 国家和地区	2009	2010	2011	2012	2013	2014	2015	2016	2017
澳大利亚	-26.40	-58.10	-114.26	-156.30	-177.27	-119.28	-88.28	-42.75	-28.35
巴西	-192.46	-300.27	-370.43	-398.49	-463.72	-481.07	-369.46	-304.47	-338.51
加拿大	-143.23	-215.08	-220.25	-226.39	-224.32	-219.27	-199.94	-175.88	-192.97
中国	-234.16	-150.63	-467.97	-797.24	-1236.02	-2137.42	-2169.07	-2425.68	-2394.99
芬兰	4.96	5.22	-2.14	-23.83	-17.94	-33.27	-30.75	-30.62	-17.83
法国	178.49	204.49	333.88	319.39	260.44	202.17	98.78	0.32	90.01
德国	-274.09	-382.65	-451.39	-421.11	-549.37	-335.97	-206.31	-234.70	-195.89
希腊	161.97	171.10	199.73	191.81	209.14	242.41	187.79	169.37	199.16
印度	123.37	21.40	132.39	156.06	222.73	288.34	327.11	282.87	299.67
意大利	-122.96	-121.54	-85.81	-1.58	5.89	-13.49	-29.70	-30.53	-41.52
日本	-348.69	-302.90	-348.33	-477.62	-356.43	-286.33	-159.50	-105.52	-61.19
韩国	-95.90	-142.38	-122.79	-52.14	-64.99	-36.79	-149.17	-177.37	-344.72
俄罗斯	-176.01	-261.20	-334.56	-465.87	-582.59	-552.78	-369.20	-238.27	-308.18
英国	825.04	865.48	1115.26	1189.85	1319.70	1419.89	1317.80	1247.28	1357.42
美国	1259.21	1540.20	1920.20	2043.98	2403.68	2611.58	2614.10	2477.14	2427.65
阿拉伯国家	-976.44	-1064.07	-1343.20	-1466.65	-1571.52	-1684.00	-1404.39	-1208.46	-1025.46

数据来源：根据 WTO 网站数据整理计算。

注：中国 2009 年服务贸易差额数据与中国商务部网站数据有差异。

从中国服务贸易结构来看，旅行、运输和其他商业服务是服务贸易中最重要的组成部分，其贸易额较大，均超过了千亿美元，这三类服务贸易

额占中国服务贸易总额的比重达 75.86%，超过 3/4。其中，旅行占比最大，达 42.18%；其次是运输，占比达 18.68%，再次是其他商业服务，占比达 15.00%。出口方面，其他商业服务占比最高，达到 26.96%；其次是旅行，占比为 16.97%；再次为运输，占比 16.26%。进口方面，旅行所占比重最高，达 54.47%；其次是运输，占比 19.86%；再次是其他商业服务，占比 9.17%。知识产权使用费进口额也较大，达 286 亿美元，占比 6.11%。在这 12 个服务大类中，处于顺差的是加工服务，维护和维修服务，建筑，金融服务，电信、计算机和信息服务，其他商业服务。其中，其他商业服务顺差额最大，为 186 亿美元；其次是加工服务，为 179 亿美元。运输，旅行，保险和养老金服务，知识产权使用费，个人、文化和娱乐服务，别处未提及的政府服务均处于逆差，其中旅行、运输和知识产权使用费这三类服务逆差额较大，分别为 2161 亿美元、558 亿美元和 238 亿美元。

表 3.14　2017 年中国服务贸易分类进出口额

服务类别	进出口		出口		进口		贸易差额（亿美元）
	金额（亿美元）	同比（%）	金额（亿美元）	同比（%）	金额（亿美元）	同比（%）	
总额	6959.0	5.0	2281.0	9.0	4678.0	3.4	−2397.0
加工服务	183.0	−2.7	181.0	−3.0	2.0	12.3	179.0
维护和维修服务	82.0	16.1	59.0	18.0	23.0	12.4	36.0
运输	1300.0	13.7	371.0	10.0	929.0	15.3	−558.0
旅行	2935.0	−3.9	387.0	−13.0	2548.0	−2.4	−2161.0
建筑	326.0	55.2	240.0	89.0	86.0	3.6	154.0
保险和养老金服务	144.0	−15.3	40.0	−3.0	104.0	−19.3	−64.0
金融服务	53.0	1.3	37.0	15.0	16.0	−20.5	21.0
知识产权使用费	334.0	32.6	48.0	308.0	286.0	19.2	−238.0
电信、计算机和信息服务	470.0	20.0	278.0	5.0	192.0	52.5	86.0
其他商业服务	1044.0	3.0	615.0	6.0	429.0	−1.3	186.0
个人、文化和娱乐服务	36.0	21.8	8.0	2.0	28.0	28.6	−20.0
别处未提及的政府服务	52.0	26.3	17.0	41.0	35.0	20.3	−18.0

数据来源：中国商务部网站。

3.3.2 阿拉伯国家服务贸易规模及结构

根据 WTO 数据，2009 年阿拉伯国家服务贸易额为 3260.36 亿美元，2012 年突破 4000 亿美元关口，2014 年达到历史最高水平，为 5268.17 亿美元。自 2015 年以来，阿拉伯国家服务贸易额出现下降趋势，2017 年服务贸易额为 4846.27 亿美元，比上年下降 0.3%。从出口来看，阿拉伯国家服务出口额呈现出持续上升趋势，2009 年为 1141.96 亿美元，2015 年达到 1812.73 亿美元，2017 年进一步增长，达到 1910.41 亿美元，同比增长 4.6%。阿拉伯国家服务贸易出口额占世界服务贸易出口总额的比重一直在 3% 左右徘徊，2016 年该比重为 3.6%，2017 年下降为 2.74%。从进口来看，从 2009 年到 2014 年阿拉伯国家服务贸易进口额持续增加，2014 年达到了 3476.09 亿美元。但从 2015 年起，阿拉伯国家服务贸易进口额出现下降趋势，2017 年下降为 2935.87 亿美元，同比下降 3.2%。总体来看，阿拉伯国家服务贸易一直呈逆差，2014 年逆差额达到最高，为 1684 亿美元，2017 年为 1025.46 亿美元，比 2016 年下降 100 多亿美元。

表 3.15 2009~2017 年阿拉伯国家服务贸易进出口额

年份	阿拉伯国家进出口		阿拉伯国家出口		阿拉伯国家进口		差额（亿美元）
	金额（亿美元）	同比（%）	金额（亿美元）	同比（%）	金额（亿美元）	同比（%）	
2009	3260.36	–5.2	1141.96	–4.7	2118.40	–5.5	–976.44
2010	3516.71	7.9	1226.32	7.4	2290.39	8.1	–1064.07
2011	3788.23	7.7	1222.52	–0.3	2565.72	12.0	–1343.20
2012	4077.73	7.6	1305.54	6.8	2772.19	8.0	–1466.65
2013	4220.32	3.5	1324.40	1.4	2895.92	4.5	–1571.52
2014	5268.17	24.8	1792.08	35.3	3476.09	20.0	–1684.00
2015	5029.84	–4.5	1812.73	1.2	3217.12	–7.5	–1404.39
2016	4859.74	–3.4	1825.64	0.7	3034.10	–5.7	–1208.46
2017	4846.27	–0.3	1910.41	4.6	2935.87	–3.2	–1025.46

数据来源：根据 WTO 网站数据整理计算。

在阿拉伯国家中，巴林、埃及、黎巴嫩、摩洛哥、卡塔尔、沙特和阿联酋是主要的服务贸易出口国。2012 年，出口额位居前五位的国家依次是埃及、阿联酋、摩洛哥、黎巴嫩和沙特，它们的出口额分别为 217.67 亿美元、160.65 亿美元、153.47 亿美元、151.25 亿美元和 110.50 亿美元。2017 年，阿联酋是该地区服务贸易出口规模最大的国家，出口额达到 704.97 亿美元；埃及居第 2 位，出口额为 200.33 亿美元；沙特和卡塔尔后来居上，位列第 3 和第 4，出口额分别为 180.21 亿美元和 177.06 亿美元；摩洛哥位居第 5，出口额为 172.61 亿美元。2012 年科摩罗、吉布提、利比亚和毛里塔尼亚服务出口额比较低，仅为 0.70 亿美元、3.39 亿美元、1.52 亿美元、1.45 亿美元，2017 年则数据缺失。2017 年出口最少的国家为索马里，出口额为 3.93 亿美元。总体来看，近年来以阿联酋为首的海合会国家在服务贸易出口方面增长速度较快，所占比重较高，2017 年占阿拉伯国家服务出口总额比重达到 64.13%①。

表 3.16　2012~2017 年阿拉伯各国服务贸易出口额

单位：亿美元

国别和地区＼年份	2012	2013	2014	2015	2016	2017
阿尔及利亚	37.49	37.73	35.44	34.55	34.33	32.61
巴林	83.32	85.01	85.71	91.13	109.98	111.30
科摩罗	0.70	0.80	0.85	0.84	—	—
吉布提	3.39	3.66	3.82	4.55	4.06	—
埃及	217.67	182.62	218.98	185.39	136.06	200.33
伊拉克	28.33	32.98	41.31	62.60	48.35	—
约旦	64.21	63.15	71.40	62.69	60.35	67.20
科威特	88.37	61.80	62.68	60.56	55.29	51.63
黎巴嫩	151.25	157.20	147.51	159.10	151.93	160.80
利比亚	1.52	1.80	0.79	4.83	0.86	—

① 阿曼 2017 年服务出口数据缺失。

续表

年份 国别和地区	2012	2013	2014	2015	2016	2017
毛里塔尼亚	1.45	1.86	2.79	2.46	2.70	—
摩洛哥	153.47	143.53	162.36	146.74	153.79	172.61
阿曼	26.87	29.55	31.30	33.79	36.04	—
卡塔尔	99.22	111.75	135.26	149.97	151.76	177.06
沙特	110.50	118.45	125.16	144.74	172.53	180.21
索马里	—	1.99	3.37	3.55	3.73	3.93
苏丹	10.59	12.58	15.68	17.27	15.45	15.17
叙利亚	—	—	—	—	—	—
突尼斯	50.77	48.31	47.34	32.94	32.49	32.60
阿联酋	160.65	212.39	583.25	607.76	655.96	704.97
也门	15.77	17.26	17.07	7.28	—	—
阿盟	1305.54	1324.40	1792.08	1812.73	1825.64	1910.41
世界	45376.57	48298.30	51900.42	49292.05	49533.86	53048.09
阿盟所占比重	2.74%	3.45%	3.68%	3.68%	3.60%	2.74%

数据来源：根据 WTO 网站数据整理计算。

注:“—”代表数据缺失。

从进口来看，2012 年沙特、阿联酋、卡塔尔、科威特和埃及服务进口位居前五，进口额分别为 734.07 亿美元、632.54 亿美元、239.06 亿美元、210.97 亿美元和 164.50 亿美元。2017 年，阿联酋超过沙特位居第 1，沙特位居第 2，卡塔尔位居第 3，科威特和埃及分别位居第 4 和第 5，这几个国家的服务贸易进口额分别为 855 亿美元、768.18 亿美元、314.27 亿美元、285.66 亿美元和 173.99 亿美元。显然，这些国家服务贸易进口额都比 2012 年有所上升，其中海合会依然是占阿拉伯国家进口总额比重最高的经济体，占比达到 78.33%①。2012 年，进口额最少的国家是科摩罗和吉布提，仅分别为 1.04 亿美元和 1.60 亿美元，2017 年这两个国家进口额数据缺失，该年度进口额最少的国家为索马里，仅为 14.52 亿美元。

① 阿曼 2017 年进口数据缺失。

表 3.17　2012~2017 年阿拉伯各国服务贸易进口额

单位：亿美元

年份 国别和地区	2012	2013	2014	2015	2016	2017
阿尔及利亚	108.73	107.95	118.03	110.77	108.81	115.99
巴林	60.45	70.51	67.64	65.92	75.30	76.42
科摩罗	1.04	1.09	0.99	0.83	—	—
吉布提	1.60	1.68	1.94	2.30	1.99	—
埃及	164.50	164.08	175.50	175.19	170.32	173.99
伊拉克	132.91	146.58	147.90	126.20	100.37	—
约旦	45.44	46.12	46.34	45.28	45.65	46.70
科威特	210.97	210.04	237.87	237.96	263.48	285.66
黎巴嫩	115.06	130.02	132.16	136.93	132.80	138.53
利比亚	69.96	84.72	74.56	46.58	28.83	—
毛里塔尼亚	10.17	9.99	9.00	6.41	6.05	—
摩洛哥	81.36	75.71	88.72	79.13	86.04	97.94
阿曼	87.85	97.98	100.14	102.14	99.46	—
卡塔尔	239.06	274.79	328.59	307.75	315.41	314.27
沙特	734.07	766.52	1005.45	880.36	702.67	768.18
索马里	—	10.17	12.24	13.28	13.35	14.52
苏丹	21.09	20.30	20.75	17.79	15.07	19.06
叙利亚	—	—	—	—	—	—
突尼斯	31.96	33.04	34.00	30.76	30.11	29.62
阿联酋	632.54	621.92	846.83	818.79	838.39	855.00
也门	23.41	22.72	27.43	12.75	—	—
阿盟	2772.19	2895.92	3476.09	3217.12	3034.10	2935.87
世界	44309.29	46960.67	51060.99	48230.43	48383.17	50803.23
阿盟所占比重	6.26%	6.17%	6.81%	6.67%	6.27%	5.78%

数据来源：根据 WTO 网站数据整理计算。

注："—" 代表数据缺失。

从服务贸易差额来看，大部分阿拉伯国家服务贸易处于逆差，只有巴林、吉布提、埃及、约旦、黎巴嫩、摩洛哥和突尼斯是顺差，但顺差额不大。顺差额最大的是摩洛哥，2017 年为 74.67 亿美元，比 2016 年增长 6

亿多美元，比 2012 年增长 2 亿多美元。逆差额较大的主要是沙特、科威特、阿联酋、卡塔尔和阿尔及利亚，2017 年其逆差额分别为 587.97 亿美元、234.03 亿美元、150.03 亿美元、137.21 亿美元和 83.38 亿美元。其中，沙特 2014 年逆差额达到最高，之后又开始下降；科威特是自 2012 年逆差额一直逐步上升，到 2017 年达到最高；阿联酋 2012 年逆差额最高，之后逐步下降；卡塔尔 2014 年逆差额达到最高，2017 年又下降到 137.21 亿美元；阿尔及利亚逆差额是先增加，后下降再上升，2017 年比 2012 年增加了 12.14 亿美元。

表 3.18　2012~2017 年阿拉伯各国服务贸易差额状况

单位：亿美元

国别＼年份	2012	2013	2014	2015	2016	2017
阿尔及利亚	−71.24	−70.22	−82.59	−76.22	−74.48	−83.38
巴林	22.87	14.5	18.07	25.21	34.68	34.88
科摩罗	−0.34	−0.29	−0.14	0.01	—	—
吉布提	1.79	1.98	1.88	2.25	2.07	—
埃及	53.17	18.54	43.48	10.2	−34.26	26.34
伊拉克	−104.58	−113.6	−106.59	−63.6	−52.02	—
约旦	18.77	17.03	25.06	17.41	14.7	20.5
科威特	−122.6	−148.24	−175.19	−177.4	−208.19	−234.03
黎巴嫩	36.19	27.18	15.35	22.17	19.13	22.27
利比亚	−68.44	−82.92	−73.77	−41.75	−27.97	—
毛里塔尼亚	−8.72	−8.13	−6.21	−3.95	−3.35	—
摩洛哥	72.11	67.82	73.64	67.61	67.75	74.67
阿曼	−60.98	−68.43	−68.84	−68.35	−63.42	—
卡塔尔	−139.84	−163.04	−193.33	−157.78	−163.65	−137.21
沙特	−623.57	−648.07	−880.29	−735.62	−530.14	−587.97
索马里	—	−8.18	−8.87	−9.73	−9.62	−10.59
苏丹	−10.5	−7.72	−5.07	−0.52	0.38	−3.89
叙利亚	—	—	—	—	—	—
突尼斯	18.81	15.27	13.34	2.18	2.38	2.98
阿联酋	−471.89	−409.53	−263.58	−211.03	−182.43	−150.03
也门	−7.64	−5.46	−10.36	−5.47	—	—

数据来源：根据 WTO 网站数据整理计算。

注："—"代表数据缺失。

由于海合会服务贸易的进出口占阿拉伯国家绝大部分，一下将以海合会国家的服务进出口结构为例说明阿拉伯国家服务贸易的结构。

出口方面，2017 年海合会在四大类服务中运输出口额最高，为 452.83 亿美元、其次是旅行，为 451.61 亿美元，其他商业服务（包括建筑、保险和养老金服务、金融服务等）为 332.60 亿美元。与 2016 年相比这几类出口额都有所增加，运输增速最高，达到了 12.68%，其他商业服务增速最低，仅为 2%。

表 3.19 2017 年海合会国家服务贸易分类出口额

单位：亿美元

项目 \ 年份	2012	2016	2017
商业服务	539.71	1153.86	1241.38
与商品有关的服务	2.94	4.29	4.34
维护和维修服务	2.94	4.29	4.34
运输	171.88	401.86	452.83
空运	56.88	317.14	353.97
旅行	237.89	421.74	451.61
其他商业服务	127.01	325.97	332.60
建筑	—	25.05	26.14
保险和养老金服务	55.73	79.33	80.16
金融服务	3.32	27.68	29.32
知识产权使用费	—	34.85	36.22
电信、计算机和信息服务	48.78	102.73	103.50
电信服务	46.32	52.92	51.66
计算机服务	—	—	50.89
信息服务	—	—	0.94
其他商业业务	16.22	52.54	54.35
研究和发展服务	10.28	11.29	10.54
个人、文化和娱乐服务	8.89	3.79	2.91

数据来源：根据 WTO 网站数据整理。

注："—" 代表数据缺失。

根据 UNCTAD 划分方法，服务被分为四个主要的项目：与商品有关的服务，运输，旅行和其他服务。其他服务进一步可分为建筑，保险和养老金服务，金融服务，知识产权使用付费，电信、计算机和信息服务，其他商业业务，个人、文化、娱乐服务，政府商品，别处未提及的服务和未划分的服务。

进口方面，2017 年海合会服务贸易进口额最大的是其他商业服务，为 1015.10 亿美元，占全部进口额的 47.61%，运输和旅行也是海合会国家进口的主要项目，这两大类服务进口比重超过了 50%。

总体来看，海合会国家在运输上具有一些优势，运输的逆差额不大，但是在建筑、保险和养老金服务和金融服务及旅游等方面逆差额比较高，表明该市场对这些项目进口需要较大。

表 3.20　2017 年海合会国家服务贸易分类进口额

年份	2012		2016		2017	
项目	进口额（亿美元）	比重（%）	进口额（亿美元）	比重（%）	进口额（亿美元）	比重（%）
商业服务	1691.61	100	2054.81	100	2131.95	100
与商品相关的服务	2.45	0.1	1.03	0.05	0.66	0.03
运输	799.01	47.2	512.33	24.93	507.74	23.82
旅行	491.02	29.0	592.4	28.83	608.46	28.54
其他商业服务	399.12	23.6	949.05	46.19	1015.10	47.61

数据来源：根据 WTO 网站数据整理。

第 4 章　中阿科技合作进程专题报告

中阿科技合作是中阿全方位合作的重要内容，中阿科技合作有力支撑了中阿经贸关系的进展。中阿技术转移是中阿科技合作的主要内容。近年来，中阿科技合作尤其是中阿技术转移快速推进，中阿科技合作在合作机制、合作内容、合作前景等方面取得了重大成果。

4.1　合作机制

中阿科技合作是伴随中阿经贸合作的发展而推进的。受制于科技合作的特殊性、长期性、无形性，合作机制非常重要。目前，中阿科技合作机制主要有官方机制和民间机制两种。

4.1.1　官方合作机制

官方合作机制主要包括中阿合作论坛、中阿博览会、中阿技术转移中心。

中阿科技合作的首要官方机构是中阿合作论坛。2004 年 1 月 30 日，中国国家主席胡锦涛访问阿拉伯国家联盟总部，会见了阿盟秘书长阿姆鲁·马哈茂德·穆萨和 22 个阿盟成员国代表。会见结束后，李肇星外长与穆萨秘书长共同宣布成立“中国—阿拉伯国家合作论坛”。中阿合作论坛组织机构包括部长级会议、高官会和其他机构，其中其他机构包括中阿能

源合作大会、中阿北斗合作论坛，以上会议都直接或间接的涉及科技合作。2014 年 6 月 5 日，中阿合作论坛第六届部长级会议上，中国国家主席习近平提出构建中阿“1+2+3”合作格局，即以能源合作为主轴，以基础设施建设、贸易和投资便利化为两翼，以核能、航天卫星、新能源三大高新领域为新的突破口，三大高新领域事实上已经涉及科技合作。

中国—阿拉伯国家博览会（以下简称中阿博览会）是中阿科技合作又一官方机构。中阿博览会是经国务院批准，由商务部、中国贸促会和宁夏回族自治区人民政府共同主办的大型涉外经贸与会展的活动。自 2010 年以来，已成功举办了三届中阿经贸论坛和三届中阿博览会。从 2015 年开始，中阿博览会加入了科技板块和科技合作内容。2015 年中阿博览会期间，举办中阿技术转移暨创新合作大会，中阿技术转移中心揭牌，签约了一批中阿重点科技合作项目。2017 年，中阿博览会展示活动包括中阿技术转移与创新合作大会暨高新技术与装备展。

中国—阿拉伯国家技术转移中心（以下简称中阿技术转移中心）是专业从事中阿技术合作的双边机构，中阿技术转移中心是 2014 年 6 月中阿合作论坛第六届部长级会议上由中国国家主席习近平亲自倡议，中华人民共和国科学技术部和宁夏回族自治区人民政府共同推动落实的。2015 年 1 月 5 日，科技部正式批复，由宁夏牵头集成全国科技创新要素和技术资源，打造中国对阿拉伯国家技术转移和创新合作的高效务实平台。宁夏回族自治区党委政府高度重视，要求按照国家所需、宁夏所能抓紧建设，并于 9 月 9 日印发《自治区人民政府办公厅关于印发中国—阿拉伯国家技术转移中心建设总体方案的通知》（宁政办发〔2015〕133 号）。2015 中阿博览会期间，宁夏回族自治区科技厅以中阿技术转移中心名义邀请到了阿拉伯联盟助理秘书长白德尔・丁・阿拉里，以及沙特阿拉伯、埃及、阿尔及利亚、阿曼、摩洛哥等 9 个阿拉伯国家的 90 名政要嘉宾。科技板块系列活动取得显著成效，中阿之间达成了 37 项合作协议意向，在国内外形成广泛影响，有效提升了宁夏在中阿科技合作中的地位。

2016 年 1 月 13 日，中国政府发表首份《中国对阿拉伯国家政策文件》

明确提出要“利用中阿技术转移中心，构建覆盖中国和阿拉伯国家的一体化技术转移协作网络”。2016 年 1 月 21 日，习近平出访埃及在阿拉伯国家联盟总部，宣布中阿技术转移中心正式成立，进一步确立了中阿技术转移中心在体现中阿务实合作方面的地位和作用。2016 年 9 月 2 日，由中华人民共和国科学技术部、发改委、外交部、商务部共同印发的《推进“一带一路”建设科技创新合作专项规划》，再次明确了中阿技术转移中心的重要使命。2017 年 5 月 14 日，习近平在“一带一路”国际合作高峰论坛开幕式上的演讲中，“启动‘一带一路’科技创新行动计划，开展科技人文交流、共建联合实验室、科技园区合作、技术转移 4 项行动”。

2018 年 7 月 10 日，中阿合作论坛第八届部长级会议在北京召开，中阿双方达成并签署了《中阿合作论坛第八届部长级会议北京宣言》、《中阿合作论坛 2018 年至 2020 年行动执行计划》和《中阿合作共建“一带一路”行动宣言》三份重要成果文件。中阿技术转移中心、中阿技术转移与创新合作大会等工作均进入上述三份文件，明确提出了要求。同时，中华人民共和国科学技术部国际合作司，也是中阿科技合作的重要推动机构，其主要工作包括搭建平台、项目撮合、信息发布、组织会议或论坛等工作。

4.1.2　民间合作机制

中阿科技（尤其是技术）合作的民间机制：一是中国公司跟阿拉伯国家相关机构自行进行技术转移，如华为公司、中国铁建、中国高铁等。二是一些市场化的技术转移机构，如中阿国际科技产业合作联盟。中阿国际科技产业合作联盟以中国企业园区国际合作联盟、宁夏国晨实业有限公司、中国—阿拉伯国家青年创业管委会、北京水木春锦资本管理有限公司、中农科产业发展基金、泰华集团、北京京鹏环球科技股份有限公司等 14 家国内外企业及商会为核心单位，近百余家企业为联盟成员。产业涉及金融、智能制造、智能高效农业、科技人才交流培训基地、国际贸易服务平台等领域。其成员囊括了国内各领域的大型企业，吸收了“丝绸之路经济带”沿线部分国家实力企业与商会组织。2017 年 10 月

19~20 日，中阿国际科技产业合作联盟与阿曼巴哈万集团在京洽谈合作事宜，双方拟在金融、新能源、高效科技智慧农业产业、特色产业园区（小镇）、健康产业合作研发、双向国际贸易合作、智慧科技、冷链仓储物流、科教文化、国际跨境电商合作及其他领域进行合作，并签署了合作备忘录。

4.2 合作内容及进展

4.2.1 科技合作内容

基于中阿友好交往传统和中阿合作论坛等机制性推动，中阿科技合作进展快速。中阿合作论坛第八届部长级会议，相继通过了《中国—阿拉伯国家合作论坛第八届部长级会议北京宣言》《中阿合作共建“一带一路”行动宣言》《中国—阿拉伯国家合作论坛 2018 年至 2020 年行动执行计划》，在三个文件中，都提到了科技合作的内容，具体合作范畴及内容如下。

表 4.1 中阿科技合作的近期规划

范畴	内容	依据文件
继续推进中阿“1+2+3”合作格局	以能源合作为主轴，以基础设施和贸易、投资便利化为两翼加强双方合作，提升双方在核能、航天卫星和新能源等高科技领域的务实合作水平，落实促进稳定、创新合作、产能对接、增进友好四大行动计划，强调根据双方法律法规和相关国际义务，重点开展相关合作	《中阿合作共建“一带一路”行动宣言》
科技创新合作	开展科技人文交流、共建联合实验室、科技园区与技术转移等；共同实施“一带一路”科技创新行动计划	《中国—阿拉伯国家合作论坛第八届部长级会议北京宣言》
卫星导航系统	中国卫星导航系统管理办公室与阿拉伯信息通信技术组织根据北斗卫星导航合作的谅解备忘录，依托中阿北斗 /GNSS 中心，在北斗增强系统等基础设施建设、教育培训、联合研发及应用产业化领域加强合作。加强在气象卫星领域的合作	《中国—阿拉伯国家合作论坛第八届部长级会议北京宣言》
水资源方面	加强在水务技术、水资源利用和节约、雨水收集、废水处理再利用和干旱地区水资源管理等领域的合作，加强双方水资源研究中心的合作关系。特别是在技术转移领域举办培训班	《中国—阿拉伯国家合作论坛 2018 年至 2020 年行动执行计划》

数据来源：中阿合作论坛官网，http://www.chinaarabcf.org/chn/。

4.2.2　合作进展

1. 总体进展

服务于中阿整体合作战略，中阿科技合作进展顺利；合作的内容包括技术转移、技术合作开发、技术人员交流、科研合作、共建技术交易与研发平台；合作领域包括航空航天、信息通信、高铁基建、水资源利用、现代农业、食品生产、医疗卫生、能源与环保等。

中阿技术转移中心挂牌成立，阿拉伯和平利用核能培训中心、中阿清洁能源培训中心取得积极进展。阿尔及利亚一号通信卫星成功发射，首届中阿北斗论坛成功举办。2018 年 4 月，突尼斯中阿北斗卫星导航系统卓越中心启动。中国企业中标迪拜哈翔清洁燃煤电站项目。

2017 年 5 月 24 日，首届中阿北斗合作论坛在上海召开。论坛由中国卫星导航系统管理办公室、中阿合作论坛中方秘书处、阿盟秘书处、阿拉伯信息通信技术组织联合主办，旨在为中阿卫星导航合作建立多边平台和长效机制，促进北斗系统服务阿拉伯国家。来自 21 个阿盟成员国和国际组织的代表及中国外交部、商务部、工业和信息化部、国家互联网信息办公室、中国卫星导航系统管理办公室等相关政府部门和企业代表出席了论坛。

2017 年 10 月 17 日，2017 迪拜投资论坛平行论坛——“中阿科技合作创新论坛”举办，由迪拜投资促进署、中国高科技产业化协会联合主办、中阿国际科技产业合作联盟协办、中融国投集团和 MERAAS 联合承办，论坛以“科技助力实业 · 创新引领未来”为主题，深度讨论“‘一带一路’政策背景下基础设施及能源类中国企业在海外的投资机遇”“PPP 模式下的互利共赢”“大数据及云科技在中东及北非地区的发展方向”“人工智能对未来生活的影响及新技术下的投资机会”“中国企业如何加大在中东及北非地区的商业影响力”。论坛首次面向中国企业，作为中阿科技创新的重要交流平台，邀请了国内外知名企业领袖、战略专家、学术精英，共同探讨“一带一路”倡议下中阿科技创新领域的发展机遇和合作商机。

2. 平台建设

中阿技术转移中心进行主要的平台建设。一是中阿技术转移协作机构网络初步形成。以构建覆盖整个区域的中国—阿拉伯国家技术转移协作网络为目标，联合国内外有关企业、科研机构、高等院校、中介服务机构等单位组建了中阿技术转移协作机构网络，积极开展各类技术转移对接活动。目前，入库协作网络成员已达4264家，其中国内2778家，国外1486家。先后主办或协办技术转移协作网络高层论坛10多次，受众3000多人次。二是技术转移综合信息服务平台正式启动。以构建大网络、应用大数据、形成大平台、提供大服务为宗旨，以为中阿双边国家间技术转移供需双方提供数据推送、在线对接、信息检索等服务为任务，构建形成以“一站、三库、五系统”为基本框架的中阿技术转移综合信息服务体系。该平台上线试运行以来，已收录技术供需数据70多万条，实现供需对接80余次，达成对接意向50多次，实现协议额12.1亿元人民币，已成为国内技术数据最丰富、更新最快、对接效果最好的对阿技术转移综合信息平台。三是一批双边技术转移中心的作用开始显现。相继建立了阿盟、沙特、约旦、阿曼、阿联酋（迪拜）、埃及、苏丹、摩洛哥8个双边技术转移中心，通过整合双边国家科技资源，共建联合研发中心、联合重点实验室、联合技术转移示范基地等国际科技合作基地，开展系列科技活动。如：依托阿盟秘书处共建技术转移中心，通过阿盟科技与埃及海运学院开展“发展中国家对外援助技术培训”、技术对接推介等工作；依托阿曼科委与卡布斯大学组建分中心，联合共建“宁夏（中阿）旱区资源评价与环境调控重点实验室”和100亩示范基地；依托沙特国王科技城创新发展中心组建分中心，推动红棕象甲防治、农业物联网、节水、食品生产等方面技术合作；依托约旦中东大学组建双边技术转移中心，在信息资源共享、创新平台培育、技术转移、高校职业培训等方面开展合作。四是承办大型国际博览会的能力得到提升。2017中阿博览会科技板块主要组织实施了中阿技术转移暨创新合作大会、高新技术及装备展、技术对接专场推介会等三个方面活动。其中，2017中阿技术转移与创新合作大会580名参会嘉宾中，外籍嘉宾占到了一

半。大会签约了涵盖共建中阿技术转移分中心、中阿科技创新平台和中阿技术合作等三个方面的 19 个科技合作项目。在科技部的大力支持下，高新技术及装备展首次将国家“十二五”科技创新成就展引入宁夏，参观者近 8 万人次。展会还同步举办中阿现代农业、半导体及智慧城市、工业领域、中科院专场、中阿共建科技合作平台、羲和系统等 6 场次专题技术推介对接会，通过对接共达成合作意向 30 余项，签署合作协议或合作备忘录 12 项，意向交易额 3 亿多元。

3. 科技人才合作

依托阿盟秘书处共建中阿技术转移中心，积极同阿拉伯科技与海运学院合作，共同在埃及举办技术推介对接会，在中国举办发展中国家技术培训班、阿拉伯国家创新创业培训班，培育中阿技术转移的“种子”。中阿技术转移中心先后与科技部国际合作司、中国科技交流中心、上海科技管理干部学院等一批机构密切合作，围绕北斗卫星、旱作节水、防沙治沙等专项技术转化应用和技术转移专业经理人培育，先后主办、承办或协办了“科技政策与管理国际研修班”等 20 期培训班，对来自埃及、沙特、摩洛哥、伊拉克、伊朗、泰国等国家近 300 名学员进行了专题培训。应埃及科研与技术院、苏丹非洲科技城、摩洛哥阿卜杜拉马利克大学等阿方机构邀请，中阿技术转移中心组织了上海交通大学、宁夏遥感测绘勘查院等区内外机构赴国外举办了 4 场技术推介对接会，在两届中阿博览会期间举办专场技术对接会 9 场，促进中阿双方技术代表面对面交流，对接成效显著。逐步构建中阿技术转移人才队伍。围绕解决技术转移服务人才严重缺乏问题展开培训，通过培训，为推进中阿技术转移合作培养了一批专业人才。

4. 技术转移

借助相关中阿合作论坛、中阿博览会、中阿技术转移中心等机构，中阿技术转移取得了阶段性成果。已启动中阿科技创新项目 20 多个，在椰枣、清真食品、农业物联网、绿色智能节水装备、卫星数据服务、马铃薯食品开发等领域培育了宁夏（中阿）椰枣工程技术研究中心、宁夏（中阿）植物饮品工程技术研究中心、宁夏（中阿）旱区资源评价与环境调控重点

实验室等一批中阿科技创新平台，推动红棕象甲防治、农业物联网、节水、马铃薯种植、食品生产等方面技术在阿拉伯国家得到了示范和推广。①

另外，依托沙特国王科技城创新发展中心组建分中心，推动华为公司在沙特国王科技城共建联合创新 4G-LTE 实验室。固原新月清真食品有限公司与沙特阿布加达叶尔餐饮有限公司在沙特建设食品生产线，输出先进的食品加工技术设备。依托迪拜园林农业局和阿联酋国家农业学会组建分中心，围绕椰枣产业、农业物联网、节水技术应用等领域开展合作。宁夏农业物联网工程技术研究中心与阿联酋农场主合作实施的 700 多棚设施农业智能管理项目，已经产生了积极的示范效应。依托约旦中东大学组建分中心，双方在信息资源共享、创新平台培育、技术转移、高校职业培训等方面开展合作。与约旦企业、大学建立产业技术转移合作关系，在约旦建立了 1500 亩马铃薯种薯与商品薯示范基地。依托阿曼科委与卡布斯大学组建双边技术转移分中心，联合共建“宁夏（中阿）旱区资源评价与环境调控重点实验室”和示范基地，开展应用基础研究和新技术、新装备研发。已实现向阿曼出口节水技术及装备 1.1 亿元。依托埃及科研与技术院组建双边技术转移分中心，组织区内外大学、科研机构及企业参加了第四、五届开罗国际创新展，在国际人才培训、共同举办技术对接活动、共建联合实验室等方面有多项合作。依托苏丹非洲科技城、摩洛哥高教部国际合作与伙伴司分别在苏丹、摩洛哥建立双边技术转移分中心，已掌握了阿方技术需求，分别在参加中阿博览会、国际人才培训、共同举办技术推介对接会等方面开展合作。

4.3 合作前景

4.3.1 规划前景

按照中阿合作论坛第八届部长级会议精神，尤其是会议通过的文件内

① 《宁夏推动中阿科技合作取得丰硕成果》，中华人民共和国科学技术部官网，http://www.most.gov.cn/dfkj/nx/zxdt/201801/t20180102_137328.htm，2018 年 1 月 3 日。

容，中阿双方规划了广阔、务实、优势互补的战略性合作前景，这包括以下几个方面。

加强科技人文交流合作，增进中阿政产学研各界的相互了解和交流，鼓励双方在共同感兴趣的领域开展多种形式的科技合作。举办知识产权领域的研讨会和培训班，促进尊重专利、商标、著作权和邻接权等知识产权的文化建设。中方与阿拉伯国家联盟就知识产权和竞争力领域共同关心的议题在国际场合进行协调。探讨合作开展阿拉伯国家和中方知识产权状况及知识产权制度对比研究。中方与阿拉伯国家就知识产权促进遗传资源、传统知识和民间文艺保护及发展等方面开展探讨和合作。

中方欢迎阿方青年科研人员通过“杰出青年科学家来华工作计划”来中国进行短期研究工作，邀请阿方科技管理和技术人员参与中国科技部每年举办的“先进适用技术与科技管理培训班”。

在共同感兴趣的重点领域共建联合实验室，支持双方产学研各界建立长期稳定的合作关系。探讨开展科技园区合作，中方愿与阿方分享中国科技园区建设和发展经验，在园区规划建设、政策咨询、人才培养、产业对接等方面开展务实合作。继续支持“中国—阿拉伯国家技术转移中心”和双边技术转移分中心建设，构建覆盖中阿各国的一体化技术转移网络，根据双方技术需求，通过培养专业技术人才，安排科技专家互访，组织多种形式对接交流活动，开展技术示范与培训等，促进先进实用技术的转移与推广，同阿拉伯青年就中国航天计划开展培训、交流经验。欢迎突尼斯教育和科研部在论坛框架下于 2019 年在突尼斯举办第二届中阿北斗合作论坛，欢迎根据中国卫星导航系统管理办公室与沙特王国阿卜杜勒·阿齐兹就国王科技城、阿拉伯信息通信技术组织签署的谅解备忘录，在突尼斯启动中阿北斗 / GNSS 卓越中心，建设中沙北斗 / GNSS 中心，在北斗增强系统等基础设施建设、教育培训、联合研发及应用产业化等领域加强合作；欢迎中国卫星导航系统管理办公室与阿拉伯科技海运学院签署关于北斗卫星导航合作的谅解备忘录，在海运、内河运输等领域开展北斗教育培训、应用推广等合作；欢迎中国卫星导航系统管理办公室与阿拉伯信息通信技

术组织、阿拉伯科技海运学院等单位联合发起阿拉伯地区北斗用户体验评价计划。①

4.3.2 市场前景

在经济全球化的今天，发展中国家积极对接世界，融入全球，发展开放型经济，中阿双方顺应世界新趋势，持续推进包括科技在内的全方位合作，实现政治、经贸、能源、科技、人文等领域的深度合作，金融优先、技术优先、人文优先显得十分迫切。当前，阿拉伯国家已成为中国第一大原油供应方和第七大贸易伙伴。中国提出的中阿共建“一带一路”，构建以能源合作为主轴，以基础设施建设和贸易投资便利化为两翼，以核能、航天卫星、新能源三大高新领域为突破口的“1+2+3”合作格局，加强产能合作等倡议得到阿拉伯国家积极响应。

科技合作是中阿合作的重要部分。不同于世界上一般的科技转移，主要是发达国家向发展中国家转移，中阿技术转移是发展中国家之间的技术转移。中阿科技合作是政府推动，市场主导。中国具有国际竞争力的高速铁路、航天通信、核能、新能源、现代农业等高新技术及装备，都是阿拉伯国家需要的。阿拉伯国家能源丰富，面临着经济社会发展的机遇和动力，尤其是海合会国家都有自己的振兴计划，发展以信息技术为龙头的“知识经济”。阿曼明确将信息技术产业列为新五年计划的重点发展产业。巴林计划斥资35亿美元建立高科技城。沙特2008年和2009年共投资400亿美元用于信息和通信技术产业的开发，成为全球在该领域投资最多的国家。同时，中国政府十分重视加快中阿政府间科技创新合作机制建设，实施中阿科技伙伴计划，不断提高阿拉伯国家的科技能力。

基于双方的传统友谊、发展阶段、技术能源需求，中阿科技合作的前景乐观。

---

① 《中国—阿拉伯国家合作论坛2018年至2020年行动执行计划》。

第 5 章　中阿金融投资合作专题报告

5.1　阿拉伯国家间接投资[①]

根据国际货币基金组织（IMF）统计数据，截至 2017 年 12 月底，阿拉伯国家资产组合投资虽非国际资本市场上的主流，但呈快速增长态势。此外，在阿拉伯国家的对外间接投资中，沙特（1569.67 亿美元）、巴林（395.01 亿美元）、科威特（169.24 亿美元）、黎巴嫩（39.63 亿美元）、埃及（15.57 亿美元）五国依然为主体投资（见表 5.1），其投资目标主要为欧美相关市场，美国约占 30% 份额，超过了阿拉伯国家对欧洲相关市场投资总和的 1/3（见图 5.1）。总体而言，沙特由于王储变更，2017 年投资总额有所下降。至于中国大陆市场，在中国香港市场有所收缩的同时基本表现稳定，沙特依然是阿拉伯国家对中国的最大投资国，相当于投资美国额度的 10%。此外，我国台湾市场也吸引了来自阿拉伯国家的投资。同时，其他国家也不同程度地吸收了来自阿拉伯国家的资产组合投资。至于阿拉伯国家投资主体，则为债券且主要集中于海湾国家，其中以阿联酋为首，巴林和卡塔尔则依此占据第二和第三的地位（见表 5.2 和表 5.3）。另据中国人民银行国际司报道，2017 年 12 月 27 日，中国人民银行行长周小川会见了来访的沙特财政大臣贾达安，双方就加强中沙金融合作交换了意见。[②]

---

① 本节只考虑资产组合投资，数据仅限于 2016 年与 2017 年。

② http://www.pbc.gov.cn/goujisi/144449/144464/3449938/index.html.

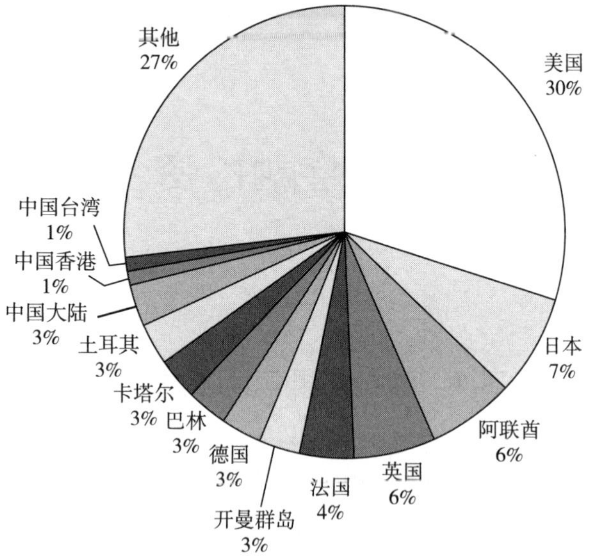

图 5.1　2017 年阿拉伯国家对外资产组合投资目标主体状况

数据来源：国际货币基金组织（IMF），截止日期 2018 年 3 月 18 日。

表 5.1　2017 年阿拉伯国家资产组合投资目标主体状况

单位：百万美元

投资来源国 / 投资目标主体	巴林	埃及	科威特	黎巴嫩	沙特	合计
阿尔及利亚	..	..	..	0	0	0
巴林	..	12	4168	226	2042	6448
巴勒斯坦	..	..	..	..	..	..
科摩罗	..	..	..	0	0	0
吉布提	..	..	..	0	0	0
埃及	418	..	108	9	2300	2835
伊拉克	16	..	11	1	0	28
约旦	878	2	37	113	61	1091
科威特	354	15	..	20	668	1057
黎巴嫩	..	13	44	..	88	145
利比亚	25	..	..	0	0	25
毛里塔尼亚	..	..	..	0	0	0
摩洛哥	95	..	5	0	5	105
阿曼	270	..	541	7	382	1200

续表

投资来源国 / 投资目标主体	巴林	埃及	科威特	黎巴嫩	沙特	合计
卡塔尔	2795	9	1045	32	2416	6297
沙特	1841	394	2059	38	..	4332
索马里	..	..	..	0	0	0
苏丹	2	2	14	4	0	22
叙利亚	..	1	80	1	28	110
突尼斯	117	2	8	0	34	161
阿联酋	5502	45	2483	112	5787	13929
也门	3	..	1	0	0	4
中国香港	1040	4	13	8	1837	2902
中国澳门	..	..	..	0	0	0
中国台湾	4	..	..	0	2177	2181
中国大陆	61	52	75	12	5598	5798
巴西	1534	0	..	16	1389	2939
开曼群岛	3253	..	944	139	2745	7081
法国	668	442	32	392	6119	7673
德国	510	92	28	82	5690	6402
印度	1421	0	23	2	877	2323
日本	194	9	3	3	15730	15939
韩国	513	..	67	1	3572	4153
卢森堡	347	1	21	228	511	1108
马来西亚	487	25	835	4	1484	2779
荷兰	405	2	17	62	2211	2753
巴基斯坦	259	..	2	10	548	829
俄罗斯	225	..	..	1	960	1186
南非	206	..	..	59	1271	1536
西班牙	136	2	2	18	2453	2611
瑞典	109	3	98	8	1283	1501
瑞士	168	6	80	179	2735	3168
土耳其	4090	0	401	49	2045	6585
英国	1636	56	737	388	9934	12751
美国	5145	251	1768	1327	55449	63940
合计	39501	1557	16924	3963	156967	218912

数据来源：International Monetary Fund，Coordinated Portfolio Investment Survey（资产组合投资协作调查）。

注：由于四舍五入，所以总投资额与细分金额不完全相等；0 表示金额少于 500000 美元或者为零；.. 表示无数据。

5.2 阿拉伯国家吸引外国间接组合投资

从世界各国对外投资状况来看，较之2016年（见表5.5），2017年阿拉伯国家吸引外国组合投资总额有所提升，但依然并非国际资本流入的热门地区，约占世界总投资的0.4%（见表5.2、表5.3、表5.4）。从2017年资金流入的构成情况来看，阿拉伯国家资金来源呈多元化，投资主体为各类债券（见表5.3），且主要来自欧美（见表5.4）。相比2016年（见表5.5），世界各国对阿拉伯国家的资产组合投资总额1689亿美元，2017年约为2265亿美元，增幅7.5%。此外，表5.2显示，阿联酋为投资热点国，同比增长7.4%，埃及、伊拉克、卡塔尔分别增长3.4%、7.1%、10%，但黎巴嫩则同比下降7.2%（2016年为144.22亿美元）。同时，除吉布提、巴勒斯坦、索马里外，利比亚、苏丹、也门依次为相关投资最低国。2017年，来自美国、卢森堡、英国、爱尔兰、瑞士、德国、开曼群岛、法国、荷兰的资金分别占22%、12%、7%、6%、5%、4%、3%、2%、2%的市场份额（见图5.2）。截至2017年底，美国、日本、卢森堡、英国、韩国、德国、瑞士、法国、爱尔兰、开曼群岛、荷兰分别向阿拉伯国家投资494.85亿美元、54.18亿美元、259.66亿美元、148.36亿美元、20.54亿美元、94.93亿美元、87.59亿美元、52.14亿美元、145.28亿美元、68.24亿美元、36.06亿美元，占全部资产组合投资的65%。中国大陆、香港、澳门分别投资26.82亿美元、21.57亿美元、7.37亿美元，占全部资产组合投资的2.5%（见表5.4）。由此可见，欧洲仍是向阿拉伯国家投资最多的地区。2017年阿拉伯区域内的资金流动依然十分活跃，巴林、科威特和沙特仍为主体投资国，从而说明阿拉伯国家内部的经济合作进一步加强。总之，虽然阿拉伯地区对外投资的规模高于外来投资，但出现的新趋势是资金双向流动，流入速度依然呈上升趋势。

表 5.2　2017 年巴林、埃及、科威特对阿拉伯国家及中国总体金融投资状况

单位：百万美元

投资项目／投入主体	巴林					埃及					科威特				
	股权投资与投资基金总额	债券投资总额			资产组合投资总额	股权投资与投资基金总额	债券投资总额			资产组合投资总额	股权投资与投资基金总额	债券投资总额			资产组合投资总额
			长期债券	短期债券				长期债券	短期债券				长期债券	短期债券	
阿尔及利亚	..	..	..	..	..	..	..	..	..	..	..	..	..	..	..
巴勒斯坦	..	..	..	..	..	..	..	..	..	..	..	..	..	..	..
巴林	..	..	..	..	..	12	..	..	..	12	3663	504	486	18	3867
科摩罗	..	..	..	..	..	..	..	..	..	..	..	..	..	..	..
吉布提	..	..	..		..	..	..	..	..	..	..	..	..	..	..
埃及	8	410	399	12	418	..	..	..	..	..	107	0	0	0	107
伊拉克	..	16	16	..	16	..	..	..	..	..	11	..	..	..	..
约旦	299	578	578	..	877	..	..	..	..	..	37	0	..	..	37
科威特	182	172	169	3	354	..	15	15	..	15	..	..	..	..	..
黎巴嫩	..	..	..	..	..	6	8	..	8	14	44	0	0	0	44
利比亚	25	..	..	..	25	..	..	..	..	..	..	..	..	..	..
毛里塔尼亚	..	..	..	..	..	..	..	..	..	..	..	..	..	..	..
摩洛哥	..	95	95	..	95	..	..	..	..	..	4	0	0	0	4
阿曼	72	197	197	..	269	..	..	..	..	..	218	323	311	12	541

续表

投资项目 / 投入主体	巴林					埃及					科威特				
	股权投资与投资基金总额	债券投资总额	长期债券	短期债券	资产组合投资总额	股权投资与投资基金总额	债券投资总额	长期债券	短期债券	资产组合投资总额	股权投资与投资基金总额	债券投资总额	长期债券	短期债券	资产组合投资总额
卡塔尔	374	2421	2326	95	1506	..	9	9	..	9	220	825	649	176	1045
沙特	709	1132	1070	62	1841	318	80	51	29	398	1542	517	502	16	2059
索马里	..	..	..	..	..	..	..	..	..	..	..	..	..	..	..
苏丹	2	..	..	..	..	2	..	..	..	..	14	..	..	..	14
叙利亚	..	..	..	..	..	1	..	..	..	..	80	..	..	..	80
突尼斯	38	79	79	..	..	2	1	..	1	1	8	..	..	..	8
阿联酋	565	4937	4628	309	5502	10	47	46	1	57	1263	1220	1181	39	2483
也门	3	..	..	..	3	..	..	..	..	..	1	..	..	..	1
中国香港	52	988	988	..	1040	..	4	..	4	4	2	10	10	0	12
中国澳门	..	..	..	..	..	..	..	..	..		..	..	..	..	..
中国台湾	4	..	..	..	..	..	..	..	..		..	..	..	..	..
中国大陆	61	..	..	..	..	1	51	..	51	52	11	64	64	0	75
合计	8262	37239	29627	1613	45501	1074	483	353	130	1557	11169	5754	4802	952	16923

数据来源：International Monetary Fund, Coordinated Portfolio Investment Survey（资产组合投资协作调查）。

注：由于四舍五入，所以总投资额与细分金额不完全相等；0 表示金额少于 500000 美元或者为零；.. 表示数据不可得。

表 5.3　2017 年黎巴嫩和沙特对阿拉伯国家及中国总体金融投资状况

单位：百万美元

投资项目 / 投入主体	黎巴嫩					沙特				
	股权投资与投资基金总额	债券投资总额			资产组合投资总额	股权投资与投资基金总额	债券投资总额			资产组合投资总额
			长期债券	短期债券				长期债券	短期债券	
阿尔及利亚	0	0	0	0	0	0	0	0	0	0
巴勒斯坦	..	..	..	..	..	..	..	..	..	0
巴林	214	12	12	0	226	336	1706	1657	49	2042
科摩罗	0	0	0	0	0	0	0	0	0	0
吉布提	0	0	0	0	0	0	0	0	0	0
埃及	3	6	6	0	9	25	2275	72	2204	2300
伊拉克	0	1	1	0	1	0	0	0	0	0
约旦	112	1	1	0	113	0	61	61	0	61
科威特	14	5	5	0	19	23	645	377	269	668
黎巴嫩	..	..	..	..	..	26	62	62	0	88
利比亚	0	0	0	0	0	0	0	0	0	0
毛里塔尼亚	0	0	0	0	0	0	0	0	0	0
摩洛哥	0	0	0	0	0	0	5	5	0	5
阿曼	0	7	7	0	7	1	381	363	18	382
卡塔尔	2	30	30	0	32	20	2396	1930	466	2416
沙特	37	0	0	0	37	..	..	..	..	..
索马里	0	0	0	0	0	0	0	0	0	0
苏丹	4	0	0	0	4	0	0	0	0	0
叙利亚	1	0	0	0	1	28	0	0	0	28
突尼斯	0	0	0	0	0	0	34	34	0	34
阿联酋	33	79	79	0	102	265	5522	4435	1086	5787
也门	0	0	0	0	0	0	0	0	0	0
中国香港	4	4	0	0	8	1579	258	258	0	1837
中国澳门	0	0	0	0	0	0	0	0	0	0
中国台湾	0	0	0	0	0	2177	0	0	0	2177
中国大陆	10	3	3	0	0	5401	197	197	0	5607
合计	2004	1959	1926	34	3963	95897	61069	41820	19249	156966

数据来源：International Monetary Fund, Coordinated Portfolio Investment Survey（资产组合投资协作调查）。

注：由于四舍五入，所以总投资额与细分金额不完全相等；0 表示金额少于 500000 美元或者为零；.. 表示数据不可得。

表 5.4 2017 年阿拉伯国家资产组合投资流入主体

单位：百万美元

投资来源主体 / 投资目标国	美国	日本	卢森堡	英国	韩国	德国	瑞士	法国	爱尔兰	开曼群岛	荷兰	中国香港	中国澳门	中国台湾	中国大陆	合计
阿尔及利亚	..	0	0	29	0	0	15	254	0	0	0	9	..	..	0	539
巴勒斯坦	..	..	..	..	..	..	..	..	..	..	..	..	..	..	..	..
巴林	976	32	1037	245	4	215	131	346	150	0	16	259	..	..	10	10442
科摩罗	..	0	0	0	0	0	0	..	0	0	0	0	..	..	0	0
吉布提	..	0	0	0	0	0	0	..	0	0	0	0	..	..	0	0
埃及	8418	167	5296	6223	29	798	194	85	1831	539	884	30	..	..	133	29908
伊拉克	..	15	735	12	318	83	34	30	279	119	55	0	..	..	35	2005
约旦	4630	20	580	247	3	164	51	1	211	56	76	0	..	..	18	8367
科威特	..	113	1070	315	111	277	28	46	541	174	15	17	5	..	12	4901
黎巴嫩	4124	52	2421	650	6	342	152	53	552	373	426	7	..	..	65	10376
利比亚	..	0	1	16	0	0	0	..	0	0	0	0	..	..	0	96
毛里塔尼亚	..	0	28	53	0	0	5	..	0	5	0	0	..	..	0	91
摩洛哥	2249	56	1540	200	19	973	279	1142	258	24	165	285	..	..	81	8492
阿曼	1791	82	1190	109	47	788	275	57	520	52	316	20	..	..	19	7141
卡塔尔	7541	1254	1221	1692	385	907	699	70	1015	966	422	996	242	..	42	29444
沙特	..	809	1039	1237	389	793	214	1523	1028	495	19	132	94	..	55	17001
索马里	..	0	0	0	0	0	0	..	0	0	0	0	..	..	0	0
苏丹	..	0	0	0	0	0	0	..	0	0	0	0	..	..	0	26
叙利亚	..	0	0	0	19	0	0	..	0	0	0	0	..	..	0	130
突尼斯	1934	1038	417	25	0	416	56	308	324	45	145	6	..	..	10	5495
阿联酋	17822	1780	9391	3783	724	3737	6901	1299	7819	3976	1067	4012	396	..	2240	92073
也门	..	0	0	0	0	0	0	..	0	0	0	0	..	..	0	4
合计	49485	5418	25966	14836	2054	9493	8759	5214	14528	6824	3606	2157	737	..	2682	226532

数据来源：International Monetary Fund, Coordinated Portfolio Investment Survey（资产组合投资协作调查）。

注：由于四舍五入，所以总投资额与细分金额不完全相等；.. 表示无数据，0 表示金额少于 500000 美元或者为零。

表 5.5　2016 年阿拉伯国家吸引外国投资总体状况

单位：百万美元

年度 / 投入国	2016 年	年度 / 投入国	2016 年
阿尔及利亚	612	阿曼	3202
巴林	8014	巴勒斯坦	—
科摩罗	1018	卡塔尔	29142
吉布提	0	沙特	11933
埃及	10165	索马里	0
伊拉克	1433	苏丹	29
约旦	6287	叙利亚	108
科威特	1324	突尼斯	4400
黎巴嫩	14422	阿联酋	68134
利比亚	51	也门	47
毛里塔尼亚	73	阿拉伯国家合计	168877
摩洛哥	8483	世界各国和地区总计	52088314

数据来源：International Monetary Fund, Coordinated Portfolio Investment Survey（资产组合投资协作调查）。

注：由于四舍五入，所以总投资额与细分金额不完全相等；0 表示金额少于 500000 美元或者实际为零，— 表示无数据。

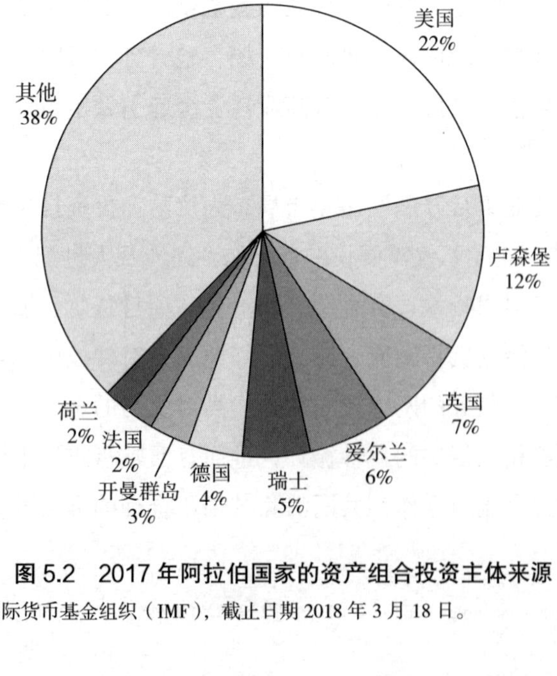

图 5.2　2017 年阿拉伯国家的资产组合投资主体来源

数据来源：国际货币基金组织（IMF），截止日期 2018 年 3 月 18 日。

5.3 “一带一路”中阿金融合作①

据中国人民银行报道，周小川在“一带一路”国际合作高峰论坛“促进资金融通”平行主题会议上表示，“一带一路”的核心是共商、共建和共享，需要沿线国家共同努力才能搞好投融资合作。同时，政府的资源是有限的，需要加强政府和市场的分工协作，坚持以企业为主体，市场化运作，才能保证投融资的可持续性。中国本着开放包容、平等互利的原则，将与有关国家加强“一带一路”投融资领域的合作，主要体现在以下几点。

一是运用开发性金融，助力“一带一路”资金融通。“一带一路”建设具有项目回收周期较长、资金需求规模巨大等特点，开发性金融可以在其中发挥重要作用。长期以来，世界银行、欧洲复兴开发银行和泛美行等开发性金融机构为发展中国家提供了大量融资。近年来，中国的开发性金融机构在此领域也做出了积极尝试。根据中国经验，开发性金融是指服务国家战略、依托信用支持、不靠政府补贴、市场运作、自主经营、注重长期投资、保本微利、财务上有可持续性的金融模式。实践证明，开发性金融业务具有多重优势，既可连接政府与市场、整合各方资源，又可为特定需求者提供中长期信用支持，还能对商业性资金起引领示范作用，以市场化方式予以支持。

二是推动商业银行开展网络化布局，为贸易和投资提供更好的金融服务。“一带一路”建设不仅需要投融资合作，还涉及大量配套金融服务，包括代理行关系、银团贷款、资金结算和清算、项目贷款、账户管理、风险管理等。无论是促进贸易融通，还是更好地服务对外投资，均需要加快推进金融机构和金融服务的网络化布局，提高对贸易的金融服务能力，才能形成金融和经济相互促进的良性循环，进而盘活整盘棋。中国正与各国金融监管当局加强交流与合作，共同消除各种不合理的准入壁垒和限制，提

① http://www.pbc.gov.cn/goutongjiaoliu/113456/113469/3307453/index.html.

供开放、公平、有序的监管环境，从而更好地推进金融机构和金融服务网络化布局，助力“一带一路”建设。

三是加强金融基础设施互联互通，推动以社区银行、互联网 / 电信支付为代表的普惠金融发展。“一带一路”沿线国家金融基础设施联通有助于保证金融市场高效运行和整体稳定。近年来，中国在这方面已经有一些进展，比如中国银联的跨境支付网络已遍布 160 个国家和地区，包括众多“一带一路”沿线国家，为各国的企业和居民提供了优质、安全、高效的支付服务。

四是积极发挥本币在“一带一路”建设中的作用。在“一带一路”建设中，积极使用本国货币有助于有效动员当地储蓄、有利于降低换汇成本、有利于维护金融稳定等。使用本币推动“一带一路”建设已有可鉴经验，中国在签订本币互换协议、货币直接交易、人民币清算行和人民币跨境支付系统方面也进行了一些有益尝试。中国愿与沿线国家分享相关经验，共同探索扩大本币在“一带一路”合作中的使用，更好地满足市场需求和经济发展需要。此外，中国还希望进一步推动股票和债券市场等资本市场发展，扩大股权、债券融资市场的连通性。

5.4　中阿金融自由度

据《金融自由指数》①（见表 5.6），在全球 185 国家和地区中，有 4 个阿

① 该《金融自由指数》基于不同国际金融组织，例如世界银行、国际货币基金组织（IMF）、安永会计师事务所（EY）、普华永道（PWC）和德勤公司等公布的数据而进行的分析。在本小节中，笔者根据 2014/2015 版的《金融自由指数》，对中阿金融自由度进行归纳和类比。该《指数》通过 15 项指标和子指标，对各国金融自由度进行了整体分析。其中，6 项“税率”指标包括最高所得税税率、公司税率、增值税、资本利得税率、遗产税率和最惠国待遇税率（某国的总体“税分”越高表示该国的税收总体发生率就越低）；3 项国际税收指标包括公民与居民、外国居民和非居民分别应纳的世界所得税，并将上述 6 项指标与 3 项国际税收指标合并为一个“总体税收分数”；1 项“投资者保护强度”指标是以世界银行 3 项衡量指数为组合，即公开程度指数、董事责任范围指数和股东诉讼缓解指数；1 项“法定权利强度”指标是以世界银行通过某国抵押和破产法专门衡量对借款人和贷款人的权利的保护；1 项“货币兑换”指标是指可自由　（转下页注）

拉伯国家排名金融自由度前十，其中巴林位居世界之首，紧随其后的是阿联酋，沙特名列第五，阿曼排名第八，中国香港位居第九。排名前十说明其金融市场开放程度较高，资本流动相对自由。在22个阿拉伯国家中，金融自由度达到中上水平的有17个，其中14个处于世界前100位。除上述国家和地区外，科威特和卡塔尔分别名列12和38位。此外，阿尔及利亚名列162，利比亚虽无排名，但依数据则处于全球倒数第二。同时，毛里塔尼亚和吉布提分别名列150和182，索马里处于倒数第一。中国澳门虽无排名，依数据应处于叙利亚（59）和埃及（65）之间，中国台湾位于埃及之后（67），中国大陆名列159。其次，从表5.6中可看出，阿拉伯地区国家金融法定自由开放度水平普遍波动较大，开放水平呈分化特点，其中只有科摩罗的“法定权利强度”指标超过了0.5，而其他阿拉伯国家的法定自由开放度则处较低水平。至于“投资人保护强度”指标，只有3个阿拉伯国家达至中上水平，即沙特0.69、科威特0.61和突尼斯0.57。这些国家在金融危机前将大量资金投入美国衍生品市场，监管部门出于资本流出管制的考虑，在这一时期对资本项目下的跨境资本流动制定了较多限制。金融危机爆发后，这些国家为规避损失，开放了相关资本跨境流动管制，尤其针对资本流入。除去金融危机这一特殊时期，这些国家保持较高金融法定自由度的原因在于其保持了较为稳定的内外部环境、较为完善的金融法制和市场。此外，在这些国家中，巴林、科威特、卡塔尔、沙特、阿联酋为OAPEC成员国，出于石油贸易原因保持了对货币自由兑换及资本流动的较高自由度，同时，也对私人资产转移和银行跨境业务保持了较高的法定自

（接上页注①）兑换货币的国家，使其公民和外部投资者更容易在国际上进行贸易、投资和流动资本；1项“不动产所有权”指标是指外国投资者在无公民身份的国家获得永久（即非租赁）产权的能力，该产权在此是指对建筑物和土地的所有权；1项“生活成本”指标，即世界银行将GDP数字调整为全球价格水平差异，以便更好比较各国的国家产出，而GDP对本地价格的调整需要使用所谓的“PPP转换因子与市场汇率比率”，所以通过PPP转换因子衡量某个经济体中生产的所有商品和服务的成本，从而衡量某个国家的生活成本；最后1项“通货膨胀”指标应用基金组织世界经济展望数据库对2011至2017年的年度通货膨胀率估算的平均数字。同时，由于一些国家缺乏数据，所以在并未将所有国家都列入排名。每项指标根据不同国家金融组织的相关详细分类描述进行平均评分，得到0到1之间的一个分数为最终评级指数。

由度。其他国家，如伊拉克、利比亚、叙利亚和索马里等国由于长期战乱及社会动荡，导致相关制度及法律缺失，表现为法定金融自由度的大幅下降，但随着近两年重建步伐的加快，这些国家（除了叙利亚）也相继制定了跨境资本管理制度，同时其法定金融自由度也有所上升。

根据《经济自由度指数》[①]，中国香港和巴林一直保持着比较高的金融自由度，摩洛哥、卡塔尔、科威特和苏丹在 2017 年的金融自由度也有所上升。另外，中国台湾和澳门的金融自由度保持不变，中国大陆有所下降。表 5.7 显示，中国香港获 90 分，说明政府干预最小，金融机构的监管极少，但可能超出执行合同义务和防止欺诈；巴林获 80 分，反映出政府名义性干预，政府对金融机构的所有权在总体资产中所占份额很小，金融机构对其提供金融服务的能力几乎无任何限制；中国澳门保持在 70 分水平，为政府有限性干预，信贷分配受政府影响，私人信贷分配几乎不受限制，政府对金融机构的所有权较大，外国金融机构受到的限制很少，同时摩洛哥也升至这一水平。处于 60 分水平的分别为中国台湾、约旦和阿曼，表明政府干预，银行和金融法规有负担，政府对金融机构的所有权和控制权进行管理，在整体资产中占有相当大的份额，金融机构提供金融服务的能力受到一些限制。同时，阿联酋、卡塔尔和科威特也达到并保持着这一水平。沙特和吉

---

① 在本小节中，笔者以美国“传统基金会”历年公布的《经济自由度指数》来分析中国与阿拉伯国家的金融自由度。在该《经济自由度指数》中，金融自由指数被置于“开放市场”类别之下，是衡量银行效率的一项指标，也是衡量政府对金融部门控制和干预的一项指标。按照该《指数》来理解，国家对银行和其他金融机构（例如保险公司和资本市场）的所有权减少了竞争，并普遍降低了获得信贷的水平。在以最低程度的政府干预为特征的理想银行和融资环境中，中央银行对金融机构的监管仅限于执行合同义务和防止欺诈。信贷是按市场分配，政府则不拥有金融机构。所有金融机构向个人和公司提供各种类型的金融服务。银行可以自由地扩展信用，接受存款和以外币进行操作。外国金融机构自由经营，与国内机构一样对待。该《指数》通过考察五个广泛领域来评估一个国家的金融自由度，即政府监管金融服务的程度，国家对银行和其他金融公司通过直接和间接所有权的干预程度，政府对信贷分配的影响程度，金融和资本市场的发展程度，以及对外方竞争的开放程度。这五个领域被认为是评估一个国家金融自由的总体水平。此外，该《指数》为百分制，通过从 0 分到 100 分来体现中国大陆及港澳台地区与阿拉伯国家的金融自由度。该《指数》数据来源：经济学家、国际货币基金组织、经济合作与发展组织经济调查、美国商务部、世界银行等。

布提两国近年来一直保持着50分的水平，说明政府干预金融程度相当大，信贷分配受到政府显著影响，私人信贷分配面临重大障碍，金融机构提供金融服务的能力受到重大限制，外国金融机构受到一些限制，同时黎巴嫩也降至这一水平。保持在40分水平的国家为埃及和毛里塔尼亚，反映出政府干预强，央行受政府影响，对金融机构监管严格，其执行合同和防止欺诈的能力较强，政府对金融机构拥有所有权和控制权，在整体资产中占有份额很小。保持在30分水平的国家分别为突尼斯、科摩罗和阿尔及利亚，表明政府干预广泛，信贷分配受到政府的广泛影响，政府拥有或控制大多数金融机构或处于支配地位，金融机构受到严重限制，银行的形成面临重大障碍，外国金融机构受到重大限制。

另据世界银行2017年《世界发展指数》①（见表5.7），相比2016

---

① 在本小节中，笔者以世界银行2017年《世界发展指数：金融准入、稳定性和效率》11项指标反映出的各国金融状况来分析中国与阿拉伯国家的金融自由度。首先，信用获取通过法律权利的强度和信用信息的深度来体现；其次，金融准入与外联通过商业银行储户、借款人、分行和自动柜员机来反映；其他指标分别为：银行资本与资产比例、银行不良贷款、国内银行向私营部门贷款利率差和贷款风险溢价等。具体而言，1. 法定权利强度指数用以衡量抵押和破产法保护借款人和贷款人权利的程度，从而促进贷款。该指数范围从0到12，分数越高表明设计良好的法律是来扩大信贷的获得。2. 信用信息深度指数用以衡量影响通过公共或私人信用登记系统提供的信用信息范围、可访问性和质量规则。该指数范围从0到8，其中较高的值数表示来自公共或私人注册局更多信用信息的可用性，以便决定贷款。3. 商业银行的存款人是指商业银行和其他非金融公司（公共和私人）与家庭存款账户持有人的报告数量。对于许多国家，由于缺少账户持有人的信息，所以本数据只涵盖了存款账户的总数。存款的主要类型包括支票账户、储蓄账户和定期存款。4. 商业银行的借款人是指非金融公司（公共和私人），以及从商业银行和其他银行获得贷款的居民客户数量。对许多国家来说，由于缺少贷款账户持有人的信息，数据只涵盖了贷款账户的总数。5. 商业银行分行是指常驻商业银行和其他居民银行的零售地点，作为商业银行，为客户提供金融服务，与主要办公室物理上分离，但不是作为合法分立的子公司组织。6. 自动柜员机是指为金融机构的客户提供在公共场所进行金融交易的设备。7. 银行资本与资产是指银行资本和储备与总资产的比率。资本和储备包括所有者提供的资金、留存收益、普通和特别准备金，以及准备金和估值调整等。资本包括一级资本（缴足股份和普通股），这是所有国家银行体系中的一个共同特征；此外，总监管资本包括几种特定类型的次级债券，如果资金不足则无须偿还，而是需要维持最低资本水平（包括二级和三级资本），而总资产则包括所有非金融和金融资产。8. 银行不良贷款占总贷款比率是指不良贷款的价值除以贷款组合的总价值（包括扣除特定贷款损失准备之前的不良贷款）。记录为不良贷款的贷款额应为资产负债表上记录的贷款的总值，而不仅仅是逾期的金额。9. 银行向私人部门提供的国内信贷是指其他存款 （转下页注）

年，在所有阿拉伯国家中，科摩罗依然保持着相对较高的法律权利自由度，表明该国国际资本流动绕开法规的数量较少。巴林、埃及、沙特和阿联酋保持着信用深度较高的水平，反映出其金融业一直保持着较快的发展势头。其对金融市场与国际资本流动的法律较为完善，管制措施也相对较少。尤其是巴林和阿联酋，两国为海湾地区的金融中心，拥有技能熟练的双语人才、经过反复检验的管理框架、低廉的运营成本和联通方便的地理位置，特别是紧邻地区第一大经济体沙特，这些优势使得巴林成为金融企业进入海湾地区建立长期并有一定规模机构的理想的投资国。因此，其法定自由度与事实金融自由度保持着相对的一致性。而埃及的法定金融自由度与事实自由度，则呈现出一定的差异。这种差异产生的原因在于埃及对衍生品、房地产、金融机构对外金融活动制定了严格的管制措施，而这些管制措施使得想进入埃及境内的国际资本绕过法律规定限制通过投资、贸易等渠道进入埃及境内。此外，科威特、黎巴嫩、摩洛哥、阿曼和卡塔尔近年来保持着较高的信用信息深度，表面其资本市场较为活跃。至于在金融准入与外联、银行资产与不良贷款等方面，相比 2016 年，2017 年阿拉伯国家整体有所改善。同时，中国香港处于法定自由度和信用信息深度很高的水平，从而说明其金融市场的完善性和活跃性，而中国大陆也保持着较高的水平，这表明其资本市场仍有很大的发展潜力。近年来，中国大陆更是逐步确定了开放金融市场、积极参与国际金融活动的大方向，开始逐渐减少对国际资本流动和外国投资的限制。相比之下，中国大陆虽不靠前，但是呈稳步上升趋势，

（接上页注①）公司（中央银行以外的存款公司）提供给私营部门的财政资源，如通过贷款，非物质证券的购买以及贸易信贷和其他应收账款，建立索偿。对于一些国家来说，索赔包括对公共企业的信贷。10. 利率差是指银行对私人部门客户贷款减去商业或类似银行为需求，时间或储蓄存款支付利率所收取的利率。利率附带条款和条件因国家不同而各异，从而限制了可比性。11. 贷款风险溢价是指银行对私人部门客户贷款的利率减去短期政府证券在市场上发行或交易的“无风险”国库券利率。在一些国家，这种利差有可能是负的，表明市场认为其最好的客户的风险低于政府。然而，贷款利率附带的条款和条件因国家而异，从而限制了可比性。

表 5.6　2017 年中国及阿拉伯国家金融自由指数

国家和地区	排名	平均分	总体税收分	法定权利强度	投资人保护强度	货币兑换	不动产所有权	生活成本	通货膨胀
巴林	1	0.856	0.992	0.22	0.49	是	是	0.78	1.00
阿联酋	2	0.830	0.992	0.33	0.38	是	是	0.65	1.00
沙特	5	0.796	0.753	0.44	0.69	是	是	0.84	0.85
阿曼	8	0.769	0.956	0.33	0.46	否	是	0.83	0.86
中国香港	9	0.756	0.819	1.00	0.92	是	否	0.65	0.81
科威特	12	0.737	0.947	0.22	0.61	是	否	0.70	0.80
黎巴嫩	25	0.671	0696	0.22	0.46	部分	是	0.76	0.78
卡塔尔	38	0.651	0962	0.22	0.46	否	否	0.69	0.82
约旦	53	0.631	0.636	0.11	0.38	否	是	0.89	0.87
也门	55	0.628	0.679	0.11	0.34	否	是	0.93	0.30
叙利亚	59	0.622	0.703	0.00	0.43	否	是	0.76	0.78
中国澳门	N/A	0.621	0.856	N/A	N/A	否	部分	0.74	0.61
埃及	65	0.615	0.563	0.22	0.49	否	是	0.99	0.34
中国台湾	67	0.604	0.588	N/A	0.61	否	是	0.78	1.00
突尼斯	92	0.571	0.432	0.22	0.57	否	是	0.91	0.71
伊拉克	93	0.570	0.693	0.22	0.38	否	否	0.87	062
摩洛哥	102	0.559	0.398	0.22	0.46	否	是	0.89	1.00
苏丹	108	0.533	0.537	0.33	0.26	否	是	0.86	0.05
科摩罗	146	0.513	0.526	0.56	0.34	否	否	0.79	0.76
毛里塔尼亚	150	0.507	0.507	0.22	0.31	否	否	0.93	0.64
中国大陆	159	0.494	0.461	0.44	0.46	否	否	0.78	0.92
阿尔及利亚	162	0.484	0.432	0.22	0.49	否	否	0.90	0.67
吉布提	182	0.429	0.407	0.11	0.15	否	否	0.80	0.92
利比亚	N/A	0.41	0.83	0	N/A	否	部分	N/A	0.57
索马里	N/A	0.116	0.289	N/A	N/A	否	否	N/A	N/A
巴勒斯坦	…	…	…	…	…	…	…	…	…

数据来源：Financial Freedom Index（金融自由指数）。

注：金融自由指数基于 15 个指标和子指标。对于整个指数的表格概览，6 种税率和 3 种国际税收指标合并为一个“税收分数”；其他 6 个主要指标显示在“指标”页上。N/A 表示无数据；…表示数据不可得；1.00 分为最佳，即 1.00“税分”转化为低税，因为 1.00“生活成本”转化为低生活成本。

表 5.7　2014~2017 年中阿金融自由度指数

	2014~2017 年中国与阿拉伯国家金融自由度				2017 年综合排名	
国家和地区 \ 年度	2014	2015	2016	2017	世界排名	区域排名
中国香港	90	90	90	90	1	1
巴林	80	80	80	80	44	4
中国澳门	70	70	70	70	N/A	N/A
中国台湾	60	60	60	60	11	5
约旦	60	60	60	60	53	5
阿曼	60	60	60	60	82	8
摩洛哥	60	60	60	70	86	9
黎巴嫩	60	60	50	50	137	11
阿联酋	50	50	60	60	8	1
卡塔尔	50	50	60	60	29	2
科威特	50	50	50	60	61	6
沙特	50	50	50	50	64	7
吉布提	50	50	50	50	171	43
埃及	40	40	40	40	144	12
毛里塔尼亚	40	40	40	40	131	25
突尼斯	30	30	30	30	123	10
也门	30	30	30	N/A	N/A	N/A
中国大陆	30	30	30	20	111	24
科摩罗	30	30	30	30	121	22
阿尔及利亚	30	30	30	30	172	14
利比亚	20	20	N/A	N/A	N/A	N/A
叙利亚	20	20	20	N/A	N/A	N/A
苏丹	N/A	N/A	N/A	20	164	40
伊拉克	N/A	N/A	N/A	N/A	N/A	N/A
索马里	N/A	N/A	N/A	N/A	N/A	N/A
巴勒斯坦	…	…	…	…	…	…

注：N/A 表示无数据；…表示数据不可得。

表 5.8　2017 年金融准入、稳定性和效率矩阵

	获取信用		金融准入与外联				银行资本与资产比率	银行不良贷款占总贷款比率	国内银行向私营部门贷款	利率差	贷款风险溢价
	法律权利力度指数	信用信息深度指数	商业银行储户	商业银行借款人	商业银行分行	自动柜员机				贷款利率减去存款利率	主要借贷利率减去国库券利率
	0~12（弱至强）	0~8（低至高）	每 1000 名成年人	每 1000 名成年人	每 100000 名成年人	每 100000 名成年人	百分比	百分比	占 GDP 百分比	百分点	百分点
阿尔及利亚	2	0	544	39	5.2	8.67	9.8	11.4	23	6.3	6.8
巴林	1	8	..	..	..	..	..	..	73.7	4.2	5.1
科摩罗	6	2	136	11	3.1	5.03	..	20.5	26.2	8.8	..
吉布提	1	0	167	35	5.9	9.61	..	..	30.5	9.6	..
埃及	2	8	440	100	4.5	13.45	..	..	34.1	5.7	5.4
伊拉克	0	0	..	..	4.1	1.88	..	..	9.2	7.4	..
约旦	0	5	534	..	15.1	27.12	..	..	75	5.1	..
科威特	1	6	..	211	14.3	62.17	..	..	103.6	2.9	..
黎巴嫩	2	6	1046	234	24.1	39.05	..	4.9	102.9	2.4	3.9
利比亚	0	0	..	..	..	..	..	..	..	3.5	..
毛里塔尼亚	2	3	147	67	8.3	9.7	..	..	..	..	..
摩洛哥	2	7	933	..	24.7	26.7	..	..	64	..	..
阿曼	1	6	1105	..	13.6	34.23	..	..	75.5	1.9	..

续表

	获取信用		金融准入与外联				银行资本与资产比率	银行不良贷款占总贷款比率	国内银行向私营部门贷款	利率差	贷款风险溢价
	法律权利力度指数	信用信息深度指数	商业银行储户	商业银行借款人	商业银行分行	自动柜员机				贷款利率减去存款利率	主要借贷利率减去国库券利率
	0~12（弱至强）	0~8（低至高）	每1000名成年人	每1000名成年人	每100000名成年人	每100000名成年人	百分比	百分比	占GDP百分比	百分点	百分点
卡塔尔	1	6	..	252	11.7	60.73	..	..	79.3	1.6	..
沙特	2	8	1141	166	8.6	74.42	14.8	1.4	58	..	..
索马里	0	0	..	..	..	..	..	..	..	..	..
巴勒斯坦	..	..	..	..	..	..	..	..	..	..	..
苏丹	3	0	..	..	3.4	4.75	..	..	8.9	..	..
叙利亚	1	2	..	..	..	..	..	..	..	..	..
突尼斯	3	6	..	218	20.5	27.44	..	..	77	..	..
阿联酋	2	8	1222	266	12.4	65.68	..	5.3	85.9	..	..
也门	0	0	124	13	1.6	6.28	..	..	..	..	..
中国大陆	0	0	34	384	8.8	81.45	8.4	1.7	156.7	2.9	..
中国香港	8	8	..	..	21.4	50.59	9.8	0.9	203.8	..	4.3
中国澳门	..	7	..	..	37.5	282.32	4.6	0.2	118.1	5.2	..
中国台湾	..	..	..	..	..	..	..	..	..	..	..

数据来源：世界银行。

注：.. 表示无数据。

说明中国的真实金融开放程度也在逐步提高，并且在法律限制范围之外有着更为活跃的资本流动。从数据上看，虽然在趋势上中国真实金融开放程度正在不断加深，法律限制也正在逐渐放开，但从利用外资的绝对数据上来看，近三年则有减退趋势，说明中国在吸引外资增速方面有所放缓。至于法律限制外的资本流动，一般来讲，当法律限制较为宽松，该国的真实金融一体化程度将在优越的法律制度条件下稳步上升；反之，当法律限制较严时，则说明其他国家可能更多选择以其他方式绕过该国的法律制度限制，从而进行资本注入或其他金融活动（见表5.6）。

第6章 “一带一路”背景下的中阿旅游合作专题报告

2015年，中国国家旅游局首次提出“旅游外交”[①]的概念和“开拓旅游外交，构建旅游对外开放新格局”等目标。[②]旅游业作为推进“丝绸之路经济带”的先导产业，对促进“一带一路”沿线各国贸易畅通、民心相通具有重要意义。发展旅游业，使人流带动物流、信息流和资金流，有利于消除各国间在意识形态、经贸、行政和产业壁垒，促进贸易纵深发展。

6.1 中阿旅游合作的动力机制

6.1.1 中阿旅游合作是阿拉伯国家旅游业发展的内在需求

阿拉伯国家旅游业在过去20年经历了逐步“离西向东”的过程，“9·11”事件是一个转折点。在“9·11”事件以前，阿拉伯人开展境外旅游的首选目标为英国、法国、意大利、西班牙等欧洲国家，这些国家拥有大量的阿拉伯移民，加之地缘距离较近，深受阿拉伯游客青睐。从入境游客源市场来看，欧美游客也是阿拉伯地区入境游的主力军。

“9·11”事件发生后，全球性反恐浪潮的高涨，以及由此催生的“伊斯兰恐惧症”使西方国家与阿拉伯国家间的政治冲突日益加剧，直接对阿

① 《2015年全国旅游工作会议代表热议工作报告》，中国国家旅游局，2015年1月16日，http://dj.cnta.gov.cn/html/2015-01/1712.shtml。

② 《“515战略”——52项举措》，中国国家旅游局，2015年5月13日，http://www.cnta.gov.cn/ztwz/515zl/52xjc/201505/t20150513_644.html。

拉伯地区旅游业造成了消极影响。一方面，前往阿拉伯国家旅游的西方游客数量出现断崖式下降，当地旅游业受到重创，其中以突尼斯、摩洛哥、埃及等国损失最为严重，这些国家不得不采取压低旅游价格、缩减旅游项目建设经费等措施应对危机；另一方面，以欧美为代表的西方国家不断收紧签证政策，导致前往西方国家旅游的阿拉伯游客数量不断下降。

在走不出去也请不进来的情况下，埃及和约旦等国逐渐将入境游客源国目标从西方国家转向周边阿拉伯国家，尤其是人均收入较高的海湾阿拉伯国家。短短数月，这些国家的入境旅游人数便恢复到了“9・11”前水平。2002 年，在欧洲和美国入境游客人数降幅达 30% 和 50% 的情况下，中东地区游客数量创下增幅 16.7% 的历史最高水平。也就是从这一时期开始，阿拉伯地区入境游客源国结构逐渐由以欧美国家为主转向以阿拉伯国家，特别是海湾阿拉伯国家为主，区域旅游流动性呈现大幅上升趋势，不少学者将这一现象称为“中东旅游业发展的悖论”。①

20 世纪 90 年代初，迪拜率先确立了以金融、贸易、房地产和旅游四大产业为支柱的多元经济发展战略，并成功将自身打造为全球知名旅游目的地。2001 年的“9・11”事件和 2010 年底爆发的“阿拉伯之春”不仅未对迪拜旅游业造成冲击，反而帮助其逆势增长。到 2017 年迪拜旅游对 GDP 的总贡献率已达到了 12%。②或许是受到迪拜模式的鼓舞，近五年来，几乎所有的海湾阿拉伯国家都表达了他们在发展旅游业上的决心。沙特阿拉伯 2030 愿景将旅游业定位为朝阳产业和未来沙特经济发展的新支柱，确立了到 2020 年旅游业对沙特 GDP 贡献比重达 18%，旅游收入达到 316.8 亿美元的目标，使旅游业成为仅次于石油的第二大收入来源③；卡塔尔“2030 国

---

① Ala Al-Hamarneh and Christian Steiner, “Islamic Tourism: Rethinking the Strategies of Tourism Development in the Arab World After September 11: Comparative Studies of South Asia,” *Africa and the Middle East*, Vol.24, No.1, 2004, pp.18-27.

② Travel & Tourism Economic Impact 2017: UAE, World Travel & Tourism Council, https://www.wttc.org/-/media/files/reports/economic-impact-research/countries-2017/unitedarabemirates2017.pdf.

③ 《沙特阿拉伯王国 2030 愿景》，沙特政府官网，http://vision2030.gov.sa/。

家旅游发展战略”表示，到 2030 年卡塔尔将吸引 700 万国际游客入境旅游；阿曼旅游部表示到 2040 年，其国际游客数量将达到 500 万人次。

要如期实现上述目标，阿拉伯国家面临着不小的挑战。除了动荡的地区安全局势外，基础设施建设落后、国际油价波动剧烈、旅游投资不足等因素都制约着地区旅游业的发展。而近年来中国境外游市场规模增长快速，加之“一带一路”背景下中阿双边关系持续向好，为阿拉伯国家旅游业的发展带去了难得的机遇。

6.1.2 中阿旅游合作是深化中阿经贸合作的重要途径

近年来，阿拉伯国家“向东看”与中国“西进战略”存在利益交会点，这为深化中阿经贸合作提供了有利条件。2004~2014 年，中阿双边贸易额从 367 亿美元增长至 2512 亿美元，[①] 增长近 6 倍。目前，中国已成为包括沙特在内的 9 个阿拉伯国家的最大贸易伙伴。

中阿经贸关系不断深化的同时，双边贸易中深层次的结构性问题也逐渐凸显。当前，中阿经贸合作主要集中在能源、进出口贸易、工程承包和劳务合作四大领域，合作主体以国家及地方政府为主，缺少成熟市场机制的导入，致使合作领域相对单一、合作水平较低，贸易结构性失衡现象长期存在，双向投资增长乏力。[②] 中阿旅游合作有利于培育中阿经贸合作新的增长点，通过旅游业带动航空、运输、基础设施建设、餐饮、住宿、文化创意等产业，引导经贸合作逐渐从政府走向企业和民间。

阿拉伯国家旅游市场发展潜力巨大。从全球增速来看，未来中东旅游市场，尤其是海湾阿拉伯国家将成为世界范围内中东阿拉伯旅游人数增长最快的地区。2015 年海合会游客境外旅游消费总额超过了“一带一路”沿线阿拉伯境外旅游消费总额的 60%。[③] 海湾阿拉伯国家的游客因逗留时间长、

---

① 李伯牙：《“一带一路”助推中阿贸易　十年内有望达 6000 亿美元》，《21 世纪经济报道》2015 年 9 月 11 日，第 9 版。

② 王猛：《中阿经贸的发展与问题》，《宁夏社会科学》2012 年第 5 期，第 74~80 页。

③ 数据来自迪拜伊斯兰经济中心与第纳尔标准公司联合发布的《2016–2017 全球伊斯兰经济发展报告》（State of the Global Islamic Economy Report 2016–2017）。

人均消费水平高、旅游服务要求高等特点，成为各国争抢的优质旅游客源。加强中阿旅游合作，对推动中国现有旅游产业升级、优化入境游客源结构、促进中国旅游业多样化发展和进一步提升中国旅游产业国际化水平具有重要的现实意义。

6.1.3　中阿旅游合作有利于增强中国在中东的软实力

旅游产业是中国推进“一带一路”建设的先导产业，在促进沿线各国贸易畅通、民心相通方面发挥着独特的作用。正因为此，中国的《“十三五”旅游业发展规划》中首次提出了旅游外交战略，希望借助旅游深化与“一带一路”沿线国家的文化交流与合作，提升中国的软实力和对外影响力。

阿拉伯地区知名媒体《阿拉伯人》对此评论道：“中东地区中国游客的不断增多可视作其软实力的一种象征。相比美国通过派遣舰队、建设军事基地扩大在中东影响力的做法，中国与海湾阿拉伯国家的旅游合作是一种性价比更高的策略。”①

6.2　中阿旅游双边交往现状

6.2.1　中阿旅游合作机制建设情况

中阿旅游往来已久，但政府层面的旅游合作机制直到2010年才建立。2010年，中阿文化旅游产业合作对接会在宁夏银川举行，后更名为中阿旅行商大会。当前，双方政府主要依托这一机制开展双边旅游合作。

近年来，宁夏政府利用“一带一路”建设契机，着力打造面向阿拉伯国家的旅游目的地。2015年，中阿旅行商大会在宁夏召开，主宾国就共同成立“一带一路”旅游发展联盟发布《宁夏宣言》，大会以“走进美丽中国、感受魅力丝路、畅游神奇宁夏”为主题，坚持“传承友谊、深化合作、

---

① 《旅游—中国扩大其在中东影响力的计划》，《阿拉伯人》新闻网站，2018年4月15日，http://alarab.uk/السياحة -خطة-الصين-لتوسيع-نفوذها-في-منطقة-الشرق-الأوسط。

共同发展”的宗旨，加强中阿双方在旅游资源推介、航空线路开辟、旅游平台建设等方面的旅游合作。[①]

6.2.2 中阿互为旅游客源国情况

1. 阿拉伯国家游客来华旅游情况

《中国入境旅游发展年度报告 2018》显示，2017 年中国（除香港、澳门、台湾地区外）入境旅游客源国仍以近程客源市场为主，排名前 10 的客源国除美国外，都是中国周边邻国或距离较近的东南亚国家。[②]来自阿拉伯国家的游客数量很少，甚至找不到详细可靠的官方统计数据。有关调查显示，阿拉伯国家特别是海湾游客不愿意来华旅游的原因主要是对中国的认知度低，文化交流少，这与中国在阿拉伯地区的宣传少，不重视中东旅游客源市场的开发有直接关系。

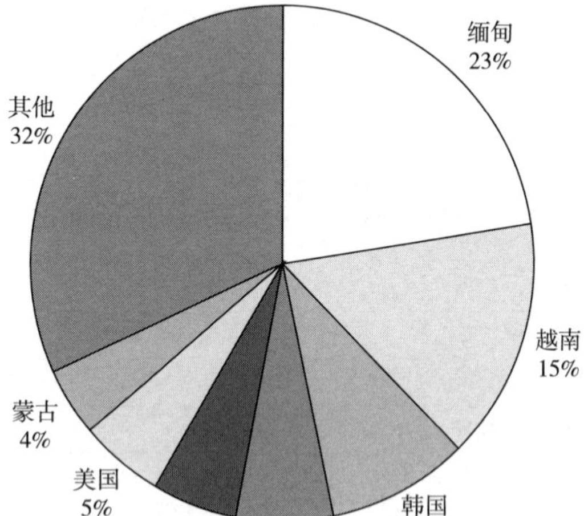

图 6.1 2017 年中国入境旅游主要客源结构

数据来源：中国旅游研究院。

① 李徽：《中阿旅行商大会将向世界营销宁夏》，《宁夏日报》2015 年 7 月 1 日，第 2 版。

② 中国旅游研究院：《中国入境旅游发展年度报告 2018》，旅游教育出版社，2018，第 19 页。

2. 中国游客赴阿拉伯国家旅游情况

21 世纪以来，中国出境游进入快速发展期。国人出境游目的地不断从周边近距离国家向欧美等远距离游国家扩展。自“一带一路”倡议提出以来，出境游目的地又呈现出了新变化，“一带一路”沿线国家的小众旅游目的地逐渐受到青睐。在此背景下，中国游客赴阿拉伯国家旅游人数也显著增长。其中以阿联酋（迪拜）最具代表性。近五年来，前往迪拜旅游的中国游客人数翻了一番（见表 6.1）。截至 2018 年上半年，中国已成为了迪拜第四大旅游客源国。

尽管前往迪拜的中国游客的人数不断增加，但据胡润百富榜与亚洲国际豪华旅游博览会（ILTM Asia）合作每年发布的《中国奢华旅游白皮书》，迪拜作为最受中国富人青睐的境外旅游目的地排名已从 2014 年的第三位下降至 2017 年的第九位。① 这表明近年来前往迪拜旅游的中国客源人群结构正在发生变化，迪拜逐渐从精英旅游向大众化旅游目的地转变。未来，阿拉伯国家如想更好地吸引中国游客，特别是高端游客，应不断在优化旅游线路、提升旅游目的地形象以及提高旅游服务质量上下功夫。

表 6.1　2014~2017 年中国游客赴迪拜、埃及旅游情况

国家 \ 年份		2014	2015	2016	2017
迪拜	中国游客数量（万人）	35	45	54	76.4
	占入境游客总数比例（%）	2.7	3.2	3.6	4.8
	入境游客源国排名	9	9	7	5
埃及	中国游客数量（万人）	6.5	13.5	17.9	28.7

数据来源：迪拜统计中心（Dubai statistics centre）。

埃及是仅次于阿联酋的接待中国游客人数最多的阿拉伯国家。近年来

① “Dubai Ranks in Top 3 Preferred Destinations for Rich ChineseTravellers,” Emirates 24|7, June 17, 2014, http://www.emirates247.com/news/emirates/dubai-ranks-in-top-3-preferred-destinations-for-rich-chinese-travellers-2014-06-17-1.553290, accessed November 20, 2015.2017 年数据来自：http://www.hurun.net/cn/article/details? num=dd1b436cb86e。

埃及旅游业发展并不理想，受“阿拉伯之春”影响，入境游人数在震荡中持续下行，但中国赴埃及旅游的游客人数始终保持着每年 30% 以上的增幅，从 2014 年的 6.5 万人次到 2017 年的 28.7 万人次，增长了 4 倍多，截至 2017 年中国已成为埃及的第七大旅游客源国。

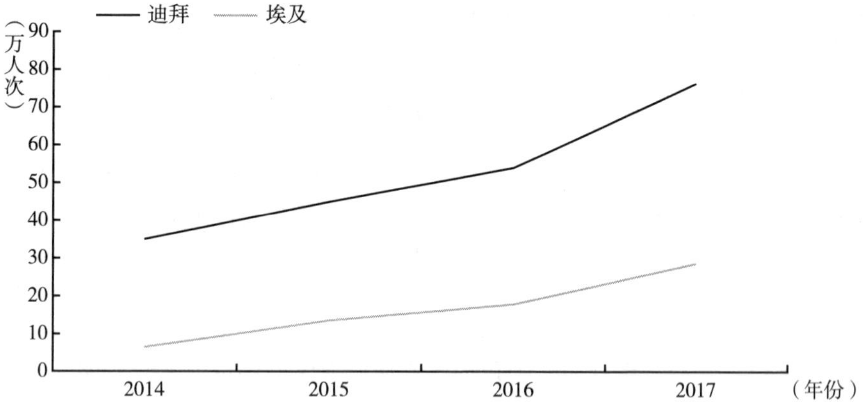

图 6.2 2014~2017 年中国赴迪拜和埃及旅游人数增长曲线

除迪拜和埃及外，近年来中国游客人数增长较快的阿拉伯国家还有摩洛哥、突尼斯和阿曼等国。阿曼自 2006 年与中国签订旅游谅解备忘录以来，每年前往阿曼的中国游客以超过 30% 的速度增长[①]；摩洛哥自 2016 年 6 月向中国游客开放落地签证以来，中国赴摩洛哥旅游人数已从 2016 年的 4.3 万人暴涨至 2017 年的 10.7 万人；突尼斯 2017 年 2 月向中国游客实施免签政策，当年中国入境游客人数同比增长超过 150%，中国成为突尼斯增长最快的客源市场。[②]

截至目前，已有 10 个阿拉伯国家对中国实行了免签或落地签政策[③]，越来越多的阿拉伯国家意识到“一带一路”背景下中国旅游业发展给他们带来的新机遇。

---

① 刘钢:《中国赴阿曼游客快速增长》,《京华时报》2010 年 8 月 12 日，第 D02 版。

② 《中国赴突尼斯游客数量剧增》，人民网，2018 年 9 月 28 日，http://travel.people.com.cn/n1/2018/0928/c41570-30317828.html。

③ 包括阿联酋、摩洛哥、突尼斯、黎巴嫩、巴林、卡塔尔、约旦、埃及、科摩罗和毛里塔尼亚。

6.3 中阿旅游合作的制约因素

6.3.1 阿拉伯地区局部动荡

阿拉伯地区局部动荡是影响地区各国旅游业发展的首要因素。“阿拉伯之春”导致地区旅游业客源整体萎缩。据世界旅游组织统计，2011 年前往中东地区的游客人次较 2010 年下降 8.4%。“阿拉伯之春”期间经历政局动荡的埃及、黎巴嫩、突尼斯等国旅游业受损严重，入境游客数量呈现大幅下降。2010 年埃及入境游客人数为 1400 万人，旅游收入占 GDP 的 13%；2011 年，埃及入境游客数量下降至 950 万。同年，巴林国内饭店入住率下降 40%，约旦旅游业收入缩水约 10 亿美元，黎巴嫩游客数量同比下降约 25%，突尼斯国际游客数量下降约 1/3。①

“阿拉伯之春”爆发后，阿拉伯国家旅游业发展两极分化日趋明显，中东旅游业格局经历深刻调整。叙利亚、埃及、黎巴嫩、约旦等国 2011 年入境游客数量分别减少了 41%、32%、24% 和 13%；摩洛哥、阿联酋、沙特等局势稳定国家旅游人数持续上涨：2011 年摩洛哥入境游客数量增长 4%②，阿联酋游客增幅达 9%，沙特入境游客增幅更是达到了 60%。③ 未来阿拉伯国家旅游业的发展预期很大程度上仍取决于地区政治安全局势的走向。

6.3.2 双边旅游合作机制建设尚不完善

目前，中阿旅游合作仍以行政手段主导机制建设为主，缺乏市场调节、

---

① “Tourism in Egypt: Arab Spring Break,” *The Economist*, May 4, 2013, http://www.economist.com/news/business/21577089-turmoil-has-scared-all-rugged-and-russians-arab-spring-breakaccessed December 2, 2015.

② Mark Johanson, “Post-Arab Spring Travel And Tourism In The Middle East: A Country-By-Country Look,” *International Business Times*, June 1, 2012, accessed December 2, 2015.

③ Gordana Kovjanic, “Islamic tourism as a factor of the middle east regional development”, *Turizam*. Vol.18, No.1, 2014, pp.33-43.

协商解决、人文融合及法律规范等多重合作机制的保障，立体合作机制构建尚不完善。合作主体以中央政府及地方政府为主，旅游企业影响力弱，行业协会存在缺位。合作层次较为单一，缺乏次区域旅游协同合作战略。今后，应主要从以下三方面完善合作机制。

1. 理顺国家与地方政府的职责分工

国家作为中阿双边旅游合作的主导者，主要承担制定旅游合作框架协议、消除各国旅游签证壁垒、搭建旅游合作平台、加强对外旅游基础设施建设投资等方面的工作；地方政府主要承担制定符合本地旅游发展实际的旅游发展规划与政策，保护和开发地方旅游资源，协调和促进地区内旅游业的发展合作，完善地区基础旅游设施建设，培育地区旅游人才等方面的工作。因此，明确国家与地方政府的职责分工，有利于协调和促进中国对阿开展旅游合作。

2. 发挥旅游企业的主体作用

旅游企业和旅游机构主要承担开发旅游产品和旅游线路、联合旅游营销以及提升旅游服务等方面的职责。未来可以考虑通过成立中阿跨国旅游企业，或加强与阿拉伯国家旅游企业合作的方式来加速中阿旅游合作进程，尤其是那些具有地区和国际影响力的大型跨国旅游企业，这些企业在制定当地旅游行业标准与规范上享有重要话语权。

3. 加强次区域旅游合作

从近年来中国开展国际旅游合作的实践来看，次区域旅游合作是跨国跨境旅游合作的主要模式之一，如澜沧江—湄公河区域旅游开发、图们江旅游合作开发、中俄旅游边境合作开发等项目，其共同点是合作双方经济都处于发展中国家水平，推行全面一体化的旅游合作模式尚存在难度。中阿双方幅员辽阔，区域旅游资源多样，地区旅游发展水平参差不齐，次区域旅游合作模式不啻为合作初始阶段的最佳选择。未来应充分发挥中国各级地方政府的主体作用，依据地方旅游资源特色、发展规划及发展水平，分层次推进中国相关区域的旅游圈和旅游板块与阿拉伯国家开展“一对一”的次区域旅游合作，提高旅游双边合作的针对性。

阿拉伯国家的旅游区域主要分为北非马格里布地区、尼罗河流域地区、沙姆地区和海湾地区等，中国的旅游区域主要分为三大区域旅游合作圈（长三角、珠三角和环渤海区域旅游合作圈）和五大区域旅游合作板块（西南区、西北区、东北区、中原区和华中区）。从现阶段中国旅游发展水平来看，应重点探索中国长三角、珠三角及西北区板块与海湾地区的次区域旅游合作。长三角、珠三角地区总体经济水平发展较高，基础设施建设较为完善，具备旅游经济优区①的优势，与阿拉伯国家的经贸往来密切。以宁夏为代表的西北区板块在发展对阿旅游方面具有天然优势，同时又是中国实施“向西开放”战略的重点区域。海湾地区国家经济发展和人均收入水平高、政治相对稳定，具备开展对外旅游合作的基础，中阿旅游合作应先考虑中国长三角、珠三角等地区与海湾地区阿拉伯国家的次区域旅游合作，待积累经验后再逐层推进。

6.3.3 中国对阿旅游基础薄弱

由万事达卡和新月评级机构合作发布的全球阿拉伯穆斯林旅游指数（GMTI）是当前衡量世界各国旅游目的地对该地区游客吸引力的权威指标，由目的地交通便利度、旅游生态环境、旅游发展意识及旅游业对当地社会的影响四个维度构成。②总的来说，GMTI指标将一个地区开发中东旅游市场的潜力归纳为两大因素：一是当地旅游业的发展基础，即是否为旅游经济优区；二是该地区开拓中东旅游市场的生态环境与发展意识。

对照指标体系可以看出，当前中国开发阿拉伯国家旅游客源市场的主要劣势在于以下诸方面。

第一，缺乏针对阿拉伯国家（主要是海湾阿拉伯国家）旅游客源市场的开发意识，缺乏专门针对该地区游客的旅游产品和旅游线路设计，缺乏

① 旅游经济优区是指旅游经济较为发达、旅游业收入较高的特定区域。

② 在这四项指标中，目的地交通便利度是指为入境阿拉伯游客提供司机服务；阿拉伯旅游生态环境是指为阿拉伯游客提供相应的旅游服务与设施建设；阿拉伯旅游发展意识是指与阿拉伯旅游相关新闻报道、事件数量等；旅游业对当地社会影响是指旅游业为旅游目的地创造的就业岗位数量。

针对性营销策略和渠道。

第二，针对阿拉伯游客的基础设施建设和服务水平低下。旅游基础设施建设的薄弱主要指餐饮，适合阿拉伯游客入住的酒店、旅游景点和活动设施，机场、景点、商场等公共区域相关措施建设不足；旅游服务水平较低主要指出行相关旅游信息获取渠道的不畅，缺乏具有阿拉伯旅游相关行业从业素质的人员等。

在诸多制约因素中，“餐饮”和“旅游信息获取”是两大核心问题。阿拉伯游客在饮食方面须遵守相关规定，能在旅游目的地足够便利地找到适合的餐厅对阿拉伯游客来说至关重要。

目的地旅游信息获取的重要性在于海湾阿拉伯国家游客大都不采用组团游的方式，而是以家庭为单位自助游模式。然而，目前中国绝大多数城市和景点的旅游网站都不提供阿拉伯游客旅游相关信息服务，国内也尚未出现一个专门针对阿拉伯游客开发的旅游网站或 App。

西北区旅游板块虽具有开拓中东国家旅游客源市场的意识，但区域旅游总体发展水平较低，旅游业基础薄弱，基础设施建设不足。而东南沿海地区虽为旅游经济优区，但长期以来欠缺开发阿拉伯旅游客源市场的意识。为此，中国各地区可根据自身旅游发展现状及特点，取长补短。如东南沿海地区应积极转变观念，吸取新加坡、日本等国和中国台湾地区开拓东南亚旅游客源以及 GCC 国家旅游客源市场的经验，推进中国“丝绸之路文化旅游经济带”建设。

6.4 中阿旅游合作领域

6.4.1 旅游客源市场

旅游市场合作是国际旅游合作的常见形式。全球经济一体化的推进，令旅游市场经历了由国内向国外、由局部向全世界的发展过程。旅游市场合作主要指旅游客源市场领域的合作，包括共同开拓旅游市场和互为旅游目的地及客源地两种方式。中国和阿拉伯国家在地理上并不相邻，双方旅游资源禀

赋不同，旅游特色迥异，因此宜采取互为旅游目的地及客源地的合作方式。

中国和阿拉伯国家均蕴含巨大的旅游发展潜力。“一带一路”倡议为中国对外开展旅游合作提供了新机遇，2015 年 3 月，中国国家发改委、外交部、商务部在博鳌亚洲论坛期间发布《推动共建丝绸之路经济带和 21 世纪海上丝绸之路的愿景与行动》，规划推动“一带一路”沿线国家及城市旅游业的长足发展。据中国国家旅游局预计，“十三五”期间中国将为“一带一路”沿线国家输送 1.5 亿人次中国游客和 2000 亿美元旅游消费。[①] 中国庞大的出境游消费将对整体提振和发展阿拉伯国家旅游业注入强劲动力。不少阿拉伯国家已意识到“一带一路”倡议对当地提供的历史性机遇，积极做出回应。2015 年开始，摩洛哥、埃及、突尼斯、黎巴嫩、卡塔尔等国纷纷采取放宽签证政策、开通直达航线、开展对华旅游推介活动等措施开拓中国客源市场。中东地区出境游客源市场体量虽不大，但增幅位列全球第一。

加强与阿拉伯国家的旅游合作将有利于中国进一步开拓“一带一路”沿线其他国家的阿拉伯旅游客源市场。2016 年全球阿拉伯游客的旅游消费总额超过了 1960 亿美元，占全球旅游市场份额的 11.8%。据预测，到 2022 年，旅游消费将达 2830 亿美元，占全球旅游市场的 14%。[②]

未来，中阿双方应积极通过互推旅游线路和开发旅游产品，共同确定旅游促销原则和促销计划，联手搭建区域性旅游宣传平台，创新签证及货币兑换政策等方式，推动双方互为旅游客源国和目的地。

6.4.2 阿拉伯旅游相关产业

受宗教信仰和风俗习惯影响，阿拉伯游客在旅游目的地选择、出行方式、消费偏好等方面具有不同于其他游客的特殊性。为满足阿拉伯游客的这些特殊的需求，相关酒店业、餐饮业、航空业和旅游信息产业在全球范

① 《“一带一路”的旅游愿景如何实现》，中国国家旅游局，2015 年 4 月 7 日，http://dj.cnta.gov.cn/html/2015-04/1824.shtml。

② Thomson Reuters，State of the Global Islamic Economy Report 2016/2017，Halal Focus，https://ceif.iba.edu.pk/pdf/ThomsonReuters-stateoftheGlobalIslamicEconomyReport201617.pdf.

围内兴起并迅速发展。这些产业依托庞大的阿拉伯旅游客源市场，致力于为阿拉伯游客提供体现特色的旅游服务。

近年来，阿拉伯旅游相关产业的发展呈现品牌化、标准化和全球化的趋势。以接待阿拉伯游客的酒店业为例，经过数年发展已形成数个具有全球知名度的行业领军品牌，如阿联酋的阿姆拉（Almulla）饭店集团。2007 年 10 月，该集团启动了首个专门针对阿拉伯游客的酒店建设项目，精心打造了旗下三个著名品牌。至 2013 年，集团在全球范围内投资 20 亿美元新建了 150 家专门针对阿拉伯游客的酒店，坐落在沙特、阿联酋、约旦、埃及和马来西亚等国，并将在伦敦、巴黎等阿拉伯游客聚集的欧洲城市继续开设 35 家分店。此外，阿联酋还拥有凯宾斯基（Kempinshi）旗下的沙赞（Shaza）品牌、瑞兹多（Rezidor）、罗塔那（Rotana）以及康富（KM）集团旗下的塔玛尼（Tamani）等多个酒店品牌。①

除阿拉伯国家外，其他国际知名旅游目的地也逐渐将目光投向阿拉伯旅游客源市场。截至 2011 年，新加坡已向本国的 366 家酒店和度假村颁发了行业证书，认定其具备接待阿拉伯游客的资质，其中 289 家由新加坡宗教部门直接认定，包括雅高（Pullman）和提斯特尔（Thistle）等知名饭店业品牌。2009 年，阿拉伯游客在英国的旅游消费总额超过 13 亿美元，英国、俄罗斯、法国等阿拉伯游客众多的国家越来越重视相关酒店业的发展。②

中国通过加强与阿拉伯国家跨国旅游集团的合作，有利于稳步提升国内接待阿拉伯游客的旅游基础设施建设和服务水平，提高中国作为阿拉伯旅游新兴目的地的知名度，以及中国文化旅游业的多样性及国际化水平。

6.4.3 旅游信息技术领域的合作

中阿旅游信息技术合作主要包括互联网旅游产业合作和旅游数据信息的共建与共享两大领域。

---

① Mohamed M. Battour et al., “Toward a Halal Tourism Market,” *Tourism Analysis*, Vol. 15, No.4, 2010, pp.461–470.

② Marcus L. Stephenson, “Deciphering ‘Islamic Hospitality’: Developments, Challenges and Opportunities,” *Tourism Management*, Vol. 40, 2014, pp.155–164.

互联网信息技术对旅游业产生重要影响，以互联网为平台的旅游信息服务已成为全球旅游业务拓展及旅游营销的重要手段。2014 年，中国国家旅游局正式提出“智慧旅游”发展概念，加快推动旅游在线服务、网络营销、网上预订、网上支付等智慧旅游业务。

阿拉伯国家早在2004年就制定了地区电子旅游产业“三步走”发展规划：第一步，协调阿拉伯各国旅游主管部门，实现旅游相关数据及旅游企业信息资源的公开和共享；第二步，通过建立网络信息平台，实现各国旅游企业的网上交易和财务结算，旅游产品的在线购买与支付；第三步，实现地区电子旅游产业与其他金融产业的全面融合。2008 年至今，阿拉伯国家每年都召开电子旅游及电子营销国际会议（IFITT），以推进地区旅游业的在线发展。①

通过互联网开展旅游联合推广及营销、双边旅游资源与产业链的整合、游客互联网使用习惯的培育，从而实现传统旅游营销模式与网络营销的有机融合，可成为未来中阿借助互联网信息技术拓展旅游合作的目标与方向。

新加坡在利用互联网开拓阿拉伯旅游客源市场方面值得中国借鉴，其经验可概括为，利用互联网整合国内旅游资源，为阿拉伯游客提供一站式旅游服务（Packaged Travel）。新加坡阿拉伯旅游专营企业领英（Crescent Rating）公司在 2013 年 12 月推出了“阿拉伯旅游”② 在线旅游预订网站，依据行业标准对饭店、度假村及旅游景点进行排序，提供酒店、机票、旅行社等旅游信息和预订服务，为来自阿拉伯国家及其他地区的阿拉伯游客提供了巨大便利。2014 年，领英公司与万事达（Mastercard）公司签署协议，通过数据联合分析，为阿拉伯旅游业投资者提供专业金融咨询与服务。近年来，前往新加坡旅游的阿拉伯游客人数增长迅速，在 2014 年发布的全球阿拉伯旅游发展指数中，新加坡位列第三，成为仅次于马来西亚和阿联酋的第三大阿拉伯境外旅游目的国。

中阿旅游数据信息的共建与共享是指双方在国家及地方政府牵头下，

---

① 哈桑埃米尔：《电子旅游及电子营销国际会议近日将在沙姆沙伊赫度假村举行》（阿拉伯文），《利雅得报》2008 年 10 月 13 日，http://www.alriyadh.com/380553。

② 该网站网址为：http://www.halatrip.com/。

建立旅游数据统计体系和旅游舆情监测网站。旅游产业作为社会化服务产业，需要建立在相关统计数据基础上才能有效推进旅游产品的设计、规划及旅游服务的改进。中阿双方可通过硬件平台的搭建，对旅游统计数据进行多渠道更新和多模式应用，通过大数据提升双边旅游合作。

6.4.4 人才培养和联合研究领域

联合人才培养是推进中阿旅游合作的基础条件。一方面，旅游行业涉及面广，对从业人员综合素质要求较高；另一方面，阿拉伯国家与中国在文化、语言、民俗方面差异较大，开展中阿旅游合作亟须培养一批掌握中阿双语、熟悉双方文化的旅游从业人员，包括外语翻译、旅游营销与管理人员、信息技术人员等人才。

为此，中阿双方可通过合作建立专科学校，根据市场需求设置专业方向，面向区域内各国招收生源，在中阿之间开展交叉教学和实践，实现短期内高素质旅游管理人才的培训和交流。

此外，中阿双方还应重视开展旅游领域的联合研究。目前，中国关于中阿旅游合作的理论研究，无论从广度还是深度上都无法满足中阿旅游实践开展的需要，遵循“理论研究先行”的理念，有助于更好地推进中阿旅游快速、有序和健康发展。

第 7 章　中阿产业园区建设专题报告

经贸合作区（包括产业园区）是推进中国与阿拉伯国家产能合作的主要平台和工作抓手。2016 年 1 月中国政府公布的《中国对阿拉伯国家政策文件》中指出:“坚持企业主体、市场主导、政府推动、商业运作的原则，对接中国产能优势和阿拉伯国家需求，与阿拉伯国家开展先进、适用、有效、有利于就业、绿色环保的产能合作，支持阿拉伯国家工业化进程。”2018 年 7 月 10 日，中阿合作论坛第八届部长级会议在北京召开，会议讨论通过了《中阿合作论坛 2018 年至 2020 年行动执行计划》，在第三条经济合作中强调，“应发挥经贸合作区等对深化双方产能与投资合作的平台和集聚作用，支持中阿企业在合作区建设领域开展更多合作”。

为积极响应国家政策，国家发展改革委、商务部等国家部委，以及宁夏回族自治区等地方政府，高度重视与阿拉伯国家的国际产能合作，先后与阿曼、沙特、埃及等“一带一路”沿线国家的政府部门和相关机构合作，设立了一批产业园区。经过不懈努力，阿曼杜库姆中国产业园、中国沙特（吉赞）产业园建设取得了积极进展，中国阿联酋（迪拜）食品工业园、中国埃及曼凯纺织产业园建设正在稳步推进。

7.1　阿曼杜库姆中国产业园

7.1.1　基本情况

1. 项目背景

2015 年 9 月 10 日，宁夏回族自治区人民政府与阿曼杜库姆经济特区政府利用 2015 中阿博览会平台，在宁夏银川签订了投资合作框架协议；2016 年 5 月 23 日，举行阿曼杜库姆中国产业园签约暨揭牌仪式；国家发展改革委已经将阿曼杜库姆中国产业园列为 2016 年重点推动建设的 20 个产能合作示范园区之一；商务部也将阿曼杜库姆中国产业园列为推进国际产能合作的 16 个重点境外经贸合作区之一，2018 年又列入“打造丝路明珠”重点项目。

2. 规划和产业定位

阿曼杜库姆中国产业园以企业运作为主，由部分在产业园投资企业成立中阿万方投资管理有限公司对园区进行规划、建设和运营。阿曼杜库姆中国产业园规划占地 11.72 平方千米，拟建项目规划总投资 670 亿元人民币，包括石油化工、建筑材料、电子商务等 9 个领域。产业园区将分为重工业区、轻工业综合区、五星级酒店旅游区，预计投产项目 35 个，包括原油冶炼、建筑材料生产等重工业项目，以及太阳能光伏项目、物流、汽车组装等轻工业项目，还有培训中心、学校、医院等配套服务设施。

3. 优惠政策

拥有长达 50 年的土地使用权，并可续签 50 年；可享受长达 30 年的企业免税期；可建立 100% 的外资独有公司；进口到特区内的商品将享受免税待遇；资金和利润可自由汇出，无最低投资额要求；无币种限制；入驻企业的环评指标与中国相当；在本地产值占比达到 33% 以上的商品可发放原产地证。

阿曼作为海湾六国之一，享受出口到海湾合作委员会国家及其他签订自由贸易协定国家的相关权益。海合会国家与澳大利亚在 2007 年签订自由

贸易协定，阿曼与美国在2009年签订自由贸易协定，海合会国家与新加坡在2013年签订自由贸易协定、海合会国家与欧洲自由贸易联盟（挪威、冰岛、瑞士及列支敦士登）在2014年签订自由贸易协定。

此外，投资者进行注册、取得营业许可和环境许可等均可享受国际上流行的方便、快捷的“一站式”服务，且项目所需工作签证不受限。

7.1.2　进展情况

1. 完成园区规划和可研报告，基础设施建设已启动

委托中国国际工程咨询公司先后完成了《阿曼杜库姆中国产业园可行性研究》《阿曼杜库姆中国产业园总体规划》《中阿曼杜库姆中国产业园市政详细规划》三份报告。规划在10年左右的时间里，大力发展石油化工、天然气化工、建筑材料、可再生能源、油田器械、现代农业、跨境电商、生活服务和海产品加工等九大产业，计划投资30余个项目，总投资约670亿人民币，用地1.2万亩，用工1万人。目前主要项目已完成了可行性研究报告，多批专业人员赴现场进行了考察调研，其余项目也已出具了项目建议书。产业园现场已运抵宁夏施工机械18台（件），注册公司3家，员工50余人，已在园区修建了3千米道路，完成园区临时水、电、路等工程。目前正在进行产业园区主干道路基和外籍劳工营地的施工和建设。

2. 签订开发协议，取得多项优惠政策

2016年5月23日，宁夏回族自治区人民政府与杜库姆经济特区政府就建设中国产业园的协议在阿曼首都马斯喀特正式签约。根据协议，中方已取得了多项优惠政策：（1）免除所有税收30年；（2）占有土地12平方千米，50年时限并可续签；（3）取消任何金融管制；（4）工作签证按工作需要不受限制；（5）国务院关于开展国际产能合作文件中涉及的能源、冶金、化工、建材等12个产业均可以落地；（6）可以建设自备电厂和自备水厂；（7）允许中方设立百分之百的独资企业，阿曼籍公民占员工总数的10%，以及其他政策。

3. 举行奠基典礼仪式，签订多项投资入园项目

2017 年 4 月 19 日，在阿曼杜库姆经济特区举办了中国产业园奠基典礼仪式，宁夏回族自治区人民政府 60 余人参加了典礼。本次活动受到了阿曼苏丹国高度重视，阿曼王子殿下、杜库姆经济特区主席、阿曼城市发展和水资源部部长、商务部次长、中部省省长等 5 名部级官员参加了典礼。有 10 家中国企业同阿曼万方有限公司签订了入园协议，总投资 220 多亿人民币。目前，产业园轻工业区一期基础设施建设项目已完成土地平整。累计签约项目 13 个，包括天然气化工、火力发电、光伏组件、建材市场、人才培训等。项目进展方面，一是职业学历教育项目，目前已完成第一批 37 名阿曼籍留学生的培训工作，第二批 30 名阿曼籍留学生已于 2018 年 9 月进入宁夏职业技术学院接受培训。二是 2018 年 4 月 15 日，由阿曼万方有限公司全额投资的综合商住楼项目开工。该项目总投资 2 亿元人民币，由宁夏住宅建设发展（集团）有限公司建设，预计 2019 年 7 月完工。三是 2018 年 4 月 23 日，建材城项目股东协议正式签署，该项目由阿曼万方有限公司与 Al Thabat Holding（阿曼内务部养老基金 100% 控股下属公司）和 Tatweer（阿曼杜库姆特区政府下属投资公司）共同组建成立杜库姆建材城股份公司（Duqm Material Market SAOC），进行建材城项目开发和运营，目前该项目已进入招标阶段。

4. 筹建产业园专项基金，推动产业园建设重点事项的落实

一是宁夏政府已经同意政府产业引导基金投向对外合作产业领域子基金 1 亿元，采取市场化运作和基金引导方式，确保撬动社会资金比例不低于 1∶3。目前，已初步确定东源（天津）股权投资基金管理股份有限公司、太仓市若森投资管理有限公司、宁夏中阿万方投资管理有限公司等单位配资 3.35 亿元，共同成立阿曼杜库姆中国产业园专项基金，进一步推动产业园建设。二是国家发展改革委支持阿曼杜库姆中国产业园发展的 1000 万元前期工作费用已划拨宁夏回族自治区财政账户，目前正按照相关规定对中国阿曼杜库姆产业园入园企业前期工作经费给予补贴。

5. 加大产业园宣传推广力度，积极对接第二批入园企业

一是受宁夏回族自治区人民政府邀请，阿曼杜库姆经济特区主席叶海

亚·贾比利一行于2017年9月5~9日访宁并参加2017中阿博览会。其间，力方公司与国内有关企业共签署了13项合作协议，涉及天然气加工、火力发电、海水淡化、新能源和建材等领域。二是连续举办阿曼杜库姆中国产业园招商推介活动。2017年9月9~12日，阿曼杜库姆经济特区主席叶海亚·贾比利一行赴大连、上海两地出席了阿曼杜库姆中国产业园招商推介活动，重点对接洽谈石油化工、天然气化工、港口、电厂、干船坞、园区配套等合作项目，项目对接取得良好效果。2018年9月下旬，自治区博览局（贸促会）联合有关单位，在济南、杭州、广州三地连续组织举办了多场推介宣传活动，与阿曼杜库姆经济特区政府就油气资源配置、水电供给、政策支持、融资渠道、项目推进等重要问题达成基本共识；与京能集团、中国石化宁波公司、浙江省远洋渔业有限公司、广汽集团、山东石油化工协会等企业和协会进行了项目对接；与中国进出口银行陕西分行、点炻金融控股集团、丝路（中国）集团有限公司等金融机构展开对接，为产业园融资提供新路径。

7.2 中国沙特（吉赞）产业园

7.2.1 基本情况

1. 项目背景

2016年1月19日，在国家主席习近平访问沙特并和沙特国王萨勒曼共同见证下，银川开发区所属的银川育成投资有限公司（以下简称银川育成）、广州高新区投资集团、沙特阿美石油公司（以下简称沙特阿美）共同签订合作备忘录，商定三方组建合资公司。

2016年4月，沙特政府公布了《沙特阿拉伯王国2030愿景》，提出在具备条件的地方建立特别发展区，实行有别于其他经济城、工业城的特殊优惠政策，以吸引更多投资，加快经济城的发展。依据这一愿景，按照中沙产能合作双方高层达成的共识，沙方提出在吉赞基础工业城设立中国企业特别发展区，并实行对中资企业更加优惠的投资政策。

2016 年 8 月 31 日，在中沙高级别委员会首次会议期间，银川育成、广州高新区投资集团、沙特延布和吉赞基础工业城皇家管理委员会（以下简称皇家委员会）、沙特阿美在北京签订了关于在吉赞基础工业城设立合资公司的框架协议。

吉赞基础工业城是沙特政府为了加快国内非石油产业的发展而建设的四个经济城之一，于 2005 年 11 月 5 日正式奠基建设，基础工业城距吉赞市区 81 千米，规划面积 106 平方千米，计划基础设施总投资额 300 亿美元，2025 年建设完成。截至 2017 年末，已由沙特阿美石油公司完成投资约 180 亿美元，其中路网、港口、供水、供电、污水处理等基础设施计划于 2018 年初完成，届时将由沙特阿美石油公司移交给延布和吉赞皇家委员会管理运营。

2. 规划和产业定位

中国企业特别发展区（中国沙特吉赞产业园）总规划面积 32 平方千米，包括无固定物理边界的 30 平方千米工业区和封闭管理的 2 平方千米生活区。按照吉赞基础工业城的产业布局规划，从南到北依次布局为重工业、制造业、轻工业、住宅区和商业区等。重工业方面，重点开发能源站、海水净化站、燃油储藏厂、发电站等；轻工业方面，重点发展原材料、电子产品、现代服务、垃圾处理、工业部件、生物技术、农业技术等。2018~2020 年重点引进延伸钢铁产业、石油化工、硅产业、船舶服务业；2020~2025 年重点引进食品产业、包装业、家电装配、机电设备装配、建筑材料等。该园区已被国家发展和改革委列为 2016 年 20 个重点国际产能示范园区之一，被商务部列为 16 个重点支持的产业园区。

3. 优惠政策

一是沙特投资总局对在经济城投资的项目，在项目资料整理、批准、建筑许可、商业注册和工业许可及环保合规等方面提供一站式的协助。二是在财政资助方面，对工业项目提供贴息贷款和拨款，主要有：由沙特工业发展基金向项目提供总投资额 50%~75%，期限为 15~20 年的贷款。其中，外资独资企业最高贷款额为 4 亿里亚尔（约合 1.07 亿美元），合资企业最高

12 亿里亚尔（约合 3.21 亿美元）。三是在免除进口关税方面，沙特财政部对企业用于生产的进口原材料、机械和设备及其备品备件等，免除 5%~12% 的进口税。同时，吉赞经济城位于沙特的欠发达省，还可享受沙特财政部针对欠发达地区的减免天课和所得税的优惠政策，主要有：按培训沙特籍员工成本的 50% 给予补贴，按沙特籍员工年薪的 50% 给予补贴。四是在人力资源支持方面，由沙特人力资源开发基金会对企业培养沙特籍劳动力给予补贴。主要有：每月 500 里亚尔的培训补贴及每月为每名学生提供 75% 的薪水（最高 1500 里亚尔），培训上岗后补贴月薪的 50%（最高 2000 里亚尔，为期 12 个月）。

7.2.2 进展情况

1. 双向对接情况

2018 年 4 月 25 日，由沙特产业集群发展计划署、沙特延布皇家委员会（RCY）、沙特投资总局（SAGIA）、沙特基础工业公司（SABIC）和中国国家发改委国际合作中心共同举办的“中沙橡胶工业发展论坛”在上海国际会展中心举行，论坛举办的目的旨在加强橡塑行业与中国的战略合作，吸引中国企业投资沙特的橡胶加工产业，来自国内各地的 70 多家企业和金融机构参加了此次活动。应沙方邀请，银川开发区、广州开发区分别组成代表团出席论坛。在论坛交流期间，中沙办推荐的几家企业与沙特各方积极对接，其中山东临沂商城海外投资有限公司明确表示对投资沙特吉赞基础工业城有浓厚兴趣，有意推动山东新能源汽车组装项目落地吉赞；江苏中浩银河橡胶有限公司已于 2018 年初考察过沙特吉赞、达曼等城市，希望能与沙特阿美公司建立合作，利用阿美石油下游产品 EPDM 作为其原料，投资三元乙丙胶混炼厂项目。上述两家企业分别与沙特投资总局、工业集群开发署及沙特阿美石油公司进行了交流，均表示会继续保持进一步沟通。

2018 年 8 月 11~18 日，应沙特国家能矿部工业集群开发计划署的邀请，中国和沙特产能合作推进领导小组办公室，银川育成投资有限公司以及有

意愿到沙特投资的隆基绿能股份有限公司一行 8 人联合组团，赴沙特、阿联酋，推介隆基公司拟在沙特投资新能源光伏产业项目，实地考察投资环境，加快推进中国—沙特产能合作项目建设。在沙方的高度重视和积极配合下，访问务实高效、成果丰硕，达到了与沙方加深了解、增进友谊、促进合作的目的。

2018 年 9 月 8~11 日，由国家商务部主办的第 20 届中国国际投资贸易洽谈会在福建省厦门市举办。银川市经开区在厦门会议中心举办了“中国（宁夏）—阿拉伯国家境外产业园区推介会”，中沙产能合作方沙特延布和吉赞皇家委员会首席执行官纳斯夫代表中沙产能合作各方介绍了吉赞经济城规划。

2018 年 9 月 10~11 日，中沙产能合作的沙方代表沙特延布和吉赞皇家委员会首席执行官阿拉·纳斯夫博士一行四人代表团到访银川。代表团拜访了银川市领导，考察了银川市和开发区投资环境，双方就中沙产能推进工作进行商讨，进一步推进中国“一带一路”倡议和沙特“2030 愿景”的融合落实，增进互信，共同努力，实现双方共赢发展。

2. 园区建设进展情况

目前已经建成和基本建成的项目有：阿美石油公司的炼油厂、发电厂、港口和一个年产 200 万吨的炼钢厂。园区首个中资企业入园项目——广州泛亚聚酯石油化工化纤一体化项目已获沙特投资总局批复。该项目是沙特吉赞基础工业城的第一个招商引资项目，也是沙特王国建国以来首个外国独资石化项目。项目建设是以年产 250 万吨 PTA、100 万吨 PET 为生产核心的大型化工企业，并通过滚动发展，逐步实现整个聚酯产业链的覆盖。该项目占地面积约 100 万平方米，总投资 32 亿美元，建成后年产值约 48 亿美元。该项目被沙特政府列为重要招商引资示范工程，并首次在沙特使用中国技术、标准和设备，将为今后中资企业落地提供典范。

随着沙特“2030 愿景”的深入实施，沙特政府为了创建一个具有地方和国际吸引力的投资环境，以增强投资者在沙特的信心，其主要目标：一是改善行政审批环境，以促使重大投资；二是改善必要的基础设施，优化

投资环境；三是制定一个统一的国家投资愿景，以促进直接投资，支持国民经济；四是突出投资服务，提高服务满意度，这些改革举措对于今后吸引并服务中国投资者具有重要意义。

7.3 中国阿联酋（迪拜）食品工业园

7.3.1 项目背景

中国阿联酋（迪拜）食品工业园位于阿联酋迪拜酋长国“迪拜批发城”（DWSC——Dubai Whole Sale City），规划占地面积40万平方米，建筑面积30万平方米，地处迪拜马克图姆机场入口旁，距迪拜2020世博园3千米，与杰布阿里自由区隔高速公路相邻。工业园建成后将成为世界最大机场的机场餐食和航食的主供应商，世界最大主题公园的旅游快餐和酒店餐食的主要供应商，同时也将是中东人道主义救援食品的重要供应方。

7.3.2 规划和产业定位

工业园分为餐食加工区、方便食品加工区、休闲食品加工区、糕点加工区、牛羊肉加工区、冷冻食品加工区、牛羊肉加工区、速冻食品区，并配备集中的冷链仓储物流区、中央能源站、中央冷站和中央商务区，将利用集中能源供给站和冷链仓储物流区，实现能源、资源、土地的充分使用，为入园企业降低经营和管理成本。

食品工业园采用创新的基金模式发起建设，建成后将工厂整体租赁给以设备出资的食品生产企业经营；食品企业设备搬迁、工业园厂房建设、铺底流动资金均由基金公司负责；食品生产企业负责项目经营，由基金与入园企业共同确认营业目标，保证投入产能能够实现约定毛利指标。入园食品企业收入来源分为两部分：一是入园食品企业作为合伙人参与基金本身的收益分配；二是入园食品企业经营收入。食品企业除向工业园管理公司支付租金等必要费用外，其他所有收入归自己所有，工业园管理公司及基金不参与食品企业的利润分配。基金期满，食品企业可选择将工厂回购，

或续签合同继续经营。

基金将通过与迪拜王室、阿联酋主要销售商（包括阿联酋航空的主要供应商）合作，成立联合销售公司和跨境电商平台，帮助入园企业实现产品在当地销售及出口。其中：餐食加工产品、糕点甜食产品、茶叶加工产品等主要销往中东及北非市场；牛羊肉加工产品、海鲜产品、椰枣加工产品主要出口中国市场。

7.3.3　优惠政策

在入园企业以设备及技术折算现金入股“中阿食品工业合作基金”后，基金将根据企业产能规模及要求设计建设厂房，并提供设备搬迁及运营铺地流动资金，为企业提供拎包入住的服务，解决企业融资困难。如入园企业由于各项原因无力继续经营，可保留基金份额改由他人经营，其继续享受基金年收益分配，到期后退出投资。

1. 税收政策

增值税及其他税项：2018 年阿联酋迪拜向所有行业、产业及服务业开始统一征收 5% 的固定增值税。除此项税收外，迪拜不征收其他税收。关税：阿联酋迪拜普通货物关税为 5%，基础食品及食品原料享受免税政策。同时，食品工业园出口的商品免征关税。

2. 保人制度政策

根据迪拜法律规定，外资在迪拜投资开设公司时需要由当地法人或自然人为法定代表人并在法律层面上持有 51% 的股份，合资企业需要有偿邀请当地保人充当公司法人并在法律层面上持有 51% 的股份（私下协议可保证外资 100% 持有公司股份，在当地具有法律效力）的方式开设新公司。食品工业园已与迪拜政府达成协议，入园企业统一由迪拜政府担当保人，可拥有公司 100% 股份，当地政府只收取少额服务费。

3. 销售政策

联合当地主要渠道商成立联合销售公司，为入园企业提供现成的销售渠道及订单。

7.4 中国埃及曼凯纺织产业园

7.4.1 基本情况

1. 项目背景

2016 年 11 月，曼凯投资注意到埃及鼓励国内制造、鼓励外商投资埃及的商机，随后专门赴埃及考察纺织行业和国内纺织大省，决定投资埃及。2016 年 12 月，曼凯投资参加宁夏・广东经济技术合作交流座谈会，联合多家纺织行业龙头企业，决定入埃投资。2017 年中阿博览会期间，在中埃两国有关领导的见证下，曼凯投资与埃方在银川签订合作框架协议。

2. 规划和产业定位

中国埃及曼凯纺织产业园位于埃及姆努夫省萨达特市工业城，占地 310 万平方米，计划入园企业 568 家，总投资 20 亿美元。主要分为工业用地、培训学校、配套商业、配套商务、配套住宅五大板块，设置生产加工基地、原辅材料基地、培训中心、技术研发中心、仓储物流中心、品牌孵化中心、金融孵化中心、商务服务中心、网络信息服务中心、五星级酒店等功能区，逐步形成纺纱、织布、印染、洗水、成衣制造、绣花、印花、辅料、鞋帽箱包等生产及贸易，仓储物流、电子商务等关联产业（教育、医疗、金融、会展、酒店、办公、研发等）融合发展的产业格局，形成产业聚集、人与产业联动的新型现代化产业园区。

3. 优惠政策

埃及方面规定，《埃及新投资法》（2017 年 5 月）生效后设立的投资项目，根据投资区域，按照如下规定享受减税的投资激励。

A 类区域：投资成本核减 70%。包括：根据中央信息统计中心的统计报告，依据《埃及新投资法》实施条例说明的投资分布，急需开发的区域。

B 类区域：投资成本核减 50%。包括：根据中央信息统计中心的统计报告，依据《埃及新投资法》实施条例说明的投资分布，A 类区域之外的急需开发的区域。

C 类区域：投资成本核减 30%。包括：根据投资活动分布，在共和国剩余区域的大量用工项目；小微项目；使用新能源、再生能源的项目和能源生产项目；最高投资委员会确定的国家级和战略性项目；最高投资委员会确定的旅游项目等。

7.4.2　产业园建设进展情况

2017 年 3 月，宁夏曼凯投资有限公司注册成立。

2017 年 5~8 月，《中国埃及曼凯纺织产业园可行性研究报告》正式编撰完成。

2017 年 10 月，曼凯投资组织 25 家中国纺织企业到埃及实地考察，最终选定“萨达特”工业城作为产业园地址，并与埃及工业发展总局和贸工部部长塔里克・卡比尔进行正式谈判，与埃及贸工部签订土地使用框架协议。

2017 年 12 月，埃及曼凯纺织制造股份有限公司正式注册成立，并向政府有关部门交纳 5% 的土地出让金。后经埃及内阁会议和国会审批，在中国驻埃及大使馆宋爱国大使见证下，埃及贸工部部长塔里克・卡比尔亲自为曼凯投资颁发了土地正式批文。

2018 年 1 月，埃及总统塞西考察“萨达特”工业城时，贸工部部长塔里克・卡比尔亲自为塞西总统介绍曼凯纺织产业园项目，得到了塞西总统的高度重视。塞西总统高度评价该项目，表示埃及政府会全力配合曼凯投资，简化一切手续尽快促成项目落地，帮助项目的实施期限从 7 年缩减至 4 年，一期实施期限减少至一年半。

2018 年 3~4 月，曼凯投资与工业发展总局签订土地产权买卖协议（永久性产权），相继又与埃及武装工程管理局签署产业园区一期项目施工协议。

2018 年 4 月，与中冶国际工程集团有限公司在京签署施工总承包合同协议书。

2018 年 6 月以来，曼凯投资在广东、福建、浙江、江苏、湖南等纺织

大省开展专题推介活动，效果显著，目前已签署入园意向的国内企业已达70余家。

2018年10月，曼凯投资接受埃及政府部门提出的建议，由宁夏曼凯投资有限公司在埃及重新设立了投资主体——长江投资有限公司（曼凯投资全资控股），土地权属全部落在长江投资有限公司名下。